The
Inner World of
the Middle-Aged
Man

The Inner World of the Middle-Aged Man #6

Peter Chew

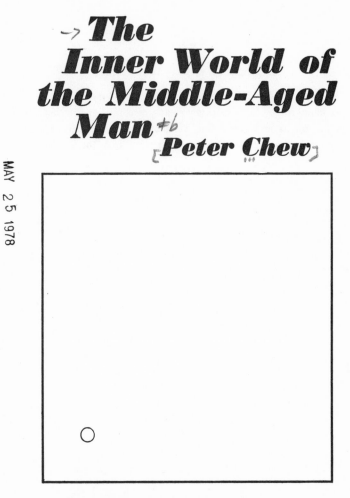

Macmillan Publishing Co., Inc.

New York

Macmillan Publishing Co., Inc.
866 Third Avenue, New York, N.Y.   10022
Collier Macmillan Canada, Ltd.

Library of Congress Cataloging in Publication Data

Chew, Peter.
   The inner world of the middle-aged man.

   Includes index.
   1. Middle-age.   2. Adulthood.   3. Men—Psychology.
I. Title.
HQ1067.C45   301.43′4   76-7455
ISBN 0-02-525000-0

First Printing 1976

Designed by Jack Meserole

Printed in the United States of America

The author gratefully acknowledges permission to reprint portions of:

"The Lamentation of the Old Pensioner" from *Collected Poems of William Butler Yeats*. Copyright 1906 by Macmillan Publishing Co., Inc., renewed 1934 by William Butler Yeats. Reprinted by permission of Macmillan Publishing Co., Inc.

The Poems of Dylan Thomas. Copyright 1939, 1946 by New Directions Publishing Corporation. Reprinted by permission of New Directions Publishing Corporation.

"The Circus Animals' Desertion" from *Collected Poems of William Butler Yeats*. Copyright 1940 by Georgie Yeats, renewed 1969 by Bertha Georgie Yeats, Michael Butler Yeats, and Anne Yeats. Reprinted by permission of Macmillan Publishing Co., Inc.

"Husbands in Crisis" by Maggie Scarf from *McCall's*, June 1972. Copyright © 1972 by Maggie Scarf. Reprinted by permission of Candida Donadio and Associates, Inc.

Something Happened by Joseph Heller. Copyright © 1974 by Scapegoat Productions, Inc. Reprinted by permission of Random House, Inc.

"Pension Act 'Cruelly' Misleads" by Merton C. Bernstein from *Cleveland Plain Dealer*, September 19 and 20, 1974. Reprinted by permission of the author.

Last of the Red-Hot Lovers by Neil Simon. Copyright © 1970 by Nancy Enterprises, Inc. Reprinted by permission of Random House, Inc.

"Prayers" by Michael Quoist. Copyright 1963, Sheed & Ward, Inc. Reprinted by permission of Sheed & Ward, Inc.

The Decline of Pleasure by Walter Kerr. Copyright © 1962 by Walter Kerr. Reprinted by permission of G. P. Putnam's Sons.

"Death and the Mid-Life Crisis" by Elliott Jaques from the *International Journal of Psycho-Analysis*. Copyright © 1965 by Institute of Psycho-Analysis in London. Reprinted by permission of the *International Journal of Psycho-Analysis* and the author.

"Male Menopause: The Pause That Perplexes," produced by National Public Affairs Center for Television (NPACT). Originally produced June 24, 1974. Reprinted by permission.

"Normal Crises of the Middle Years" a paper by Dan Levinson given at a symposium sponsored by The Menninger Foundation. Reprinted by permission.

"New Pension Reform Enacted; Law Gets Mixed Reaction" by James W. Singer from the *National Journal Reports*, August 31, 1974. Reprinted by permission of the *National Journal*.

Alone by Admiral Richard E. Byrd. Copyright 1938 by Admiral Richard E. Byrd, renewed 1966 by Marie A. Byrd. Reprinted by permission of G. P. Putnam's Sons.

To my daughter Liz

We cannot live the afternoon of life according to the program of life's morning, for what was great in the morning will be little at evening, and what in the morning was true, will at evening have become a lie. I have given psychological treatment to too many people of advancing years, and have looked too often into the secret chambers of their souls, not to be moved by this fundamental truth. . . .

—CARL GUSTAV JUNG,
Modern Man
in Search of a Soul

Contents

Preface

To DISCOVER the ubiquitous is a rare and wonderful thing, as we all know. I didn't discover it, however; I stumbled upon it. The idea of writing about middle-aged man—his foibles, fantasies, and occasional desperate triumphs—was sparked by the chance remark of a friend of mine more than five years ago.

Late one chilly afternoon in the fall of 1970, architect Hugh Jacobsen and I were watching our sons playing 100-pound football at St. Alban's School in the shadow of Washington's towering National Cathedral. After concluding that neither of our offspring would ever be Washington Redskins' material, we drifted into a lugubrious discussion of the high cost of raising children, the latest marital crackups and rumors thereof among our friends, and the morbid details of a contemporary's fatal heart attack a few nights before. Jacobsen mentioned that he'd read there was some kind of "middle age crisis" that everyone went through, and that maybe *we* were going through it.

Some time later, I stopped by the National Institute of Mental Health (NIMH), to see whether anyone there had heard of a middle age crisis, and talked with Dr. Thomas E. Anderson, then as now, a leading researcher in mental health for the aging.

Anderson was frank to say that he knew very little about middle-aged man beyond the fact that he was one himself. The midlife male was the "forgotten man" as far as behavioral science was concerned.

"We simply don't have much in the way of data yet from our research on middle-aged man," said Anderson. "We do know that middle age is a period of high suicide rate, coronary attack, a *lot* of depression, and a *lot* of alcoholism. It's a crucial time as far as marriages are concerned, especially when the children grow up and start moving away."

Anderson said that there was a psychologist up at Yale by the name of Dan Levinson who was conducting a study of "normal" middle-aged men under an NIMH grant, and perhaps Levinson would talk with me. Anderson also recommended that I talk with Dr. Nathan Shock, one of the world's foremost gerontologists, over in Baltimore. And right here in Washington there was a versatile psychiatrist-gerontologist by the name of Dr. Robert N. Butler who was a busy and effective activist in causes of the aging.

By now, I was intrigued. I went to John F. Bridge, editor of *The National Observer*, a Dow Jones property in whose vineyard I labored for a dozen years, and suggested a story on the problems of middle-aged man in our society. Bridge is a man of few words. "O.K.," he scrawled on my memorandum. With Bridge's always terse but strong encouragement, I wrote a number of articles, most of them built around a fictional middle-aged character whom I called Good Old Charlie. In time, Charlie became for me like the invisible rabbit in the old Broadway show, *Harvey*. I took him with me to interview psychiatrists and before long, I found them using his name in their replies to my questions.

Charlie is rather like Ralph Waldo Emerson's description of Montaigne, the patron saint of the inner-searching middle-aged man. In Emerson's introduction to *The Works of Michel de Montaigne* published nearly seventy years ago, he wrote:

"He pretends to most of the vices; and if there be any virtue in him, he says it got in by stealth. There is no man, in his opinion, who has not deserved hanging five or six times; and he pretends no exception on his own behalf. 'Five or six as ridiculous stories,' too, he says, 'can be told of me, as of any man living.'"[1]

Charlie, in other words, is well within the range of normal. While not without faults, he is nevertheless not evil. He is a man struggling with unseen demons.

Although, as NIMH's Tom Anderson said, there have been few major studies of male adulthood—and almost none of middle-aged man per se—a great deal of research has been carried out on the psychological and physiological aspects of the aging process; the nature of work and leisure in America; marriage; morals; and many other concerns of the man in mid-passage. In the course of researching *The National Observer* articles, and later during the years I spent expanding that research for this book, I crisscrossed the country interviewing— besides Levinson, Shock, and Butler—scores of other leading behavioral scientists: Birren, Neugarten, Menninger, Weinberg, Heath, Klemme, Martin, to name but a few.

Much of their brilliant insight into the midlife phenomenon has remained in solution, as it were, in articles in professional journals, papers delivered before learned societies, and works written for academic audiences, though all of these people are capable of making their thoughts clear to the layman when called upon to do so. *The Inner World of the Middle-Aged Man* is an attempt by such a layman to interpret their findings and theories, and pass them along to a wider audience.

I've had the fun, as well, of talking with astronauts, monks, professional football players, and no less interesting mortals in workaday life—bankers, stockbrokers, salesmen, government officials.

At the same time, I searched out the midlife theme in literature. And to my surprise and delight, I discovered that many of the great works that I had been force-fed at the Choate School, and later at Princeton, now made great sense to me. After some twenty-five years of covering revolutions, wars, labor disputes, rocket launchings, civil rights and anti-war riots, assassinations, and more mundane matters, it has been a treat to slip into the silent world of the library.

With the help of Joyce Canady Bowes, a former researcher for the American Psychological Association, I also searched the scientific literature—with sometimes mixed results. *Correlates of Extramarital Coitus* did not tell me, for example, what I was trying to find out about that subject, nor did most of the other graph- and statistics-laden abstracts that computers turned up. For such material, I had to turn elsewhere. But when I fed "Oedipus Complex" into the computer at the National Library of Medicine, it poured forth abstracts on the father-son problem in an unending printout.

Finally, there are certain practical problems that men face in this country in their forties and fifties, problems related to career, age discrimination, pensions, health, and so forth. I have pursued answers to many of these by going to the top men and women in the various fields.

I must emphasize that were it not for Jack Bridge, *The National Observer*, and the total cooperation of the brilliant scientists, Levinson, Butler, and Shock, this book could not have come into being. I must also stress that while I have had the cooperation and guidance of experts in many fields, and I have been scrupulous in reporting their exact words, the conclusions I have reached are my own, and I'm sure they want to be absolved.

This book, then, is primarily about stocktaking. The ancients said that when a man starts working out a philosophy for himself, or reworking a philosophy—as most of us do in our forties— he is preparing for death. *I* think he's preparing for life, but then again, perhaps it's all the same thing. In the words of a Latin poet:

Death plucks my ears, and says *Live*—I am coming.

PETER CHEW

Washington, D.C.

Acknowledgments

SPECIAL THANKS to Fred Honig, executive editor, Macmillan Publishing Co., Inc. and to Arthur Pine, literary agent.

Appreciation as well to the many people who have helped me with this book, including Daniel S. Rogers, information officer, the Gerontology Research Center of the National Institute on Aging, Baltimore; Legare H. B. Obear, chief of the loan division, Library of Congress, and the staff of the information office, Library of Congress; Carl Charlick, translator, librarian, scholar, The Metropolitan Club, Washington, D.C.; Mrs. Jean Jones, librarian, American Psychiatric Association; Miss Martha Guse, librarian, American Psychological Association; Mrs. Janet Hummell and James O'Neill of the Washington, D.C. public library, and staff of the Palisades branch, D.C. public library; The Menninger Foundation, Topeka, Kansas; Michael Batten and the National Council on the Aging; John Crystal; Professor Merton C. Bernstein, Washington University School of Law, St. Louis; William H. Donaldson, dean of Yale University's Graduate School of Organization and Management; and Dale Tarnowieski and Frank Doeringer, The American Management Association.

The
Inner World of
the Middle-Aged
Man

1 "God, in Six Years, I'll Be Fifty!"

Midway upon the journey of our
life
I found myself within a forest
dark,
For the straightforward pathway
had been lost.
Ah me! how hard a thing it is to
say
What was this forest savage,
rough, and stern,
Which in the very thought renews
the fear.
So bitter is it, death is little
more.

—DANTE, *Divine Comedy*[1]

MOST of us know Good Old Charlie, the stereotypical middle-aged man in the process of making a donkey of himself over a young woman not his wife. For twenty years or so, Charlie has been married to Faithful Jane, has brought up two teen-age children, and has been plugging away steadily, if with decreasing enthusiasm, at Amalgamated Widget. An occasional snootful at the country club dance is Charlie's only noticeable vice, and he's easily chastened by a stern pillow talk.

Suddenly, it happens. Charlie plunges into a hot-and-heavy affair with a cute young nurse. He'd sensed her presence when he came out of anesthesia: the musky fragrance zephyring past; the white-starched rustle of her uniform.

Charlie hasn't felt so vibrant, so *alive*, since his days at State when a beautiful coed fell for him. At the same time, he feels guilty as hell. He doesn't relish the words his minister uses on Sunday to describe the sort of thing he's up to.

Charlie's inner turmoil hasn't gone entirely unremarked at the Widget works where his mood oscillates from depression to ebullience to anger. At the sales meetings which Charlie used to chair with enthusiasm, his eyes now glaze with indifference.

Charlie hasn't the foggiest notion what's gotten into him.

"All of a sudden at my age, you realize you are mortal and that time is running out," said Charlie to a younger colleague one day. "And as time runs out, it gets more precious. It's almost an economic thing."

Charlie has embarked upon a major stocktaking, an orgy of introspection. He's begun to question everything he's worked so hard to create during his twenties and thirties.

"Do I *really* want to spend the next thirty-two-point-one years of my life [Charlie has just turned forty and he's peeked at the actuarial tables] with Jane? Sure, I still love her, I guess, but things have been dullsville for years.

"Do I *really* want to go on knocking myself out for the Widget company, in the wild hope that I'll be made financial vice-president?

"Or do I want to kick over the applecart, run off with my young gal, and buy a ranch in Idaho where I spent the happiest summers of my childhood? In a few more years, I'll be shooting blanks and it'll be too late.

"Well, Charlie, old boy, if not now—when?"

Charlie feels trapped in his marriage and in his job, caught up in an intricate web of his own—and society's—weaving.

Charlie, and he is legion, is smack in the midst of the male midlife crisis. Long preoccupied with childhood and adolescence at one end of the life cycle, and old age at the other, behavioral scientists have only recently begun to focus upon the forgotten man "midway upon the journey," to borrow Dante's immortal words.

"We act as if we know the really important things that happened in a man's childhood, the rest of his life is more or less predictable, which of course it isn't," said Yale University psychologist Dan Levinson the first time we talked in his New Haven office. "Psychologists speak of development as if it goes on to the age of six, or possibly eighteen. Then there's a long plateau, in which random things occur, and then around sixty to sixty-five, a period of decline sets in to be studied by gerontologists.

"My position is that development does occur in adulthood, that there is an underlying order to the adult course, that there are basic principles governing development in adulthood as in childhood and adolescence."

Few men know the inner world of the American male better than Dan Levinson. With funds from the National Institute of Mental Health, he recently completed a five-year study of men aged thirty-five to forty-five that has resulted in a compelling theory of adult development.

Among authorities such as Levinson, the realization has been steadily growing that man's heightened psychic activity as he moves from young adulthood into middle age at around forty, is a natural human development. How a man now faces up to the larger questions—where his marriage and career go from here; the prospect of old age and mortality—will help determine his fate in the evening of his life.

Yet so many American men work so hard in their twenties and thirties—"They have their noses and everything else to the grindstone," says Levinson with a smile—that they figuratively stumble into this thicket. Unprepared, they're thrown off stride by the psyche's mysterious motions—the emergence of sides of their nature that have lain dormant; the resurgence of childhood dreams and conflicts now demanding to be resolved; often an upsurge of erotic longings and fantasy; the mourning of lost opportunities and shrinking horizons; and the sudden questioning of values they'd thought immutable.

There are gains as well as losses, but in the beginning, Charlie can only see the losses.

How a man navigates the period obviously varies, depending upon his social class, the times in which he lives, and the variables of his particular situation. Nevertheless, behavioral science has isolated a number of things that most men, regardless of their circumstances, experience at this time.

The theme of man's search for a meaning to his life as he passes through what Joseph Conrad poetically termed "the shadow line" of forty, has been vividly portrayed in autobiography and biography, novels and poetry, the theater and motion pictures. Eugene O'Neill, who often complained of "my particular allotment of fatal forties period of physical bogdown and mental meanderings," considered man's search for meaning the *only* worthwhile theme.

"The playwright today must dig at the roots of the sickness of today as he feels it . . . the death of the old God and the failure of science and materialism to give any satisfactory new one for the surviving religious instinct to find a meaning for life in, and to comfort its fears of death with. It seems to me that anyone trying to do big work nowadays must have this big subject behind all the little subjects of his plays and novels, or he is simply scribbling around the surface of things, and has no more real status than a parlor entertainer."[2]

And in a line, Yeats has spoken volumes about one of man's unspoken fears:

> There's not a woman turns her face
> upon a broken tree[3]

An even greater fear—terror, in fact, is not too strong a word—lies at the heart of the midlife crisis. It is a fear of death that can no longer be repressed. When this clammy substance seeps through a man's being, his sensitivity to the flight of time becomes acute. This, in turn, causes him to reassess values and goals.

It's common knowledge that many men lose themselves in depression at this time, or in alcohol, promiscuity, divorce, hypochondria, suicide. Some men engage in desperate—sometimes ludicrous—attempts to cling to their youth. Others make a last heroic effort, invariably at great risk, to achieve their dream, to integrate their experience and thus give meaning to their lives. Many resign themselves to their changed circumstances and adapt. In any event, I'm convinced that man's search at midlife is ultimately a spiritual one.

"The idea of death, the fear of it, haunts the human animal like nothing else; it is a mainspring of human activity—activity designed largely to avoid the fatality of death, to overcome it by denying in some way that it is the final destiny of man," says Ernest Becker in *The Denial of Death*,[4] a philosophical work that won him a Pulitzer Prize.

Becker, who died in 1974, the year after publication of his book, had been a professor in the Department of Political Science, Sociology and Anthropology at Simon Fraser University in Canada. He argues brilliantly that man's horror of death, and of the "overwhelmingness" of a world that's beyond his comprehension, is the mainspring of his drive for success, his dreams of heroics, his everlasting busyness. Man's furious activity helps him forget that he's half god, half animal, that his fate is annihilation.

Man has a symbolic identity that brings him sharply out of nature. He is a symbolic self, a creature with a name, a life history. He is a creator with a mind that soars out to speculate upon atoms and infinity, who can place himself imaginatively at a point in space and contemplate bemusedly his own planet. This immense expansion, this dexterity, this ethereality, this self-consciousness gives a man literally the status of a small god in nature, as the Renaissance thinkers knew.

Yet, at the same time, as the Eastern sages also knew, man is a worm and food for worms. This is the paradox: He is out of nature and hopelessly in it; he is dual, up in the stars and yet housed in a heart-pumping, breath-gasping body. . . . It is a terrifying dilemma to be in and to have to live with.[5]

Becker is not alone in this emphasis upon death.

" 'Is not the fear of death natural to man?' asked Boswell.

" 'So much so, sir,' replied Dr. Johnson, 'that the whole of life is but keeping away thoughts of it.' "[6]

French psychologist Gerard Mendel believes we are able to

keep these gray thoughts away because we possess an irreducible element of irrationality:

"No individual could escape depression if he were constantly aware of his weakness. If we are able to forget up to a point—and sometimes completely—that we may be dead in an hour's time and are able to go on living, acting, and speaking, this is because of our protective armor of irrationality which makes us see our position in a more favorable and reassuring light than is really the case, and blinds us sufficiently to allow us to retain the minimum confidence in ourselves."[7]

In early middle age, however, we can no longer ignore the offstage presence of the eternal Footman.

"The simple fact of the situation is the arrival of the mid-point of life," wrote Elliott Jaques, a British psychoanalyst who was using the term "midlife crisis" more than a decade ago:

> What is simple from the point of view of chronology, however, is not simple psychologically. The individual has stopped growing up and has begun to grow old. The paradox is that of entering the prime of life, the stage of fulfillment, but at the same time, the prime and fulfillment are dated. Death lies beyond.
>
> I believe it is this fact of the entry upon the psychological scene of the reality and inevitability of one's own eventual, personal death, that is the central and crucial feature of the midlife phase—the feature that precipitates the critical nature of the period.
>
> Death—at the conscious level—instead of being a general conception, or an event experienced in terms of the loss of someone else, becomes a personal matter, one's own death, one's own real and actual mortality.
>
> As Freud so accurately described the matter: "We were prepared to maintain that death was the necessary outcome of life. . . . In reality, however, we were accustomed to behave as if it were otherwise. We displayed an unmistakable tendency to 'shelve' death, to eliminate it from life. We tried to hush it up. That is our own death, of course. No one believes in his own death. In the unconscious, everyone is convinced of his immortality."[8]

The death of a man's father can set him to thinking.

"The death of a father means, irrevocably: 'I can never turn to my father again for whatever I want,'" says Dan Levinson. "And somehow this idea intrudes: 'My father has stood between me and the grave. It looks like I'm next.'"

A contemporary dies of a heart attack; cancer strikes a friend.

"I tend to notice it in the newspapers nowadays when people my own age die," said one of Levinson's subjects to one of the research staff, "which is something you don't seem to remark on much when you're in your thirties. But then, people at that age die in accidents; in their forties, they start to keel over from heart attacks. Hardly a day goes by when I don't say—I don't mean it preoccupies me by any means—but I play the awful game. I'm sure many people do. Where you say: 'God, in six years I'll be fifty!'"[9]

Hours, days, months, and years now vanish with a rush. What the German gerontologist A. L. Vischer has termed "the silent flow and uncanny flight of time" is a universal characteristic of the midlife transition.

"The measurement of time is a creation of man for his orderliness and convenience," says Dr. Jack Weinberg, clinical director of the Illinois Psychiatric Institute. "Then he looks upon it with typical human ambivalence. It is a great friend and healer for 'time heals all wounds.' On the other hand, its ticking minutes are a tragic accompaniment to his life pulse. It is a constant reminder of his periodicity and all things temporal. It is forever running out on him; he begins to look upon it with hostility, suspicion, and anger."

Weinberg believes that the midlife transition is more of a problem for Americans than other nationalities, because of the nature of our society. We're hard-driving, success-oriented, future-oriented people. We reward youth, and pragmatism, and productivity. We mete out insults, conscious and unconscious, to the middle-aged and aging. Past forty, a man finds age discrimination in employment pervasive.

"Time enters into our entire being: past, present, and future," says Weinberg. "In our society, we value the future most. We don't get into anything without asking what the 'future' is in it. We are so busy planning for the future that when the future catches up with us, we can't enjoy it—because we are again too busy planning for the future."

Near the end of John P. Marquand's novel *The Point of No Return*, Charles Gray, the hero, learns that he's finally beaten out his rival, Roger Blakesley, for the vice-presidency of the Stuyvesant Bank.

> There was a weight on Charles again, the same old weight, and it was heavier after that brief moment of freedom. In spite of all those years, in spite of all his striving, it was remarkable how little pleasure he took in the final fulfillment. He was vice president of the Stuyvesant Bank. It was what he'd dreamed of long ago, and yet it was not the true texture of early dreams. The whole thing was contrived, as he had said to Nancy, an inevitable result, a strangely hollow climax. It had obviously been written in the stars, bound to happen, and he could not have changed a line of it, being what he was, and Nancy would be pleased, but it was not what he had dreamed. . . .
>
> Automatically, his thoughts were running along new lines, well-trained, mechanically perfect thoughts, estimating a new situation. . . . They would sell the house at Sycamore Park and get a larger place. . . .[10]

The problem begins in our educational system. "Americans have trouble being introspective, developing a philosophy for themselves," says Weinberg. "Our universities produce excellent technicians, but not thinking, educated, contemplative men. We have trained people in how to make a living, but not in how to live."

Psychiatrist Robert N. Butler, director of the National Institute on Aging, finds the average American's life stultifyingly programmed, starting with a twenty-year block of education, followed by a forty-year block of work, ending in a retirement too often characterized by emptiness.

Butler, like Weinberg, is convinced that we must somehow reorder our lives to let in a little more light and air, that we should break the work block with sabbaticals or leaves of absence to travel, rest, explore new possibilities, and continue with education. He does not believe in compulsory retirement at age sixty-five.

Men in the academic world have long enjoyed this kind of life. They have extensive vacations, sabbaticals, and, most importantly, a portable pension plan which enables them to move from one university or foundation to another without giving up their vested rights.

One great problem is that so much office work is without excitement. Robert Butler likes to make the point that for so many Americans, their forty-year block of work is stultifying. For others, the constant pressure and stress causes them, in time, to burn out. The middle-aged man, too, is constantly being pressed by younger men anxious to move up.

Manhattan psychiatrist Alexander Reid Martin has made a lifetime study of work and leisure, having served as founder and chairman of the American Psychiatric Association's Committee on Leisure Time and Its Uses. He believes that this country's dedication to the work ethic has become "a national neurosis."

"Man's innate capacity for leisure has taken a terrible beating by the work ethic," says Martin. "For too long, we have been living in a world in which our whole education, our whole philosophy, is predicated on the world of work. We push our children's education so they can find jobs. We educate them to make a good living—not to make a good life. We have completely distorted the true purpose of education."

Hard-driving industrial managers tend to forget leisure's vital role in the mind's creative process. It was the German theologian Josef Pieper who said, "The imperishable intuitions come only to a man during his moments of leisure."

Ideally, work and leisure should complement one another.

Aristotle believed that work's sole purpose was to gain the means for leisure, life's highest goal. Leisure to Aristotle meant pursuit of knowledge for its own reward, not for utilitarian purpose.

Stocktaking goes forward at midlife whether or not man has attained success in his own or society's eyes. For as Carl Gustav Jung observed, the values that have sustained a man during life's morning, do not suffice for his afternoon. He must change his life if he is to become a more whole, truly mature individual. Jung believed, in fact, that a man was rarely mature enough until around forty to become a true individual, that until that time he was largely the product of his surroundings and society's demands upon him.

Writer James Baldwin has said of stocktaking: "Though we would like to live without regrets, and sometimes proudly insist that we have none, this is not really possible if only because we are mortal. When more time stretches behind than before one, some assessments, however reluctantly, begin to be made. Between what one wished to become and what one has become, there is a momentous gap, which will now never be closed. And this gap seems to operate as one's final margin, one's last opportunity for creation."[11]

During a young man's striving for success, he must repress many qualities that are associated, rightly or wrongly, with the feminine. During his soul searching at midlife, these "other voices" in "other rooms" of the personality, as Truman Capote put it, demand to be heard. The man who has aligned his personal destiny with the corporate purpose of, say, IBM or General Motors, or Amalgamated Widget, rarely has the time or the inclination to pursue music, art, philosophy, science, religion—the things that will provide the purest happiness in later life.

"We might compare masculinity and femininity and their psychic components to a definite store of substances of which, in the first half of life, unequal use is made," said Jung. "A man consumes his large supply of masculine substance and has left over only the smaller amount of feminine substance which now must be put to use. It is the other way round with woman; she allows her unused supply of masculinity to become active."[12]

Hence we found old warriors like Winston Churchill and Field Marshal Lord Wavell taking up painting and poetry, respectively, in their later years. More recently, former Prime Minister Edward Heath—to stay with the English in this sample—joined a professional jazz band.

Jung believed that a man pays a terribly high price in his striving for success, and that his personality suffers from his enforced concentration upon the business at hand and failure to enjoy other experiences.

My friend Robert Butler has observed in his private psychiatric practice that many men as they grow older regret most the things they failed to do along the way. He often quotes the Talmud which said: "Man will be called to account for all the permitted pleasures which he failed to enjoy."

From his mid-thirties onward, man appears drawn into the gravity field of forty, like a spacecraft picking up speed as it approaches the moon. Oliver Wendell Holmes, for one, was convinced that a man must achieve fame by forty, or it would be too late. "So he pushed himself to the limit, trying to finish his book, *History of the Common Law,* before his fortieth birthday," wrote the late Catherine Drinker Bowen. "He succeeded, and with his enchanting wife Fanny, celebrated over a bottle of champagne, the cork of which still exists."[13]

One of Dan Levinson's thirty-nine-year-old subjects observed wryly one day that on his next birthday he would be ten years older. And all of the subjects had engaged in stocktaking in their late thirties. There were forty of them—forty was hit upon as both a symbolic and manageable number—including, for diversity's sake, ten business executives, ten hourly wage earners, ten writers, and ten biology professors.

Born in the 1920s, many of the men had served in World War II and had lived through their twenties and thirties in a period of prosperity. "All of them were working and relatively stable," says Levinson. "They weren't a psychiatric sample, in other words, though some had had some treatment. They were all kind of going about their lives; they all had a sense of being en route."

At one point or another, each man had lifted his nose from the grindstone, and had asked himself whether the grindstone was all there was to life.

" 'What am I *doing* here?' 'What is this thing that I have created?' They ask questions about the world they live in.

" 'Do I want to live in this neighborhood?' 'Do I want to work in this company?' 'Do I want to stay in this occupation?' 'Do I want to be in this family?' Those are questions about the environment.

" 'And what about *me*?' They ask questions about the self. 'What is it I want?' 'Would I rather be an executive in a corporation or a schoolteacher?' 'Or do something more in the public good?' 'Or do something more artistic, more aesthetic'—questions like that."

Most of the men felt trapped in their jobs, the blue collar worker especially, for he has the fewest options. The union's rigid seniority provisions, pension plans, and the like, tie the man inexorably to his lathe. Where can he go?

Similarly, the business executive fears that he has too much at stake in *his* pension plan and prerogatives to make a break—if he's fortunate enough to be covered by a pension plan at all. As for the distinguished anthropology professor: Well, what else can a professor of anthropology do? he asks himself.

A middle-aged man is squeezed between generations: his adolescent children, to whom he must play the role of parent; and his own aging parents, to whom he must play the role of son. As his parents grow older, a reversal takes place. He winds up taking care of them, thus becoming a "parent" to both generations.

The concept of fatherhood undergoes radical changes during the midlife period. The father of an infant has a feeling of omnipotence, notes Levinson. "The father says, 'I feel sort of like God; I have created something in my own image, and I can take care of it; its fate rests very much on me.' It's another thing to be the parent of a twenty-year-old: 'I can no longer have any illusion that I can determine its fate from here on. In fact, I frequently can't even get a hearing.'"

Man's decisions concerning his wife and family carry the greatest potential for heartbreak or happiness. In this connection, Levinson finds there are two conflicting views of Good Old Charlie's trek down what used to be called the primrose path.

"One view is that it's going to be terrific, because he married young and he didn't know what he wanted, but now he's really found himself and so now he's got a great love, and it's all going to be beautiful," says Levinson.

"And the other view says: There is nothing beautiful about it. He's just going through another adolescence and he has the illusion that he has found some ideal love, but you know, life isn't like that, and it's unrealistic. It's what in the mental health field is called 'acting out'—where you enact a fantasy thing but it doesn't have much to do with the realities, and that doesn't work out because there is a lot of make-believe in it.

"So what I'm saying is there is evidence of both extremes and everything in between. And that's why giving advice is tough because if you say to a person: 'Look, if you've made a lousy life for yourself, now is the time you can readily change. So don't stay in a rut: Swing! It's the Gauguin fantasy.'

"On the other hand, you can say to people: 'Look, if you're having all these particular troubles, don't be so alarmed; it is the period you are going through, and you can relate it to where you are in the life span. If you can get through the next few years, chances are you'll find some way to live and you won't be in this turmoil. Life will be a little simpler. Things may not necessarily be better, but you won't be so restless, moody, and that sort of thing.' And this sort of talk about time has a reassuring function, especially with the wife: your friend 'Old Charlie' may be noticing his young secretary a little more, but he'll get over it, and he won't be too different."

Levinson pauses. A tall, dark, forthright individual, he speaks slowly, falling silent for long seconds to frame a thought, then he gathers speed as he warms to his subject.

"But I can't help coming back to the other side once again, and that's that this transition is *not* just a little upset, like a cold that you get over. The fact is that there is something very profound happening here; or at least there is that possibility. It is important how much you do change your life. I mean: Take it seriously, man! Don't just say, 'If I can hold out, I'll be all right; now that you tell me everybody goes through the same thing, I can relax a little bit and I'll survive it.'

"There is more possibility here than just survival—in your job or whatever. And if you try for big changes, you may fail miserably. On the other hand, if you don't try for changes, you'll feel dead in a few years—because you'll be stagnant. And that's tough. What I'm trying to say is that all this *really is tough,* and if you've been getting hypochondriacal or been drinking too much, maybe you have reason to be in turmoil."

2 "... I Was Conscious of a Certain Aimlessness"

STOCKTAKING often results in a feeling of resignation. A friend of mine in his mid-forties puts it this way: "I call it the 'all of a sudden you ask yourself' syndrome. What is a marriage really about? All of a sudden you ask yourself real basic questions like that. You may have choices but you just can't think of your own short-term pleasure. You have to think of your children.

"Raising children of good sound character is damned important, as important as anything you do. If a parent cops out when faced with adversity, what's going to happen to the kids? They really are harsh critics around fourteen, you know. They suddenly realize the old man isn't what they thought he was. You purport to be one thing and here you are something else. Then again, you suddenly discover that you're *not* going to be a U.S. senator or president of the XYZ soap company. So you've got to adjust. The grail gets kind of misty. Finally you say 'to hell with it.'"

One of Levinson's subjects said one day that he was no longer counting on hitting any home runs in life; he'd be happy if he could just make it through the game without getting "beaned."

In Anne Morrow Lindbergh's felicitous phrase, a man in mid-life often tries "to evolve another rhythm with more creative pauses in it." Rear Admiral Richard E. Byrd cites this wish as his principal reason for isolating himself in a weather observation shack during the Antarctic winter of 1934—a five-month "creative pause" that nearly cost him his life from carbon monoxide poisoning. Byrd was forty-five at the time, a world-famous flyer, explorer, and scientist. In *Alone*, Byrd wrote that after fourteen years of periodic expeditions, he felt little sense of achievement.

> Rather, when I finished my stocktaking, I was conscious of a certain aimlessness. This feeling centered upon small but increasingly lamentable omissions. For example, books. There was no end to the books that I was forever promising myself to read; but, when it came to reading them, I seemed never to have the time or the patience. With music, too, it was the same way; the love for it—and I suppose the indefinable need—was also there, but not the will or the opportunity to interrupt for it more than momentarily the routine which most of us cherish as existence. This was true of other matters; new ideas, new concepts, and new developments about which I knew little or nothing. It seemed a restricted way to live.[1]

With the help of a snow tractor team, Byrd established his weather observation post 125 miles from his main base; his plan was to make meteorological and auroral observations for seven months alone, communicating with main base by radio. Even for a man of Byrd's experience, it was a risky proposition. Once winter settled in, it would be extremely hazardous—indeed, nearly impossible—for snow tractors to reach him in case of emergency.

Byrd was criticized from some quarters for leaving his expedition to go off like this. And in his book he confesses that his desire to make weather observations in this remote corner of the world only partially explained his motivation. He wanted, he said:

> to taste peace and quiet and solitude long enough to find out how good they really are. It was all very simple. And it is something, I believe, that people beset by the complexities of modern life will understand instinctively.
>
> We are caught up in the winds that blow every which way. And in the hullabaloo, the thinking man is trying to ponder where he is being blown and to long desperately for some quiet place where he can reason undisturbed and take inventory. . . .
>
> Out there on the South Polar barrier, in cold and darkness as complete as that of the Pleistocene, I should have time to catch up,

to study, and think, and listen to the phonograph; and, for maybe seven months, remote from all but the simplest distractions, I should be able to live exactly as I chose, obedient to no necessities but those imposed by wind and night and cold, and to no man's laws but my own.[2]

Byrd wrote lyrically of his first hours alone after the departure of the snow tractors for the main base.

About 1 o'clock in the morning, just before turning in, I went topside for a look around. The night was spacious and fine. Numberless stars crowded the sky. I had never seen so many. You had only to reach up and fill your hands with the bright pebbles.

Earlier, a monstrous red moon had climbed into the northern quadrant, but it was gone by then. . . .

If great internal peace and exhilaration can exist together, then this, I decided my first night alone, was what should possess the senses.[3]

In time, he was beset by severe mental and physical anguish. But even though he had come close to death, he said he did not regret what he had done.

For I read my books—if not as many as I had counted on reading; and listened to my phonograph records—even when they seemed only to intensify my suffering; and meditated—even though not always as cheerfully as I had hoped. . . .

All this was good, and it is mine. What I had not counted on was discovering how closely a man could come to dying and still not die, or want to die. That, too, was mine, and it also is to the good. For that experience resolved proportions and relationships for me as nothing else could have done; and it is surprising, approaching the final enlightenment, how little one really has to know or feel sure about.[4]

Stocktaking can result in a man's decision to seize what he conceives to be his last clear chance to achieve his dream. Levinson calls this making "the special bet," or "the magical event," and the character of this bet depends upon what developmental stage a man happens to be in when he makes it.

The special bet made by a man in his twenties or thirties generally consists of an all-out effort—within a segment of his professional sphere—to make his mark, to achieve recognition. In his striving, he becomes more specialized, more focused than ever.

The special bet made by a man in his forties or later more often reflects an attempt to reduce what Graham Greene once called "the chaos of experience" to some sort of order; an effort to become a more "whole" person. He's trying to achieve something for his own satisfaction, rather than for recognition, though recognition often follows as a matter of course if he's successful.

Ernest Becker would say that such "heroics" represent a man's attempt to transcend death, that each man's particular achievement is his "immortality formula." Be that as it may, sages spoke of the phenomenon centuries before Becker and Levinson.

Ptolemy, the great second-century Alexandrian astronomer, wrote:

"The second half of manhood . . . is governed by Mars, the evil planet, the agent of disaster. It initiates the serious side of life, bringing bitter grief and imposing on body and soul a period of worry and torment; it gives the first painful intimation that the morning of life is past, and thus forces man to devote himself to harsh labors before it is too late, to the accomplishment of some worthwhile purpose."[5]

A quiet ferocity characterizes a man once he has launched upon his harsh labors. Wife and family often take the hindmost. Such was the case of writer Robert Pirsig. In June 1972, Pirsig—then forty-three—completed a 600,000-word philosophical work that he'd spent nearly five years writing.

Pirsig was working as a technical writer for a big naval ordnance equipment firm in St. Paul, Minnesota, when he wrote his book in his spare time.

"I would go to bed at 6 P.M, get up at 2 A.M. and write until I went to work at 8," he told Tom Zito of *The Washington Post*. "I did that for two years, first at home but then my wife threw me out. I expected the kids to shut up at six so I could sleep and she didn't think that was fair. So I got a $12-a-week room at a flophouse. My boss let me come into the office and write early in the morning and I'd show up for breakfast at my own house each day. Writing this book was a compulsive act and whoever stood in the way of it was going to get hurt."[6]

Without benefit of an agent, Pirsig submitted the elephantine manuscript to many publishers, to no avail. A young editor at William Morrow & Co., took the trouble to wade through the sea of words, persuaded Pirsig to cut the manuscript to one-sixth its length, and then accepted it. Within two months of its publication on April 15, 1974, Pirsig's *Zen and the Art of Motorcycle Maintenance* had sold nearly 50,000 copies. Paperback rights quickly brought $370,000. And Book-of-the-Month Club named it an alternate September selection.

Pirsig's book amounts to a 130,000-word stocktaking, an attempt to reduce the extreme chaos of his life—he had suffered a mental collapse in the early 1960s—and to reconcile the arguments of the world's great philosophers concerning the nature and origin of human knowledge, all within the context of a motorcycle journey.

During the summer of 1968, Pirsig—then thirty-nine—drove his 305 cc. red Honda Superhawk from St. Paul to California with his eleven-year-old son Chris perched behind him. They were accompanied on another cycle by a married couple, old friends of the Pirsigs.

During the long ride, Pirsig the narrator discusses a wide range of subjects, from the importance of "caring" for a motorcycle through proper maintenance, to the arguments of Kant and Hume, Aristotle and Plato concerning the validity of human knowledge:

"A motorcycle functions entirely in accordance with the laws of reason, and a study of the art of motorcycle maintenance is really a miniature study of the art of rationality itself.... Peace of mind isn't at all superficial. It's the whole thing. That which produces it is good maintenance; that which disturbs it is poor maintenance. What we call workability of the machine is just an objectification of this peace of mind."[7]

Pirsig had taken a bachelor's degree in philosophy and a master's in journalism from the University of Minnesota, then had taught English at Montana State University in Bozeman during the late 1950s and early 1960s, before suffering a mental breakdown and undergoing shock treatments.

"Approximately 800 mills of amperage at duration of 0.5 to 1.5 seconds had been applied on 28 consecutive occasions in a process known technologically as 'Annihilation ECS.' A whole personality had been liquidated without a trace in a technologically faultless act. . . ."[8]

"I'm a Zen Buddhist and I had gotten interested in motorcycles after I was turned down for a pilot's license in 1964 because of my mental problem," he explained to the *Washington Post* reporter. "It's all 'Catch 22.' I'm a tech writer because I can't be a teacher because a teacher can't be nuts. Anyway, the motorcycle took on a special meaning to me because it was a way of overcoming the hangups of the hospitalizations. So after the trip, I started writing these essays. . . . They sounded pontifical, so I decided to put it in the mouth of a narrator who's vulnerable. . . . I'm trying to make the classic concepts more relevant today, helping people lead more imaginative, productive lives. The problem today is that one has to succeed in some terrible chain of values. The book just says, 'be true to your own interests in terms of Quality.' "[9]

When psychiatrists speak of the "Gauguin Syndrome" in connection with middle-aged man's yearning to escape, they do so advisedly. Still, the impression has been left with a wider public that Gauguin himself suddenly gave up his placid existence in Paris and, without a backward glance, abandoned his wife and children and sailed for Tahiti. And that there, in a fit of manic creativity inspired by the glories of primitive jungle and voluptuous native women, produced the canvases that were to establish him as a father of modern art.

With his *Noa-Noa, A Journal of the South Seas,* Gauguin contributed to this myth. At the same time, he doubtless succeeded in arousing the fantasies of untold Frenchmen smothering at midlife in mundane marriages and stultifying jobs:

> I was aware that on my skill as a painter would depend the physical and moral possession of the model, that it would be like an implied, urgent, irresistible invitation. She was not at all handsome according to our aesthetic rules. She was beautiful.

All her traits combined in a Raphaelesque harmony by the meeting of curves. Her mouth had been modeled by a sculptor who knew how to put into a single, mobile line, a mingling of all joy and all suffering. I worked in haste and passionately, for I knew that the consent had not yet been definitely gained.

I trembled to read certain things in those large eyes—fear and the desire for the unknown, the melancholy of bitter experience which is at the root of all pleasure, the involuntary and sovereign feeling of being mistress of herself.

Such creatures seem to submit to us when they give themselves to us; yet it is only to themselves that they submit. In them resides a force which has in it something superhuman—or perhaps something divinely animal.[10]

In this minor masterpiece of escape literature—written, some believe, to promote interest in his paintings back in France—the artist says little or nothing about the disease, poverty, and frustrations that plagued him in an Eden flawed already by civilization's incursions.

In fact, Gauguin effected the dramatic changes in his life only after years of inner turmoil. His was a lonely struggle in line with the way most lesser mortals work their way toward major mid-life changes. Moreover, Gauguin was already established among his peers in the Parisian art world before he went to the South Seas, and he was still obviously in love with his wife, Mette, when he left. He even tried to get her to join him in the islands.

From 1871 to 1883, Paul Gauguin was employed in the firm of Bertin, stockbrokers, in the Rue Laffitte, a Parisian street with numerous art galleries. Gauguin collected art on a modest scale, and became an amateur, weekend painter. In January 1883, at the age of thirty-five, he quit his job without first warning family or friends, and announced with a flourish: "From now on, I will paint every day."

Yet it was not until 1890—seven years after quitting his job—that he wrote from France to his wife, who was then living in her native Copenhagen, to say:

"May the day come, and perhaps soon, when I can flee to the woods on a South Sea island, and live there in ecstasy, in peace, and for art—far from this European struggle for money. There in

Tahiti, in the silence of the lovely tropical night, I can listen to the sweet murmuring music of my heart, beating in amorous harmony with the mysterious beings of my environment."[11]

Finally, in April 1891, Gauguin sailed for Tahiti.

According to Gauguin's biographer, Robert Goldwater,

> Each of Gauguin's decisions was long and difficult, into each went pondering and doubt, and even fear, until at last the combined pressure of character and accident, of economic circumstances and the absolute necessity to go on painting, forced him to action. At each turning point—from the slow transformation of the collecting amateur into the professional artist (the decision of January 1883 had years of built up pressure behind it) until the move in 1901 to the Marquesas (a change that had been contemplated from the beginning of the South Seas stay) and above all, the reluctant separation from his family—one sees a holding back, a desire to hold on to what he has, until the accumulation of immediate difficulties has forced the creation of a mirage that drives him forward into the future.[12]

There's a touch of Gauguin in most of us at midlife, especially when responsibilities become overbearing, and life loses its zest. As a means of coping, men fantasize, and sometimes their fantasies become reality.

On this matter, Robert Butler and Myrna Lewis have written: "Many lives have an infrastructure—hidden, secret, parallel *infra-lives*—maintained often with enormous expenditures of energy. Some hold close a secret self that, because it is revealed to no one, leads to the elaboration of a richly fantasied other life. For some, extramarital relationships may be more crucial than marriage, the avocation more salient than the vocation, the lives of one's children more highly valued than one's own."[13]

Sailing a small boat alone across the ocean is a stock daydream of weekend sailors. In the summer of 1965, the late Robert Manry lived out just such a dream when he piloted his *Tinkerbelle* across the Atlantic. Manry's infra-life had become real.

"The voyage was something I simply *had* to do, had wanted to do for a long, long time,"[14] said Manry.

During the previous twelve years, Manry had grown increasingly restless and bored with his sedentary life as a copy editor in a windowless city room of the *Cleveland Plain Dealer*. Though he said he was happily married, life for Bob Manry at age forty-seven had long since lost its zing.

As a child he had been thrilled one day by the slide lecture of a young German adventurer who had crossed the Atlantic under sail, and Manry had dreamed of taking such a voyage ever since. Not until 1958, however, could he afford to buy a boat—a thirty-year-old wooden craft, 13½ feet long with a 5¼-foot beam, which he christened *Tinkerbelle*.

Early in 1964, a friend who owned a twenty-five-foot sloop had asked Manry, half in jest, if he would sail it across the Atlantic with him. Manry was elated. He immediately sought and received a leave of absence from his newspaper for the summer of 1965. Manry's friend then had second thoughts, and finally decided against sailing his sloop across the ocean. Thereupon Manry resolved to go it alone in *Tinkerbelle*, confiding his plans only to his wife, family, and a few trusted friends. He allowed his colleagues at the newspaper to continue believing that the original scheme to sail the twenty-five-foot sloop with his friend was still in effect.

During the last half of 1964, and the first half of 1965, Manry continued to prepare secretly for his voyage. He secured equipment, studied maps and charts, and took *Tinkerbelle* for trial runs on Lake Erie.

On the sunny morning of June 1, 1965, *Tinkerbelle* slipped out of Falmouth, Massachusetts, harbor, a little white boat with a bright red mainsail. Its destination was Falmouth, in Cornwall, more than 3,000 miles away, his mission still secret.

During the next seventy-eight days, Manry was to experience in full measure the adventure that had been missing from his life for so long. He roller-coastered over the crests and into the troughs of mountainous waves. He was nearly run down in the fog by giant freighters. He was swept overboard. He suffered acute loneliness, hallucinations, and chilling fear that nearly caused him to turn back. But he also knew periods of tranquillity as he ghosted along under blue, sunny skies, and under the moon and stars, across a phosphorescent sea.

It was, as Manry described it, "A wonderfully far cry from the immobility, tedium, and sometimes harrowing predictability of a copy-desk existence. I couldn't help thinking of the gray flannel suit brigades in the big cities ashore, living in a kind of lock-step frenzy, battling noisy highway or subway traffic to get to work in the morning, and to return home in the evening, existing on pure nervous energy in between, having to be ever alert to opportunities to get ahead, or guard against the encroachment of rivals."[15]

Jung has said that, approaching the fortieth year, "you look back upon the past which has accumulated behind you; and the silent questions reproach you, stealthily or openly: Where am I standing today? Have my dreams come true?"[16]

Manry gave a similar explanation for risking his life crossing the Atlantic Ocean in a sailboat scarcely larger than a dinghy:

"There comes a time when one must decide of one's dreams either to risk everything to achieve them, or to sit for the rest of one's life in the backyard."[17]

Once word leaked out about his voyage, interest in his welfare grew worldwide, a fact that was to surprise him greatly.

Manry had left Falmouth, Massachusetts, an overweight, anonymous copy editor; by his own admission, a very dull man. When he sailed into Falmouth, Cornwall, he'd regained a measure of his youth, including his booming, infectious laugh.

"Robert Manry, riding the winds and the stars, came home last night from the sea," said a dispatch by reporter George J. Barmann in the *Cleveland Plain Dealer* datelined Falmouth, England, whence the paper had sent him to cover Manry's arrival. "In a brilliant blue evening of water and sky, with nearly 50,000 persons cheering and the late sun burning the windows of Falmouth, he came home to land after 3,200 miles of the great and lonely Atlantic. Robert Manry was terribly tired. He could hardly walk. He was waving. He was happy. . . ."[18]

Manry was also forty pounds lighter, tanned and fit, sporting a guardsman's moustache. In crossing the Atlantic, Manry said he'd "struck a blow for all the copyreaders of the world. Sitting at a desk is inclined to make a man desperate. I was becoming a crashing bore."[19] Now he was a free man at last. Book royalties and lecture fees would enable him to break his bondage to the *Plain Dealer*.

In the end, Manry's quest had spiritual overtones.

> Aside from my love of sailing, I looked forward to a small boat voyage because of an inexplicable notion I had that a voyage was a kind of microcosm of life, a life within a life, if you will, with a birth (beginning), youth, maturity, old age, and death (end) and that it was possible for a sailor to express himself in this miniature life—with his techniques, responses to changing conditions, and endurance—somewhat as an artist expresses himself with paint and canvas.
>
> It seemed to me, too, that in this abbreviated life, a sailor had an opportunity to compensate for the blemishes, failures, and disasters of his life ashore. . . .
>
> What had the voyage achieved besides making dreams a reality? I think probably the most important thing it had done for me was to enable me to stand back away from human society ashore, and look at life for a little while from a new perspective. In a sense, the Atlantic Ocean had been a personal Walden Pond on which I had lived simply, in close communion with nature, confronted by elemental dangers and necessities. It certainly had not been a place for trivialities and I think, perhaps, that fact may have done something to make me a better person inside than I had been before.[20]

Six years later, at the age of fifty-three, Manry died of a heart attack.

With astronauts, extreme courage and competitiveness are assumed. Like poets in another place and time, they blaze across the firmament and are as quickly gone. By their early forties, most astronauts find they cannot work themselves to the psychological pitch needed to undergo the mental and physical rigors of training. They seek less stressful pastures.

Not so, Alan Shepard. At age forty-seven, Shepard led *Apollo 14*, this country's third manned expedition to the moon, in early February 1971. To crown his personal triumph, he swatted a golf ball across the lunar surface with a club that he had secreted aboard the spacecraft.

The harshness of Shepard's preflight labors was considerable. Although he'd been close to the manned lunar program in his administrative capacity as astronaut training officer, he hadn't flown in space for nearly a decade.

On May 5, 1961, Shepard had become the first of the seven

original Project Mercury astronauts to rocket into space. But his fifteen-minute suborbital flight down-range from Cape Canaveral in the cramped little Mercury capsule was a primitive maneuver indeed compared with an Apollo flight to the moon.

During the intervening years, Shepard had been named as backup pilot for one flight, and pilot for another flight that had been scrubbed. Then he developed an ear condition known as Meniere's syndrome and was immediately grounded. He took over the job of astronaut training officer, and on the side, he became wealthy through shrewd investments.

In May 1968 an operation corrected his ear problem, and he stepped out of his astronaut training position so that he would be eligible for a lunar flight. As quietly as he could, he started getting up to speed. He flew to the plants of North American, Grumman, and other Apollo contractors for familiarization courses, rode centrifuges, learned to fly a helicopter, started working out in the astronauts' gymnasium, and ran two miles or more a day.

The word soon leaked out, of course, that "Shepo" was trying to make a comeback. "There are a lot of things you can do without appearing obvious, but, oh hell, I guess people knew what was going on. They'd see old man Shepard coming down and doing all these things, and they'd figure he wasn't doing it just for the fun of it. I just kept pussyfooting around doing all these little odds and ends."[21]

Shepard was ultimately selected for lunar flight. Behind his back there was resentment. A few months before blasting off for the moon, Shepard said that he was well aware of the undercurrents. "Nobody said to me: 'Look, you're too old, you've been away too long. Forget it.' Nobody said that directly, but indirectly I've sensed that there are certain people who felt that maybe the old guy shouldn't be given a chance, that it would take me longer to get up to a high level of technical competence than it would other individuals among my colleagues. I think it *has* taken me longer than it would have taken some of them. But I've been working at it quite a while now, and I feel that it's no longer a problem."[22]

As it turned out, Shepard was right.

The Chinese ideograph for "crisis" comes in two parts, they

say. One symbol stands for "opportunity," the other for "danger." There should probably be a third symbol standing for "difficulty." Psychiatrist Herbert Klemme, formerly of the Menninger Foundation in Topeka, Kansas, believes the midlife crisis "is equal in difficulty to any other period of transition in the growth and development of people." Along with many other behavioral scientists he finds that failure to cope with the multiple stresses that characterize the period accounts for the high rates of alcoholism, depression, divorce, and suicide. Not the least of the stresses is success.

During the summer of 1969, Colonel Edward E. "Buzz" Aldrin, Jr., became the second human being to leave his footprints on the surface of the moon, certainly an immortality formula to satisfy most men of thirty-nine, his age at the time. Yet the experience plunged Aldrin into a clinical depression that lasted for years, resulting in a searingly honest stocktaking in the form of an autobiography entitled *Return to Earth*.

Aldrin says that from early childhood, his parents pushed him to excel in whatever he attempted. "Besides my parents, the camp I attended for seven summers gave me another strong motivation for success. It was there I learned to compete, to strive to be the best because winners ate turkey, and losers ate beans. Winners received trophies, losers nothing. . . . This attitude is in the mainstream of the American life style, and I was one of the most willing participants in the competitive area."[23]

From summer camp on through secondary school and beyond, Aldrin's life had been a never-ending succession of goals: West Point, the Air Force, flight school, aerial combat in Korea, spaceflight. And, finally, he had reached the moon, the most important goal of all. Yet in his book, there is no expression of awe, of wonder, of elation. He *does* express considerable anger that his colleague Neil Armstrong had been selected to step onto the moon first.

Where does a programmed man like Aldrin go after he's reached the moon? For the first time in his driven life, Aldrin found himself without a goal. Having never learned to live in the present, and with nothing in the future to strain toward, Aldrin began to slip his psychic moorings.

"I was like an inert ping pong ball being batted about by the whims and motivations of others. I was suffering from what the poets have described as 'the melancholy of all things done.' "[24]

"Groupies" provided diversion for a time; the same kind of young women who flock around rock musicians, racing-car drivers, and other glamour-men. Then there was an extended love affair with a Manhattan divorcée he'd met on the banquet circuit after the lunar flight.

Aldrin tells of his distaste for the public relations tours and political appearances that he'd been pressured into making with his colleagues Neil Armstrong and Michael Collins. He recoiled at the hypocrisy of contracted magazine articles portraying the astronauts as "simon pure" family men. He describes the increasingly incapacitating depression that finally hospitalized him and put an end, in 1972, to the Air Force career he'd resumed after leaving the space program a year earlier.

Since his retirement, Aldrin has been traveling the road back, ranching in California, his marriage intact.

"Few men, particularly those who are motivated toward success, ever pause to reflect on their lives," says Aldrin. "They hurry forward with great energy, never pausing to look over their shoulders to see where they've been. . . . My depression forced me, at the age of forty-one, to stop and for the first time examine my life. The circumstances that brought about my study were extreme, but I now look upon this experience as one of the most valuable things I have done. It taught me to live again, at an age when it is very possible to begin anew."[25]

Dan Levinson believes that "one of the functions of having a hard time around forty is that it increases your possibilities of living better after that, so that the transitional period which is often a time of destructuring one's previous life, also provides the possibility of restructuring in a way that will make life more fulfilling. And the men who don't, who aren't able to restructure their lives to some degree in the early forties, may then have an age-fifty crisis where they have an opportunity to do that; or they may become stagnant and lose touch with their own vitality, which happens to some people in middle age. Or in some cases, they die. Also, there is a kind of death that occurs in the late thirties and early forties, which has to do with the difficulty of getting through the midlife transition."

There is substance to the legend that men gifted in the arts tend to have a particularly stormy midlife passage, and that many founder. Eugene O'Neill was one who nearly went under.

Malcolm Cowley has recalled a time in the late fall of 1923 when O'Neill, then thirty-four, disappeared from his country home in Ridgefield, Connecticut, for a week. He had made his way, with intervening stops, to the Golden Swan, a bar in Manhattan's Greenwich Village. There he'd drunk himself into a stupor, and the manager had put him to bed in an upstairs room.

O'Neill and other literati knew the Golden Swan as "the Hell Hole." It is believed to be one of the models he used in *The Iceman Cometh* for Harry Hope's saloon, a place peopled by men with lost dreams.

"It was the grubbiest drinking parlor west of the Bowery— the No Chance Saloon, Bedrock Bar, the End of the Line Cafe, Bottom of the Rathskeller, as Larry Slade calls it in the play," wrote Cowley. " 'Don't you notice the beautiful calm in the atmosphere?' he continues. 'That's because it's the last harbor. No one here has to worry about where he's going next because there is no farther they can go.' "[26]

After a frantic search, O'Neill's wife found him at the Golden Swan and drove him back to Ridgefield. Following a brief recuperation, O'Neill resumed his work on *Desire Under the Elms.*

A few years later, O'Neill gave up drinking for good.

Dylan Thomas was one who failed, spectacularly, to make it across the shadow line. The great Welsh lyric poet died in 1953 at age thirty-nine after a period of rampant self-destruction, pursued, wrote his widow Caitlin, by devouring American women.

We tend to think of poets peaking early and dying, romantically, in their youth, and many of them do. Thomas always believed that he'd never live to reach forty.

". . . He was convinced that time was ticking against him," says his biographer, Constantine FitzGibbon:

All the more reason, then, to come to terms, poetical terms, with his own past. As he had put it some years before:

> The ball I threw while playing in the park
> Has not yet reached the ground

When it does reach the ground, he must no longer be there, and thus all he can hope truly to comprehend is its upward flight, the first stage of the parabola. And from such comprehension much can be understood about the only vital problem, that of the relationship between birth and death. For even when he was young and easy under the apple boughs

> Time held me green and dying
> Though I sang in my chains like the sea.[27]

In a random study of more than 300 of the world's greatest poets, writers, composers, painters, and sculptors, Elliott Jaques discovered that their death rate jumped far above normal between the ages of thirty-five and thirty-nine. Jaques mentions Raphael, Chopin, Mozart, Baudelaire, Rimbaud, and Watteau.

Jaques first became aware of midlife as a universally critical period for men when he began to notice that crisis invariably marked the work of creative artists at this time. Pursuing this line of thought, he found that the creative crisis expressed itself in three principal ways: "The creative career may simply come to an end, either in a drying up of creative work, or in actual death; creative capacity may begin to show and express itself for the first time; or a decisive change in the quality and content of creativeness may take place."[28]

Jaques also discovered that many artists suffer a fallow period after the middle years, but regain their creativity later on.

The British psychoanalyst reminds us that Ben Jonson had written his plays by the age of forty-three, though he lived for two more decades; that Bach's talents as a composer did not reveal themselves until he was nearly forty; and that the sculpture of Donatello changed markedly in style after age thirty-nine.

Michelangelo was among those who survived a creative lull after age forty. Having completed his *Moses*, by that time, he was not heard from again for fifteen years, when he started to work on the Medici monument. *The Last Judgment* and the Pauline Chapel frescoes followed.

Jaques found that nearly every artistic genius reflected, in both method and content, the effect of having gone through a midlife developmental stage. He subsequently concluded that similar changes probably show up in the work of all men.

Jaques describes the output of artists in their twenties and thirties as spontaneous, "hot-from-the-fire" creativity; their past-forty output as "sculpted" creativity.

"The inspiration may be hot and intense," says Jaques of mid-life creativity. "The unconscious work is no less than before. But there is a big step between the first effusion of inspiration and the finished, created product."[29] It's a worked-over, modified, elaborated kind of creation.

Whereas the content of creative work performed in a man's twenties and thirties has a lyrical and descriptive flavor, there emerges past forty a tragic and philosophical quality which gives way, ideally, to serenity. The idealism of early adulthood is made possible only because at that age, it's still possible to deny one's eventual death and the existence of hate and destructive impulses in one's self.

Jaques believed that his thesis was borne out with dramatic emphasis in the writings of Shakespeare and Dante. Shakespeare's emphasis, for example, shifted from comedy to tragedy in his middle thirties, and thereafter, to tragicomedy. In *The Tempest*, possibly Shakespeare's last work, Prospero offers a supreme expression of life's mystery:

> Our revels now are ended. These our actors
> As I foretold you, were all spirits and
> Are melted into air, into thin air,
> And like the baseless fabric of his vision,
> The cloud-capp'd towers, the gorgeous palaces,
> The solemn temples, the great globe itself
> Yea, all which it inherit, shall dissolve
> And like this insubstantial pageant faded,
> Leave not a rack behind. We are such stuff
> As dreams are made on, and our little life
> Is rounded with a sleep.

Dante started writing *The Divine Comedy* when he was thirty-seven, after being exiled from the city-state of Florence in the year 1302. In Dante's allegory, Jaques saw

a vivid and perfect description of the emotional crisis of the midlife phase, a crisis which would have gripped the mind and soul of the poet whatever his religious outlook, or however settled or unsettled, his external affairs. . . . Even taken quite literally, *The Divine Comedy* is a description of the poet's first full and worked-through conscious encounter with death. He is led through hell and purgatory by his master Virgil, eventually to find his own way, guided by his beloved Beatrice, into Paradise. His final rapturous and mystical encounter with the being of God, represented to him in strange and abstract terms, was not mere rapture, not simply a being overwhelmed by a mystical, oceanic feeling. It was a much more highly organized experience. It was expressly a vision of supreme love and knowledge, with control of impulse and of will, which promulgates the mature life of greater ease and contemplation."[30]

> Here vigor failed the lofty fantasy:
> But now was turning my desire and will,
> Even as a wheel that equally is moved,
> The Love which moves the sun and other stars.[31]

3 *"Everywhere, Adult Brains Seem to Resemble Blighted Trees. . . ."*

"LIFE makes old men of boys who live for a sufficient number of years," said Proust. The boy in every man dies hard, especially the little boy. Sometimes it never does.

More than three decades ago, educator H. A. Overstreet called attention in *The Mature Mind* to the fact that Americans were placing a premium on prolonging immaturity. We were doing this, he said, by overindulging our young, and by failing in our later years to set an example for our children by moving forward into "zestful" intellectual activity.

It's hard to argue that things have improved since those words were written, although there appears to be a greater awareness of the phenomenon. The fact remains that we're still trying to compete with the young rather than getting on with our own lives. And it's no wonder the young often learn to look down upon adults: so many adults are bores.

"The days of youth teem with fragments of living knowledge; with daring philosophies; morning dreams; plans," said William M. Sheldon in *Psychology and Promethean Will.* "But the human mind of forty is commonly vulgar, smug, deadened, and wastes its hours. Everywhere, adult brains seem to resemble blighted trees that have died in the upper branches but yet cling to a struggling green wisp of life about the lower trunk."[1]

Overstreet observes that when a man fails to mature, havoc can result. A forty- or fifty-year-old man, fixated in childhood, is capable of behaving very badly indeed. He figuratively smashes up his toys and breaks the furniture. This is a major theme, too, of the first full-length book about the midlife male written by an American psychoanalyst: Edmund Bergler's *The Revolt of the Middle-Aged Man*, published in 1957. Bergler contends that many men regress in midlife to adolescent behavior patterns.

Robert Butler agrees that we are overly concerned with trying to stay young, but that while we think of ourselves as youth worshipers, we treat children badly in many instances.

"One may see serious problems develop," writes Butler. "There may be fantasies of juvenescence and rejuvenation, or frenetic and sometimes obscene efforts to prove one's continuing youth, strength, and virility through activities of possible physical danger to one's self.

"There may be great hostility and envy toward youth and one's own progeny. There may be longing, nostalgia. Those who have struggled to never grow up—the 'Peter Pans'—are particularly affected, if aware at all of the need to adapt to the changes life brings."[2]

There is evidence at every hand of American society's encouragement of immaturity in men and women. The advertising industry is the most visible example. Vast commercial enterprises have been erected upon woman's vanity and panic about aging. In recent years, the male's fears have been increasingly exploited.

John Revson, the cosmetics executive, says that cosmetic products for men are the fastest-growing part of the industry.

"Middle-aged men today are buying 'male cosmetics' as we're calling them here—or we call them 'grooming products'—because they're looking for that fountain of youth. Everybody is looking to maintain a youthful image today. Everything in our society is youth-oriented."[3]

A man's head of hair has ever been an emotional thing with him and the Grecian Formula man on television is cashing in on this fact. Charles Berg, a British psychiatrist, sees hair as a phallic symbol, loss of hair as a symbolic castration. From primitive times, says Berg in *The Subconscious Significance of Hair*, man has spent a good part of every day working with his hair. "Either he is making it seem longer than it really is, or else he is cutting it off, and making it seem less than it really is, or else, as in shaving, he is endeavoring to remove every trace of it."

In his celebrated *Sexual Life of Savages*, Bronislaw Malinowski tells of the Trobriand Islanders in the Southwest Pacific who cut off all their hair when a member of the tribe dies. When no one dies for a long period, the men's hair is allowed to continue growing. The men comb their hair at a certain point, sing, and walk back and forth for weeks on end while the women admire it and pronounce judgment on its quality. European observers find this pointless, notes Malinowski, but the natives find the whole thing absorbing. "In this, sex plays a considerable part. For the desire to show off, to produce an effect, to achieve 'buture' (renown) in its most valued form, that of irresistible charm, contains a pronounced erotic element."[4]

In some primitive tribes, too, the aging chiefs secretly dyed their gray hairs lest the younger men see it as a sign of weakness and start plotting their removal. Things are not all that different in today's big corporations.

Says Brian Clark, a man's hair stylist: "Well, ten years ago, most of the people who came in for hair coloring were theatrical people, whereas today businessmen have their hair colored. I would say ninety-five percent of our hair coloring business today is from middle-aged businessmen who try to look younger. I think today's society is very competitive, and in order to keep jobs, they have to look younger."[5]

Hair transplanting is yet another "growth" industry. Dr. Norman Orentreich, a Manhattan plastic surgeon, is to the hair follicle what Isaac Stern is to the violin. Twenty years ago he developed a technique for transplanting hair, and it has made him a wealthy man.

Today the eminent trichologist operates with a staff of nearly fifty individuals from a two-floor suite of pop-modern waiting rooms, offices, and research laboratories on Fifth Avenue. Lovely young attendants diddy-bop back and forth with an air of businesslike bustle. It's believed that Frank Sinatra, Joey Bishop, Hugh Downs, and the Chicago Black Hawks' Bobby Hull have all found their way to the house that hair built.

The minor operation is carried out with local anesthesia, the patient usually sitting upright on a chair. Thanks in large measure to Orentreich, most American cities have hair transplanters to-day. Their clientele, once limited to actors and the very wealthy, now include men from all walks of life.

"Men don't sneak in the back door for cosmetic surgery the way they once did," says one Maryland dermatologist with whom I talked. "They wear their head bandages as badges of honor. There's a camaraderie about the whole thing."

A few years ago, when he was in his mid-fifties, Senator William Proxmire, Wisconsin Democrat, underwent four separate hair-transplant treatments, receiving 200 plugs of hair at $7.50 per plug, or 3,000-odd individual shafts of hair for a total of $1,500. When it was all over, he cheerfully held a press conference to report on the progress of his hair-seeding operation.

Plastic surgery does not stop with hair transplants. Proxmire had his doctor remove the slightly puffy pouches beneath his eyes. Says Dr. Arthur Dick, a plastic surgeon: "There's been an enormous increase in middle-aged men coming to the plastic surgeon for help in trying to eliminate those parts of the body which make him look older than he would really like to be. We do face lifts on men. We also do the noses. We also take out some of the telltale marks around the eyelids; we take out double-chins."[6]

Today it's even possible to buy artificial chest hair.

Many men in middle age stop taking their bodies for granted, as the saying goes, and start taking care of them. Hence the growing armies of joggers huffing and puffing through the nation's parks these days. This is obviously to the good. The point remains, however, that while many men struggle to stay physically fit, not all of them make the same effort with their mental faculties.

H. A. Overstreet condemns as recklessly wasteful the billions of dollars that we spend upon education of the young while all but ignoring adult learning. In so doing—and here is his main point—we add further tacit acceptance of the idea that youth is all.

Overstreet argues that education in midlife and thereafter must go far beyond a course of study here or there, the acquiring of a hobby or handicraft to keep mind and hands busy. Only through active, systematic studies can we change the vision we now have of middle and old age as periods of stagnation and decay, hence to be feared and denigrated. Only through a wholehearted return to great literature, music, philosophy, art, and religious concerns can we mature, achieve fulfillment, and set examples for those who are coming behind us.

Dan Levinson's theory of adult development owes much to his study of the midlife theme in literature. His appreciation of great writing reveals itself in dozens of quotations and lines of poetry pinned to the bulletin boards of his small office in the Connecticut Mental Health Center in New Haven. On one of my visits, he drew my attention to two lines from Yeats' "The Circus Animals":

> I must lie down where all the ladders start
> In the foul rag and bone shop of the heart.[7]

"I think what Yeats means—God knows what he means—but I think what he means is that the 'ladder' is not what life is really all about," says Levinson. "And if you can make the ladder less important and get into yourself, then you're going to have to deal with a lot of *stuff*, but out of *that*, you can kind of sort out and decide what's important—and feel good if you come somewhere near it."

Levinson was born in 1920 and raised in Los Angeles where he took his psychology degree from UCLA in 1940, and his master's two years later. Also in 1942, he married Maria Hertz, a fellow graduate student in psychology and the daughter of an Austrian public official who'd fled Vienna with his family in 1938. They have two sons: Mark, a musician, and Douglas, a medical student.

After receiving his Ph.D. from the University of California at Berkeley in 1947, Levinson taught psychology there and at Western Reserve, before moving to Harvard in 1950, where he became an authority on career development of men in their twenties and thirties. When Levinson transferred to Yale in 1966, he became interested in studying men at a somewhat older age level, and carrying his research beyond career problems.

Throughout 1968, Levinson met informally with about a dozen

Yale faculty members in psychology, psychiatry, and sociology, who had expressed interest in the problems of men in their mid-to-late-thirties and early forties. At forty-eight, Levinson was the oldest member of the group; the others were all between thirty-five and forty-five.

As finally presented to the National Institute of Mental Health, the Levinson male midlife study was somewhat unusual in its method. A more general practice in such research is to gather test data from hundreds and sometimes thousands of individuals through questionnaires, then feed the data into computers and develop hypotheses therefrom. Instead, the Yale researchers elected to study a few men intensively, their aim being to construct nothing less than a theory of adult development—an ambitious undertaking.

The study took effect officially on January 1, 1969, and Levinson finished work on it in 1975. The forty volunteer subjects, in the 35-to-45 age range, came to Levinson's office periodically and talked on a one-to-one basis with members of the Levinson team for a total of about twenty hours apiece. These confidential, tape-recorded interviews were then transcribed into 300-page psychobiographies of each man. Recurrent themes emerged from these biographies, and it was from these themes that Levinson wove his theory.

It's my personal view that Levinson's study represents his own "special bet," an attempt to synthesize his personal and professional experience, primarily for his own satisfaction, not to draw attention to himself or advance his career at Yale. Like most such bets, Levinson's included a strong element of risk. He would be spending years, and government funds, exploring the minds of forty men, yet there was no guarantee that these minds would yield material for a coherent theory.

Furthermore, when Levinson began his work more than seven years ago, there were few detailed maps of the region he was about to explore. Freud's work, of course, has tremendous relevance to the study of midlife. But Freud, interestingly, had little personal interest in either middle or old age, in theory or in his psychiatric practice. This is ironic in light of Freud's own increasing creativity as he grew older. Freud was forty-four when he published his principal work, *The Interpretation of Dreams,* and nearly seventy before he introduced the terms id, ego, and superego.

Carl Jung and Erik Erikson provided important guideposts for the Yale researchers. Jung wrote of middle age with characteristic genius, though in general and sometimes mystical terms. Erikson was the first psychoanalyst to produce anything like a theoretical model of the life span from birth to death, but some psychiatrists find his work on middle age, per se, limited and general in character.

It is true that, from earliest times, great thinkers have concerned themselves with the mysteries of the life cycle. Aristotle, Horace, Rousseau, and Shakespeare, among many, have depicted life as an unfolding of stages. But it was not until the twentieth century that beginning efforts were undertaken to study segments of the life course in a scientific way. The heavy emphasis since that time has been upon life's morning. Courses in human development have attained a measure of popularity, but the reading list gets skimpy when the class reaches the study of midlife, then fattens again when old age becomes the subject matter.

There are practical reasons why modern behavioral scientists have until recently left midlife to Edward Albee, T. S. Eliot, Arthur Miller, John Updike, Saul Bellow, Joseph Heller, and other writers. To study modern man over his life course, or even a major portion thereof, poses nearly insuperable problems of cost and methodology.

"Unlike the seasons of the year, or even the stages of childhood, nobody sees the human life cycle more than once, and then only through a biologically ever-changing perspective," says George Vaillant, a psychiatrist at Harvard, which has conducted one of the few longitudinal or continuing studies that follow an individual over a long period of time. "Like van Leeuwenhoek gazing through his microscope for the first time, the investigators who have tried to harvest the growth studies view a phenomenon never seen before—human beings as they actually develop. Yet as the right questions were discovered, the right time to ask them had often passed."[8]

It was not until 1974, that *The Comparative Textbook of Psy-*

chiatry included a chapter on middle age. Robert Butler, who authored the chapter, complained at its outset that "professional and scientific literature has been strangely silent about middle age." Popular nonfiction has been equally silent. The first such work was Walter B. Pitkin's slim volume, *Life Begins at Forty*, published in 1932, and nothing since has caught on like that one. A quick nod must, however, be made in the direction of a fine little book by Barbara Fried entitled *The Middle Age Crisis*, published in 1967.

One reason for the sparsity of material on the American adult male, in my opinion, has been his traditional reluctance to discuss his innermost feelings with spouse, friend, clergyman, or physician. Admiral Byrd touches upon this, saying that the experience he describes in *Alone* was "so personal that for four years I could not bring myself to write it. And since my sufferings bulk so large in it and since man's instinct is to keep such things to himself, I did not see how I could write about Advanced Base and still escape making an unseemly show of my feelings."[9]

Psychologist Douglas Heath of Haverford College is among many behavioral scientists who believe that the American male's inability to express his emotions is one of his principal problems. For more than a decade, Heath has been conducting a study of nearly seventy Haverford graduates who are now in their early-to mid-thirties. Heath tells me these men are exceptionally intelligent, hard-driving, and "successful" in their careers. Their marriages, however, are another story.

One-third of the men have been divorced or have suffered disruptive marital difficulties such as separations. The wives' almost unanimous complaint is that their husbands give so much of themselves to their work that they have little emotional substance left for them. The men hardly ever tell their wives they love them. "I have *never* seen my husband cry," is a familiar observation.

For their part, the husbands complain that their wives are either unwilling or unable to provide the kind of emotional support they feel they require. Often, says Heath, the men reach out rather desperately for their daughters.

"I was puzzled, too, by the large number of men who had not

made any close friends since college," says Heath. "The typical pattern is to be exclusively preoccupied by work and by one's family. One psychological consequence may be that the burden of fulfilling one's needs for intimacy, emotional release, and support falls very heavily on one's wife."

One man with a sense of humor about himself said recently in *The New York Times* that he'd tried just about everything, including primal scream therapy but even that didn't work. "I screamed for a while, but it didn't help; everybody was screaming, and nobody was listening."

Like Heath, Dan Levinson has observed that many men seem to feel that they have no one in whom to confide. "It seems to be a problem of the times. I don't assume it's a brand-new problem, but it's a problem we've become more aware of now that people in middle life are more ready, I think, than they used to be, to recognize that their lives aren't all they want, that they would like to make life better, that they would like to reexamine their values, that they would like to consider alternatives. But a lot of things are considered undiscussable, and those that are discussable, there's no one to talk to about."

Levinson's own subjects did freely discuss undiscussables, coming to accept him and his fellow researchers as something between real friends and "paid friends," as psychoanalysts and other professional helpers are sometimes known. Herein, it seems to me, lies the study's potential. For Levinson has demonstrated, in his speaking appearances, writings, and interviews, that he's been able to integrate the study's findings with the myriad strands of his own, and his colleagues' experiences, and to express just what it means, what it feels like, to be a middle-aged man of some education and substance in this country today. At the same time, he identifies, in a general way, stages that he has found most men pass through en route to the midlife transition.

After the Yale psychologist addressed the Society for Life History Research in Psychopathology in the early 1970s, for example, the psychiatrists, psychologists, and geneticists who largely comprise the organization, jumped to their feet and cheered.

Levinson's hope is to reach an audience beyond academia with his developmental view of adulthood, so that today's forty-year-olds will understand themselves better and come to realize that if they're beset by assorted demons, they are not alone. Further, he wants them to realize that the midlife transition, crisis, call it what you will, is a natural, developmental process, and that while the losses are all too obvious at this time of life—and while the losses are going to increase—men should be equally aware of the not-inconsiderable gains, and be prepared to take advantage of them.

4 "Look How Marvelous Our Little Boy Is!"

THE TERM "middle age" is a pejorative one, just a step removed from "old age." Dan Levinson tells me he tries to avoid using it, but with mixed success. People are constantly asking him when he considers a man middle-aged. His answer is not a simple one.

"To me, 'middle-aged' is neither a descriptive nor a technical term," says the Yale psychologist. "It's really an idiomatic term. If you ask a man of thirty-eight if he's middle-aged, chances are he'll be offended. If you ask a man in his early forties, he'll say: 'I'm trying to decide if I am'; or he'll say: 'I don't like the idea.' But from forty-five on, he'll say: 'I guess I'm middle-aged.'

"If only we could relax about these terms and use them descriptively, so that middle age would refer to an appropriate age period. Middle age is generally thought to begin around forty or forty-five and go on to sixty or sixty-five.

"A term like 'youth' is much like 'middle age,' for it describes a state of mind as well as an approximate age period. You can retain your youthfulness at any age, but people generally think about youth in the twenties. Under twenty is usually adolescence. And we all know that when you reach thirty, you're over the hill, right?

"There's a question about what to do with the decade of thirty, because at thirty-two, say, one is clearly not middle-aged, yet one is no longer a 'youth' in most people's eyes."

Levinson has tried to resolve the problem by defining the period of 20 to 40 as "young adulthood"; 35 to 45 as the "midlife decade"; and 40 to 65 as "middle adulthood," or, reluctantly, "middle age." He speaks of the period beyond 65 as "late adulthood."

Throughout most of Levinson's career, he has worked the border land between psychology and sociology. And because he was just as interested in man's relationship to his outer as to his inner world, he included sociologists on his research staff. The interdisciplinary group conceived the "Individual Life Structure," which they define as "the overall pattern or character of an individual life at a given time in both external and internal aspects."

Externally, life structure refers to the ways that a man is engaged in the world—through his work, family, social class, and organizations. Internally, life structure has to do with the meaning the world holds for a man—through his personal values, aspirations, goals, and fantasies.

Within his life structure, a man works at appropriate developmental tasks at each life stage, an observation that the Levinson group shares with Erikson. A man moves on to the next stage only when he begins to concern himself with the new tasks of that stage. Therefore, Levinson sees adult development as a fluid thing.

"The life structure changes and evolves over the course of adulthood; sometimes slowly and imperceptibly; sometimes in faster, qualitative jumps," said Levinson at a symposium sponsored by the Menninger Foundation. "There are times when it is forming, times when it is destructuring and reforming to a greater or lesser degree. In our view, adult psychosocial development is the evolution of the individual life structure."[1]

Levinson believes that most men go through four basic developmental stages during the young adulthood period from the late teens to the mid-to-late thirties: "Leaving the Family," late teens through early twenties; "Getting Into the Adult World," mid-twenties; "Age Thirty Transition," late twenties through early thirties; "Settling Down," mid- to late thirties. He believes that while these changes in the twenties and thirties are important ones, this twenty-year period retains a certain character.

"But the next change, that begins near forty, is not going to be just more of the same—but something different. The midlife transition is, in our view, a *universal* period in adult life. It may take the form of a crisis, in the sense of turmoil, disruption, and dramatic change, as we've seen. It may go more smoothly. But at the end of it, the man will be different from what he was at the beginning."[2]

Levinson's study picks up the male when he is in his late teens, struggling to emerge from adolescence. "If you talk of adolescence, everyone knows what it's like," said Levinson expanding on this theme to me one day in his office in downtown New Haven. "It's generally understood that adolescence is a developmental transition; you don't even need a fancy word for it. The adolescent is something between a child and an adult.

"The problem with the adolescent is that he's got some losses, and some possible gains, and he doesn't quite know what to make of them. And he wants the pleasures of the child but the advantages of the adult—but not the responsibilities—and he goes around and around in that. He's sorting a lot out. And he has a certain amount of turmoil because that's a tough change to make. But my notion is that any developmental transition will have some of these qualities. A lot of what we attribute to 'adolescence' is not adolescence as such: It's developmental change; moving from one period to another; upsetting the applecart.

"There *are* parallels between adolescence and the midlife decade and these include the disruptions of any developmental transition. Another is, as we've said, adolescent wishes and conflicts and aspirations are often reactivated during the midlife decade. 'I feel as though I were eighteen!' There is also reactivation of even earlier wishes, conflicts, and so on. So it isn't just a matter of having another chance to settle adolescent conflicts, though that's part of it. But also, there are practical problems that have to do with being forty—and 'What am I going to do about them?' "

Levinson conceives of the "Leaving the Family" stage—starting from about age eighteen and lasting through the early twenties—as a transitional period between adolescent life in the family, and entry into the adult world. During this period, a young man starts putting physical and psychological distance between himself and his parents, though the business of trying to gain independence from parents begins, in a sense, even earlier, and lasts far beyond this particular stage—"sometimes forever," Levinson wryly observes.

Putting it another way, says Levinson, this is the start of "Becoming One's Own Man," another continuing process that he likes to call "BOOM!" when it reaches a critical stage in midlife.

When a young man goes away to college—or takes his first job, say, but continues to live at home—he gains an intermediate measure of autonomy and responsibility. He's half in the family, half out. Once he has started to make a place for himself in the world, once his center of gravity has started to shift from his family to a new home base, then he moves into the next stage, "Getting Into the Adult World," which occupies his mid-twenties.

Our hero is now busily exploring sexual, marital, and career possibilities. This is a time of provisional commitment; of starts and stops. "The young man tries to establish an occupation, or an occupational direction, consistent with his interests, values, and sense of self. He begins to engage in more adult friendships and sexual relationships, and to work on what Erikson has termed the ego stage of 'Intimacy' versus 'Aloneness.'

"The overall developmental task of the 'Getting Into the Adult World' period is to explore the available possibilities of the adult world, to arrive at an initial definition of oneself as an adult, and to fashion an initial life structure that provides a viable link between the valued self and the wider adult world."[3]

"The Dream" now becomes, if it hasn't already, a vital element in the young man's growth.

"The core of the dream is a sense of self in the world; a vision, an imagined possibility that generates excitement, aliveness, energy—hope. A major task of these first periods is to give form to the dream and put it in one's life, to start building a life structure around the dream. To the extent that one's explorations and initial choices are influenced by the dream, it makes sense to be an adult. One can enjoy the present and anticipate the future."[4]

In a research paper which he authored with four of his

colleagues, Levinson wrote that, "Where such a dream exists, we are exploring its nature and vicissitudes over the life course. Major shifts in life direction at subsequent ages are often occasioned by a reactivation of the sense of betrayal or compromise of the dream. That is, very often in the crises that occur at age thirty, forty, or later, a major issue is the reactivation of a guiding dream, frequently one that goes back to adolescence, or to the early twenties, and concern with its failure."[5]

In a man's early twenties, there's invariably a vague, romantic quality to the dream. Writer subjects in the Levinson study envisioned their works riding the bestseller crests one day; the biologists imagined themselves stepping forward to receive the Nobel Prize. The ebb-and-flow character of Levinson's view of the life cycle becomes particularly clear when he talks about the twenty-year-old and his dream.

"There's a myth that psychologists and psychiatrists have helped perpetuate and that is that development occurs in childhood and adolescence, and that, suddenly, at the end of adolescence, we all become 'adults'; that there's this crazy stuff with adolescence where we react to life in all sorts of irrational ways, but then between eighteen and twenty-one, we become adult, we become more realistic," he said in an interview.

"And my view is that those beginnings of adulthood are *very full* of the preadult self, and we don't just get away from childhood and adolescence, and that, suddenly, at the end of adoles-In every man in his early twenties, there is a little boy whose voice is strong, and who wants to rescue the fair damsel and do heroic things, to build a better mousetrap, or win the Heisman Trophy—all the forms it can take: athletic, intellectual, sexual.

"He's a little boy to the extent that he wants to be recognized by the world in general, and also, particularly, by his parents. But along with the little boy who is saying: 'Look what a big brain, or a big something, I have, Mommy, and maybe Daddy,' is also the beginnings of an adult who is saying, 'I want to be grown up and I want to pursue adult goals.' Of course I'd like to win the Nobel Prize, but mainly I want to be a biologist; that's my profession.' So he looks at things 'more realistically.' So there's all sorts of trappings of reality; to be grown up and reasonable and define success in terms of the adult world: to get promoted, to write good things, to be a professional athlete, a master carpenter, or whatever. The little boy goes on wanting his parents to say, 'Look how marvelous our little boy is!'; and the adult part of him says, 'I'd like my parents to appreciate what I'm doing, but I'm *not* their little boy anymore, and I don't want them treating me like a little boy, and telling me what a good boy I am. I'm independent now. I hope we can be friends, but if we can't, well. . . . Can't they see I'm a man?' "

Levinson continues:

"Being one's own man—that has a particular meaning in the late thirties, but the idea of being one's own man you can have at sixteen, or twenty-six, or fifty-six, in different forms. And that's one of the things that's so tricky about all this. Any issue you raise, or any phrase you apply to a particular developmental period, there are analogues to that at a lot of other times. And you've got to get beyond the phrase to the meaning of it, and its particular character."

To a lesser degree than age forty, age thirty has a psychological effect upon men. Nearing the "Age Thirty Transition," a young man generally takes pause. He reassesses his line of work, asking himself whether he has the talent and taste for it; whether he should change course, or continue on; whether his career compromises his dream.

The questions are not as urgent, or as wide-ranging, as the ones he'll ask himself ten years later. For approaching thirty, a man still has, or believes he has, time to maneuver, to compensate for false starts, mistakes, and missteps. Stocktaking at age thirty thus has, as Levinson puts it, a different character than it does at forty.

Some men do choose this time to kick over the applecart, however. C. D. B. Bryan III, whose first novel won the 1965 Harper Prize, recalled for me one day the details of his age-thirty soul-searching in the late 1960s.

"There I was one evening, sitting on my porch in Tuxedo Park," said Bryan. "I guess I had everything, even a Melnor traveling lawn sprinkler. I guess it was that sprinkler that set me to thinking about my values. Then I went back into the house and

there on my television set was a race riot and the Vietnam War
—all in living color."

Whereupon, says Bryan, he divorced his wife, remarried, and
moved to Iowa City to become involved for a time with the University of Iowa's Writers' Workshop.

Levinson finds the "Age Thirty Transition" lasts from about age
twenty-eight to thirty-two. Now, as a man starts into the "Settling
Down" stage, life becomes real.

"We are saying that it is not until the early thirties that a man
truly begins to settle down in a full sense. At this point, he has a
life structure that he will settle for with enthusiasm and excitement, or with serious misgivings, or in bland acquiescence. Life
becomes less provisional. He makes deeper commitments, takes
on more adult responsibilities, invests more of himself in family
and personal interests, and within this framework, pursues long-
range plans and goals.

"The two major tasks of the settling down period are first, to
find a niche in adult society, to make a place, build a nest, create
an order for pursuing one's interests. One joins the tribe. Second,
one works at 'making it,' planning, striving, moving onward and
upward, giving shape to his ambitions and having a timetable
that defines his path and his pace of travel."[6]

Levinson and his colleagues find that coexisting with—yet anti-
thetical to—the nest-building and ladder-climbing of this period
is man's instinct "to be free, unfettered, not tied to any structure
no matter how great its current satisfaction, nor how alluring its
future promise; always open to new possibilities, ready to soar,
wander, quest in all directions as the spirit moves one."[7]

This disposition to soar and wander has a way of surfacing during or after the midlife transition.

"The Mentor" now becomes increasingly important to the
young man on the rise, says Levinson, who has observed that
nearly all the successful men in his study had had one or more
mentors, sometimes starting when they were in their twenties.

The mentor is usually about ten years older. He may be a
senior officer in the company; an older writer or editor; the head
of a department in the university; the foreman in the plant. The
mentor has achieved Erikson's stage of generativity; he cares

about the young man's future. He becomes the younger man's informal guide and sponsor, figuratively putting his arm around him.

"But as we use the term, the mentor does much more. He supports the young man's dream, and helps him put it into the world. He regards the young man as an adult, as a younger man, not as a boy. And he relates as an older peer, not as a father; and welcomes the young man into a new, active world and defines him as a valuable, working adult. He thus helps the young man overcome the father-son polarity, the sense of being a boy dependent upon and struggling with paternal adults.

"Even with this help, however, the struggle goes on for many years. The mentor serves an essential developmental function. Through this relationship, one may in time, but only after about age forty, give up the search for the father and become a genuine 'father' and mentor to others."[8]

The young man's wife serves a similar function in that she creates a life structure "within which the dream can take place. Alternatively, she may remain unconnected to the dream, or even antagonistic to it. Of course, the relationship will be durable and further his development only if it also furthers hers."[9]

By the time an individual has reached his early thirties, he knows his trade; he's a professional; he has saleable skills and a certain freedom of movement. Consequently, he feels more "manly," more autonomous than ever before. And it is true that he is more independent than he was, say, under his parents' thumb. But he's not as independent as he thinks he is. And in a few more years this will come home to him forcefully. For no matter how successful he may have been up to this point, he's still very much a *junior* member of his enterprise.

"The most you can get by age thirty or thirty-two is the bottom rung of the ladder," says Levinson. "You may be at the top of middle-management but you're a whole world away from top management which you can see up there ahead dimly."

A man's task is now to become a *senior* member of his enterprise, a vice-president of the Stuyvesant Bank. He wants this desperately, in most cases, says Levinson. And with this urge, at about thirty-five, he enters a new phase of "Becoming One's Own

Man." Levinson sees "BOOM" as the beginning of the end of young adulthood, the culmination of "Settling Down."

Now Good Old Charlie realizes that he has not been as autonomous as he'd thought he was, that he's been too eager to please his bosses, has lacked courage on too many occasions to speak up and act as a man. He wants now to speak with authority, to try out his own ideas, to be affirmed by his organization and by society.

In the gravity field of forty now, he invariably seizes upon some key event that will symbolize his success or failure: partnership in his law firm by forty; a full professorship by forty; a best seller by forty, and so on.

Charlie now becomes hypersensitive about his masculinity. At work, says Levinson, "one is very vulnerable to feelings of being slighted, being intimidated, being dependent; anything that has to do with being a 'little boy,' having to take orders.

"The novelist suddenly feels that he's being pushed around by his editor, his publisher, his agent, his critics. He realizes that he's been telling himself he's independent when he's not.

"The businessman in his middle thirties is angry because number one is not delegating enough to him; or he knows he can do number one's job better than number one. He wants to try out *his* way of doing things. That's the rational part.

"But the irrational part has to do with the fact that along with the wish to be authoritative, innovative, creative, try his own ideas, take responsibility, there's still that little boy problem. He doesn't want to be responsible, or he may have doubts that he can make it. There is the wish to be independent *and* the wish to be dependent.

"There are Oedipal things in here. There is that little boy saying to the person symbolized as father, the number one guy, the boss, whoever it is: 'You've got what I want and I'm going to get it if I have to kill you for it,' but then there's the guilt about that. Because to succeed means knocking off the old man, and there are guilt feelings and all kinds of irrational feelings that get in the way of succeeding. It's still the little boy struggling with Daddy, fearing that he'll be wiped out, killed, castrated; and to some extent feeling he should be because what he wants is so bad. So there's that aspect: The authority at work is seen as an oppressor; he's oppressing the little boy.

"Often, in reality, the man in authority *is* oppressive, and a son-of-a-bitch, so it's a problem of sorting out the realistic appraisal of the authority, and the realistic appraisal of oneself.

"The analogue of this at home would be the projecting of various Oedipal 'bad mother' images on his wife. 'She doesn't understand me; she won't listen to me; she isn't nice to me; she won't give me the breast, or the whatever part of her I happen to want. She's oppressive; she may devour me.'

"Subjectively, there's that mother in there, and she keeps telling him, 'You're no good, or you mustn't do this or that.' Some men—I don't say this is universal—but some men come to regard their wives in this fashion. The general thing about the late thirties is that this kind of conflict is there and can come out in various forms. Some men will feel their wives are unappreciative. 'She's not sensual enough; she's not sympathetic enough; she doesn't believe in me; she doesn't understand what it is I really want, and I can't tell her what I really want. There's no way I can get through to her.' Feelings of this sort. Again, there's this mixture of rationality and irrationality, and it varies a lot."

Levinson finds that there often are real incompatibilities. "Either the choice was poor in the first place, or it might have suited both people early but over time it didn't. 'Were we ever in the same world?' Or, 'We were in the same world once, but something happened.' Frequently when a man feels that way it is terribly hard for them to work at getting together. Some kind of gulf has been created that's almost impossible to bridge. Yet in some cases, it does get worked out."

During BOOM, a man scuttles his mentor. "The person who was formerly so loved and admired, and who was experienced as giving so much, comes to seem as hypercritical, oppressively controlling, seeking to make one over in his own image rather than fostering one's independence and individuality; in short, as a tyrannical and egocentric father rather than a loving, enabling mentor."[10]

Levinson finds that the relationship lasts three or four years, ten years at the outside, and that after forty, a man cannot have mentors. The relationship ends either bitterly, or in more friendly fashion, with a gradual lessening of involvement. In any event, it generally lasts only as long as it proves useful to the younger man's purpose. And when the younger man's dependency on the mentor comes to an end, he feels rejuvenated.

"One may have friendships or significant working relationships after this, but the mentor relationship in its more developed form is rare, at least in our sample, and in our life experience. It is given up as part of 'Becoming One's Own Man.'"[11]

Sigmund Freud (1856–1939) and Carl Gustav Jung (1875–1961) left behind in their seven-year correspondence from 1906 to 1913, a remarkable chronicle of the birth, flowering, and savage death of a mentor relationship.

Jung had read Freud's *The Interpretation of Dreams* at the turn of the century, and had been overwhelmed with admiration for the work of the older man. Jung had initiated the correspondence and relationship in 1906 by sending one of his own works to Freud for his opinion.

Jung's early letters are almost servile; Freud's replies stern. "Dear Friend, you seem to recognize that I am right, which disposes of one point," wrote Freud.[12]

But with the passage of time, Jung began to question some of Freud's theories and to develop his own. Freud reacted with anger, and the men started accusing each other of being neurotic.

On January 3, 1913, Freud wrote: ". . . It is a convention among us analysts that none of us feels ashamed of his own bit of neurosis. But one who while behaving abnormally keeps shouting that he is normal gives ground for the suspicion that he lacks insight into his illness. Accordingly, I propose that we abandon our personal relations entirely. I shall lose nothing by it, for my only emotional tie with you has long been a thin thread. . . ."[13]

Three days later, Jung replied: "I accede to your wish that we abandon our personal relations, for I never thrust my friendship on anyone. You yourself are the best judge of what this moment means to you. 'The rest is silence.'"[14]

Jung was thirty-eight when, with this letter, he became his own man. "BOOM!" as Levinson would say.

When a man gives up his dependency upon his mentor, he gives up being a little boy in search of a father. He becomes an adult in an adult world. *He* now becomes a "father" to younger men in a symbolic way.

"An age difference of twelve to fifteen years is sort of a minimum for a younger person to regard an older person as a generation removed," says Levinson. "So when you get into your late thirties, there are young adults who are twenty or so who see you clearly a generation removed, and in that sense, 'paternal.' And that has at least two elements to it: One has to do with 'caring.' How does a man engage in 'caring' for other men? Well, if he's a boss, he has their interests at heart, somehow. He's concerned about their welfare, and his relationship to them is important. They can in some way turn to him, count on him. He must have qualities of that sort.

"The second element is the exercise of authority. The 'father' is in an authoritative relationship to the 'son.' But what does that mean? What is involved is the *judicious* exercise of authority. That is one of the eternal questions, and one of the least discussed. He must be neither coercive nor permissive. That question is not likely to become focal and serious for a man before his late thirties."

In his celebrated biography of Gandhi, Erik Erikson analyzes the changes the Indian leader went through from about age thirty-five to fifty, and emphasizes this business of caring. Gandhi "cared" for India; he "cared" for India's poor. He was forty when he created his doctrine of nonviolence.

" 'Caring' for the adversary is an important part of Gandhi's philosophy," says Levinson. "He's still an adversary, and you don't deny there is conflict. But you oppose him nonviolently and with caring. That is an advanced moral position which is hard to arrive at before you are around forty."

During most of the twenty-year period of young adulthood in this country, a man more or less cheerfully engages in self-denial, postponing fulfillment. He believes that he will be rewarded for hard work, loyalty, fortitude, inventiveness, productivity, and other work ethic virtues. He will be a *success*. And what is the nature of this success?

"In America, success has meant making money and translating it into status, becoming famous," says former Princeton University historian Richard M. Huber. "Success was not earned by being a loyal friend or a good husband. It was a reward for performance on the job. It is not the same thing as happiness—which is how you feel."[15]

Success always lies up ahead, just beyond the horizon. But by the time a man has reached forty in our system, he has reached the horizon, observes sociologist Charlotte Darrow of Levinson's research team. "Whatever illusions he might have had before, this is, inevitably, a time of assessment," she told *McCall's* writer Maggie Scarf. "He knows fairly clearly just where he has placed in life's battles—and just about how much further he can go.

"At this point, many beliefs and values—all of those obvious 'truths' that support a man while he is 'Settling Down'—may suddenly come into question. For he's been engaged in a huge effort, working toward the thing that was supposed to make him happy in some glorious, distant future. And now here he is, and things suddenly don't seem so clear."[16]

If a man sees himself as a failure, he must come to terms with this fact—or gird himself for a "harsh effort" later on as Manry and Pirsig did. But even if he has succeeded in reaching his goals, says Levinson, "there will still be a disparity between what he hoped for, and what life allows him." By the time a man's dream comes true, the magic has usually gone out of it.

"The midlife transition occurs whether the individual succeeds or fails in his search for affirmation by society. At thirty-eight he thinks that if he gains the deserved success, he'll be all set. The answer is, he will not. He is going to have a transition whether he is affirmed or not; it is only the form that varies.

"The central issue is not whether he succeeds or fails in achieving his goals. The issue, rather, is what to do with the *experience of disparity* between what he has gained in an inner sense from living within a particular structure and what he wants for himself. The sense of disparity between 'what I've reached at this point' and 'what it is I really want' instigates a soul-searching for 'what it is I really want.'

"To put it differently, it is not a matter of how many rewards one has obtained; it is a matter of the *goodness of fit between the life structure and the self.* A man may do extremely well in achieving his goals and yet find his success hollow or bitter-sweet."[17]

"To the possession of the self, the way is inward," said Plotinus, the Egyptian-born Roman philosopher who lived two centuries after Christ. But as Jack Weinberg has observed, American men have great difficulty in embarking upon such a journey. The American man, and woman too, for that matter, is a doer, with a low tolerance for ambiguity. Besides, our whole society conspires against the inward journey. "It lives too fast," said Thoreau.

The journey must be made, however. The man must change, and his values must change. Said Jung in *Modern Man In Search of a Soul:*

> We cannot live the afternoon of life according to the program of life's morning, for what was great in the morning will be little at evening, and what in the morning was true, will at evening have become a lie. I have given psychological treatment to too many people of advanced years, and have looked into the secret chambers of their souls, not to be moved by this fundamental truth.[18]

Early in a man's searching for values more true to himself, a process that Levinson calls "de-illusionment" takes place. "I don't mean 'disillusionment' in the sense of cynicism, although that can happen too," he explains. "I mean the shedding of illusions, the attempt to deal with the reality of oneself and the world in a more honest way."

Dr. Roy Menninger, the fifty-year-old president of the Menninger Foundation, concurs: "One of the things that makes this midlife period most interesting to me is the importance of myths, how many of us live our lives with a set of assumptions that are illusions," he said in an interview in his office on the campus-like foundation grounds in Topeka. "One of these is that we are going to live forever; the second one is that we have yet time to do what's important; and the third is that we are constantly moving forward, so that we are getting ever closer to those adolescent goals: success, wealth, and fame. And it sometimes takes a heart attack to make one realize how much we've been sustaining ourselves with fantasies.

"What is it that makes it so hard to accept today as an experience; why must everything be pegged to achieving something tomorrow in order to make today worth anything? Why can't we simply recognize that things are pretty good the way they are—and they aren't necessarily going to be better?"

Courage is required to take one's own measure. If successful, a man will emerge from this exercise with the humility that is the beginning of wisdom, with fear beneath his feet, better equipped to cope with less cosmic and more practical problems of this age period.

Freud believed that fear of self-knowledge lay at the root of much mental illness. In this vein, Jack Weinberg says:

"Each of us carries within him a legend about himself: 'I have yet to find a photograph that does me justice!' We don't want to believe what we see. It takes time to arrive at and understand the personal legend that each human carries within. I use the term 'legend' for in all of us, the concept of the self as a dynamic force interacting with the environment is often tinged with wish rather than reality, and is thus distorted and obscured.

"It is when the legend of the self is not in concert with the facts as they are that discomfort and illness make their appearance. The legend leads to the romanticizing of the self, and a poetic interpretation of reality which is not easy to discern."

Carl Jung said that to accomplish the tasks of midlife stocktaking, a man must regain a strong measure of the spiritual that he has lost, and that the loss of spiritual moorings was at the root of the mental illness among all his patients over the age of about thirty-five.

Though Jung was a stout Protestant, he criticized the church because he said its admonitions to faith and the performance of charitable works do not satisfy modern man. He was equally critical of his former mentor Freud whose ideas, he said, failed to satisfy his patients' spiritual needs.

Jung believed that neuroses spring from a failure to acknowledge that religious ideas have always been deeply embedded in the psyche. Yet he took a psychological view of religion and he called for a union between religion and behavioral science. For example, he meets the subject of death matter-of-factly.

"As a physician I am convinced that it is hygienic ... to discover in death a goal towards which one can strive; and that shrinking away from it is something unhealthy and abnormal which robs the second half of life of its purpose. I therefore consider the religious teaching of a life hereafter consonant with the standpoint of psychic hygiene. . . ."[19]

Jung encourages man to continue his striving to find his way between the blind faith demanded by the church, and intellectual rationalism that dismisses the spiritual.

If a man can emerge from all this with an honest vision of himself, then he can start being honest with others—perhaps for the first time in his life. Anne Morrow Lindbergh wrote of this greatest of midlife compensations in her durable little book, *Gift from the Sea*, first published more than twenty years ago and still selling briskly. Though addressed to women in middle age, her words are no less applicable to men, in my opinion.

"Perhaps middle age is, or should be, a period of shedding shells; the shell of ambition, the shell of material accumulation and possessions, the shell of the ego. Perhaps one can shed at this stage of life, as one sheds in beach-living, one's pride, one's false ambitions, one's mask, one's armor.

"Was that armor not put on to protect one from the competitive world? If one ceases to compete, does one need it? Perhaps one can, at last, in middle age, if not earlier, be completely oneself? And what a liberation that would be!"[20]

 5 "Your Place or Mine?"

THE FRENCH have a word for it: *démon de midi;* the "devil" that gets into men at the "noonday" of their lives when their wives have perhaps grown matronly. The Germans have a word for it too: *Torschlusspanik,* "closed-door panic"; the pursuit of young women by middle-aged men seeking a final fling "before the gates close."

Démon de midi and the *torschluss* syndrome are among the obvious signs that a man is going through disequilibrium. With one recent exception—a study by the Life Extension Institute— the few attempts that have been made to study extramarital affairs agree that the middle-aged man who hasn't wandered is a *rara avis*. The studies also conclude that the reality of infidelity differs in many respects from our stereotypical conceptions. There, agreement ends.

Some behavioral scientists see the extramarital affair as evidencing normal, healthy behavior. Others see it as an unhealthy symptom of deeper, unresolved conflicts with the spouse. Advocates of the situation ethic say that whether it is good or bad depends upon each individual circumstance. Still others see in our tolerance of adultery, pornography, and sexual obsessiveness a clear threat to the institution of the family. And when the family disintegrates, they say, history has shown time and again that civilization decays.

"The resolution of 'romantic love' and lifelong sacramental marriage is a major clinical problem of the middle-aged man," says Robert Butler. "Amazingly, there is little scientific literature available that a man can read to help him cope with his extramarital affair."

The late Dr. Alfred Kinsey's Institute for Sex Research shocked many people in the late 1940s and early 1950s with the assertion that at least 50 percent of American men and at least 25 percent of American women engaged in extramarital relations. The foundation has since speculated that the post-Pill percentages are probably closer to 60 for men and 40 for women—cause, if true, for many a sidelong glance in the nation's living rooms.

Kinsey was primarily concerned with the number of adulterous episodes, perhaps because we Americans are almost as preoccupied with statistics as we are with sex—we're a land of orgasm counters, it's been said. Sociologist John F. Cuber and Peggy B. Harroff, coauthors of *The Significant Americans: A Study of Sexual Behavior Among the Affluent,* were more concerned with the *context* in which adultery occurred. After interviewing nearly 450 upper-income Americans aged thirty-five to fifty-five, they concluded that our monogamous code was a "colossal unreality" based upon "common pretense."

Virginia Satir, the family therapist and cofounder of the Esalen Institute in Big Sur, California, has said that "Almost every study of sexual practices of married people today reports that the myth is monogamy; the fact is frequently polygamy."

Morton Hunt, author of *The Affair: A Portrait of Extra-Marital Love in America*—by far the most readable nonfiction book on the subject to date—considers adultery "the hidden reality" of American life. Says Hunt: "The most common attitude toward the extramarital affair is somewhat like the American attitude toward paying one's income tax: Many people cheat—some a little, some a lot; most who don't would like to but are afraid; neither the actual nor the would-be cheaters admit the truth or defend their views except to a few confidants; and practically all of them teach their children the accepted traditional code though they know they neither believe in it themselves nor expect that their children will do so when they grow up."[1]

Dr. Harry J. Johnson, chairman of the medical board of Life Extension Institute, Inc., a preventive medicine group, is skeptical about contentions that infidelity is widespread, and maintains that the American businessman is more upright than he's given credit for. In a confidential survey of 6,000 business executives passing through Life Extension's Manhattan offices for their annual physical examinations in the early 1970s, Johnson found that "only one in five married men engages in outside affairs either regularly or occasionally."[2]

Johnson did find that a man is most likely to wander during the 35-to-45 midlife decade after a marriage of some ten to twenty years. Not surprisingly, he also found that the incidence of such activity rises with income. Thirty-two percent of the men in the $50,000-a-year bracket and up confessed to straying from the straight and narrow.

Dr. John P. McCann, medical director of the Institute, tells me the survey confirms his observation, and that of Johnson, that "the average guy is pretty conservative" when it comes to extra-marital adventuring.

But, says McCann, the average man is exposed to so many books, magazines, and motion pictures featuring unfettered sexual activity—both within and without the marriage bond—that he feels there is something wrong with him, to say nothing of his wife.

The following excerpt from one current novel, *Month of Sundays* by John Updike is typical:

> Alicia in bed was a revelation—at last I confronted as in an ecstatic mirror my own sexual demon. In such a hurry we did not always take time to remove socks and necklaces and underthings that clung to us then like shards or epaulets, we would tumble upon her low square bed, whose headboard was a rectangle of teak and whose bedspread a quiltwork sunburst, and she would push me down and, her right hand splayed on her belly . . . whimper . . . and squirm . . . and her white-skinned joy, witnessed, forced a laugh from my chest. This laughing was unprecedented for me; under my wife's administration, sex had been a serious business. . . .[3]

The Life Extension people would have us believe that H. L. Mencken was right when he said years ago:

> The average man of our time and race is far more virtuous than his wife's imaginings make him out—far less schooled in sin, far less enterprising in amour. I do not say, of course, that he is pure

in heart, for the chances are that he isn't; what I do say is that, in the overwhelming majority of cases, he is pure in act, even in the face of temptation.

And why? For several main reasons, not to go into minor ones. One is that he lacks courage. Another is that he lacks the money. Another is that he is fundamentally moral, and has a conscience. It takes more sinful initiative than he has to plunge into any affair save the most casual and sordid; it takes more ingenuity and intrepidity than he has to carry it off; it takes more money than he can conceal from his consort to finance it. A man may force his actual wife to share the direst poverty, but even the least vampirish woman of the third part demands to be courted in what, considering his station in life, is the grand manner, and the expenses of that grand manner scare off all save a small minority of specialists in deception.[4]

Humorist L. Rust Hills recently reached much the same conclusion as Mencken, suggesting that adultery these days is just too complicated, the spontaneity gone. Take the matter of telephoning. Obviously, you can't phone Hester from your own home with your wife in residence, observes Hills,

> ... and phoning from a public phone booth, either the one on the corner near your apartment or one of the ones down in the parking area of the shopping center is no help—in fact, the opposite. Just being *seen* in one of those glass booths is enough to give you away. You figure that if people see you, they'll just think you forgot the laundry list and are phoning home. But that *isn't* what *anyone* thinks. What everyone thinks is just what's the case. "Uh-oh," is what everyone thinks.
> "What's going on in that phone booth? Must be some call he can't make from home." Being seen in a phone booth is like having a giant scarlet letter A *drip-painted* on your front and back.[5]

Apart from the risk of discovery, extramarital dalliances can be dangerous in other ways. Dr. Leonore Zohman of New York's Montifiore Hospital reported a while back on a Japanese study which revealed that eight out of ten sudden deaths that take place during sexual intercourse involve illicit relations. Doctors theorize that the risk to an out-of-shape or coronary-prone man increases because of his guilt, and his concern over his performance. And if he'd been calling for stronger wine and faster music earlier in the evening, followed by a big meal, well. . . .

Life Extension's Johnson is a spry individual in his seventies. He is the first to emphasize that he is a medical doctor, not a psychologist, but he does venture in his survey report that the minority who do engage in extramarital excursions do so for a "combination of factors including sex drive, wearing off of the initial romantic implications of marriage, perhaps a broadening of horizons socially, intellectually, and in business, along with an increasing financial security that may well make it easier for the married man to afford those additional expenses incurred in extramarital affairs. This is also a period when tensions may arise in the marriage and before they can be worked out."[6]

Forty percent of the confessed adulterers said they were seeking "new sexual experiences," nearly the same number blamed their activities in various ways on their wives, and only 17 percent said that extensive traveling had anything to do with their infidelity—the latter statistic doing violence to the image of the dashing traveling sales executive.

In his comedy *Last of the Red Hot Lovers*, Neil Simon chronicles the failure of Barney Cashman to commit adultery in his mother's empty Manhattan apartment. Barney is a fat, homely little guy, the proprietor of a seafood restaurant—a middle-aged man frantic to live before it's too late. In the following scene, Barney has struck out with a gal named Elaine. He exclaims:

> ... I'm sure it will come as no great shock to you, but you are the first "attempted" extramarital affair for me in twenty-three years of marriage. I've never even kissed another woman. In twenty-three years.
>
> I got married to my high-school sweetheart—and when have you heard that expression last—at the age of twenty-four, having gone steady with her since I was sixteen. And how many experiences with other women do you think I've had prior to getting married? ... One! I had one shot at it. When I was eighteen my brother took me to an apartment in Newark, New Jersey, where I consorted with a forty-four-year-old woman who greeted me lying naked on a brass bed reading a newspaper. It cost me seven dollars and I threw up all night.
>
> I don't smoke, I don't gamble, and you've had more to drink this afternoon than I've had in my whole life. I've never had a car ac-

cident, never had a fistfight, never had a broken bone, never had a temperature over a hundred and two. . . . Life has not only been very kind to me, it goes out of its way to ignore me. . . .

So why after twenty-three years do I write my mother's address on the back of a check, buy a bottle of Scotch with two glasses and pray to God I never get caught?

Why? I'll tell you why. . . . I don't know, I've never had the urge before. . . . Not true. I started getting the urge about five years ago. Two years ago, seriously. About a year ago, I decided to give in to it, and the last six months conscientiously. I'm forty-seven years old and for the first time in my life I think about dying. . . . I read the obituaries every day just for the satisfaction of not seeing my name there. . . . Do you know I even practice dying? I lie in bed at night trying to feel myself slipping away. . . .

. . . But it's inevitable, it's going to happen someday, maybe sooner than I think. And I ask myself, "Have you enjoyed it Barney? Was it a really terrific forty-seven years?" And you know what my answer is? "Well, I wouldn't say terrific. It was nice. . . ."

I wanted to know what it was like with another woman. Would I be successful, would she like me, would I like the touch of her? A thousand questions that I'd never know the answer to if suddenly my name were in the obituary column tomorrow morning. So I decided to indulge myself just once . . .

There is a long silence.

Elaine: "And that's why you wanted to get laid?"[7]

There are a number of Barney Cashmans—and Don Giovannis, too—among Dan Levinson's subjects, one-third of whom have been involved in extramarital affairs, with more who were in the "urge" stage during his study.

In a *McCall's* article, writer Maggie Scarf quotes from Levinson's research material. "I haven't had the nerve," said one Levinson subject of a woman toward whom he'd made a few advances. "I set these things up, and then I don't go through with it. I cannot pass her house without the most excitement and an energy change coming over me."[8]

Another man reflected a high degree of ambivalence. "My wife isn't an oversexed individual," he said. "I think we've got a good match there. If it wasn't, one way or another, my attentions would have turned a long time ago. Still, you know, sometimes

I see a movie or read a book and I think, gee, she's frigid compared to what I'm seeing, or this thing I'm reading. But in my evaluation, she is not a frigid person. She has deep feelings, she's warm, she's a devoted mother. But you never know what will happen as you get older. They say once the kids grow up, then divorces occur. I can't predict that something won't happen once the kids are gone."[9]

What Levinson's subjects did about these urges varied widely. Some left their wives and married their extramarital loves. Some went through a succession of brief affairs or flings, found the experience hollow, and settled down again. Some did nothing whatsoever about their fantasies.

That Americans especially have a lip-smacking fascination with the Eternal Triangle appears obvious from the public prints. The Seventh Commandment has always been grist for the playwright and novelist. In the mid-1970s, it bid fair to replace the latest quick-weight-loss diet and "Seven New Hairstyles for Fall" in the four-color slicks.

Thus *Town & Country* asked a while back: "Is Infidelity a Sport?" and concluded: "An affair is the winked-at pastime of the cosmopolitan elite, a natural part of the frenzied lives of the jet set."

New York Magazine wondered: "Can Adultery Save Your Marriage?" In this piece, writer Linda Wolfe revealed that half her friends were having affairs. And how did she know? Her answer is enough to make strong men panic: "Adulterous women like to brag." Of her adulterous lady friends, she said: "They have children, houses, a great fear of loneliness and economic deprivation; and feelings toward their husbands, which, if not passionate, may still be love. They aren't, I suppose, terribly different from the armies of male adulterers who are hanging on, also seeking the best of two worlds." (Ms. Wolfe recently authored *Playing Around—Women and Extramarital Sex.*)

Pageant weighed in with "Affairs: Are More Women Having Them?"

Cosmopolitan encouraged the Cosmo Girl to have affairs with married men—as long as she covered her emotional bets with a bachelor or two. "With enough good sex she's going to have the married man climbing the walls," says *Cosmo* editor Helen Gurley

Brown. "But weekends and evenings he's not around, so it's not equal." When I asked her how she would feel if *her* husband had an affair with a young Cosmo girl, Ms. Brown recoiled: "I couldn't bear it; couldn't accept it!"

Washingtonian magazine served up a juicy chronicle of past presidential and congressional adultery, and even *Lady's Circle* dealt with the subject, warning the good housewife about "the other man" and advising her to break off a tempting relationship early —while she is still strong enough to do so.

Do such magazines truly reflect life around us? It's hard to say, but I suspect they do. Ask any attractive and outgoing woman who works in an office with a lot of men. One married woman in her late thirties who worked for a year in a scientific research group says she was propositioned by nearly every man in her department. She says that it would have been more flattering if it hadn't been so cut and dried.

"These guys are all pretty damn bright," she says. "They're tops in their fields, most of them, so they don't have the excuse of dull jobs. They all complain, 'There's no excitement with my wife any more.' Then they get to this stage: 'Well, do you want to go to bed, or not?' At first I was shocked. But then I began to think: 'I guess this is the way life really is!' "

The other side of that coin is presented by a friend of mine in his early forties who recently spent a year in Washington, D.C. between marriages. He says he was dumbfounded at the number of approaches he received—some oblique, some direct—from wives of friends and acquaintances.

One of the shocks that attractive middle-aged widows have come to expect is the attentions they receive from husbands of their friends, or friends of their late husband's who are still married.

"It's the first warning I got from a friend who'd been through it twice," says a fortyish Maryland widow. "She said, 'I may as well tell you that the area of aggressive sexual activity will come from the husbands of your friends and neighbors, the people you'd least expect.' She was right: It started about four or five months after my husband died. I guess men figure, 'She must be sexually starving and need servicing—and who better than me?' "

Good Old Charlie, our middle-aged Casanova, would find—

were he to seek it—widely conflicting advice from experienced observers of human behavior. Like so many men, Charlie tells himself that he still loves his wife, Jane. He rationalizes his affair as an "escape valve" that will save his "boring" marriage. Yet Charlie wasn't born yesterday. Even though he's dancing from cloud bank to cloud bank, a romantic lover in his own eyes, he's a philanderer in the eyes of society. "Charlie, old boy, if you've learned anything in your forty years, it's that you can't have it both ways in this life."

Or can he?

Some say he probably can. Dr. Albert Ellis, a Manhattan psychotherapist, who has been advocating a freeing up of sexual customs for decades, says:

"The man who resides in a large urban area and who never once . . . is sorely tempted to engage in adultery for purposes of sexual variety is to be suspected of being indeed biologically and/or psychologically abnormal; and he who frequently has such desires and who occasionally and unobtrusively carries them into practice is well within the normal range. The good Judeo-Christian moralists may never believe it, but it would appear that healthy adultery, even in our supposedly monogamous society, *is* possible."[10]

Sociologists Cuber and Harroff say in *The Significant Americans* that most of us nourish many false stereotypes about adultery.

We have inherited a morbid legacy which vigorously asserts that because of the guilt and deception involved for the participants and the feelings of humiliation and rejection experienced by the spouse, the net effect is necessarily negative to mental health. Our non-clinical sample would justify almost the opposite conclusion. . . . Overwhelmingly, these people expressed no guilt . . . although they sometimes acknowledged regret over practical consequences.

The "offended" spouses were often not offended at all; sometimes they were even relieved to be "out from under" a relationship which was personally frustrating and, because of the adultery, they were able to maintain the marriage for other reasons.

We were struck by the sizable group of people who were involved in adulterous relationships of many years standing, who were enriched and fulfilled through the relationship in much the same way that intrinsically married people are, whose health, efficiency, and creativity remain excellent. Many of these pairings are in effect *de facto* marriages.[11]

Morton Hunt makes the same point. For his book *The Affair*, he interviewed eighty-five unfaithful men and women. Some of the affairs proved disastrous all around; some proved benign; some proved felicitous and therapeutic to the adulterers' marriages.

In Joseph Heller's best seller *Something Happened*, the middle-aged hero, Bob Slocum, is talking about his wife:

> She wants me to tell her I love her, although she has stopped asking me to (I bring her a box of chocolates every Saint Valentine's Day now, and she is pleased to receive it, although we both know it is only a box of chocolates. Still, it *is* a box of chocolates, and everybody in the family enjoys eating chocolates but me), just as she has too much pride (or good sense) to delve into the subject of my sleeping with other girls (as she does surmise about other married men we know. If *that* ever hopped out into the open between us, like that little mouse I was afraid of in our apartment in the city so long ago, *she* would have to do something about it, *she* would have to act—and I know she does not want to. I know that she, like me, prefers to keep us together until time, or life, runs out).[12]

Dr. Eleanor Hamilton, a Manhattan marriage counselor with a fashionable clientele, has advice for Good Old Charlie that would stun him. "If Charlie had any guts, he'd confront his wife with his sexual needs. He'd open up communications and let her see that this young woman is not a threat to her. Jane might react with hysterics. But after she's slept on the idea, she isn't going to throw Charlie out. The thing that frightens wives is that they'll be dislodged."

Dr. Hamilton is a handsome widow of fifty-odd years with white hair and keen, sparkling eyes. She leaves no doubt about where she stands on extramarital affairs: she's all for them under certain circumstances.

"In my opinion, it is simply too much of an emotional burden to expect one man to get all his emotional sustenance from one woman and vice versa," says Dr. Hamilton. "We are all such complicated beings that there are parts of our personality that may not be dominant, but are nevertheless quite active. Your wife might not discover that part at all, and you are enchanted to discover someone who does. Why, it's like discovering skiing!

"Marriage shouldn't be a prison. When it becomes a prison, love walks out. Jealousy and possessiveness are sicknesses. Yes, I do believe there's such a thing as a beneficial extramarital love relationship. I believe that a good marriage can be made better by an occasional affair. Maybe you're a Wall Street broker and she enables you to write poetry. It's heady medicine, I'll tell you.

"But this cannot work in secrecy. The man or woman who plays this game in secret plays an unfair game, and the secrecy will break out. It's just a matter of time. No, this only works if there's an agreement, a clearly stated agreement."

Dr. Hamilton says that more often than not, however, the agreement is unstated but understood.

In the early 1970s a book on this theme rode the best-seller lists for many months: *Open Marriage: A New Life Style for Couples,* by George C. O'Neill, a City College of New York anthropology professor, and Nena, his wife of more than twenty-five years, also an anthropologist.

"Man is not sexually monogamous by nature, evolution, or force of habit," say the O'Neills. "In societies around the world in which he has been enjoined to become sexually monogamous in marriage he has failed. He may fail gloriously, impudently, nonchalantly, regretfully, or guiltily, but he always fails—in numbers large enough to make that failure significant. And that leads us to an inevitable question: Is it the 'unfaithful' human being who is the failure, or is it the standard itself?"[13]

A key passage in the book:

"In open marriage you can come to know, enjoy, and share comradeship with others of the opposite sex besides your mate. These relationships enhance and augment the marital relationship in turn. These outside relationships may, of course, include sex. That is completely up to the partners involved."[14]

This has all been said before. Nearly twenty years ago, Bertrand Russell wrote in *Marriage and Morals:*

There is another difficulty in the way of modern marriage, which is felt especially by those who are most conscious of the value of love. Love can flourish only as long as it is free and spontaneous; it tends to be killed by the thought that it is a duty. To say that it is our duty to love so-and-so is the surest way to cause you to hate him or her. Marriage is a combination of love with legal bonds, thus it falls between two stools.

Shelley says:

> I never was attached to that great sect
> Whose doctrine is, that each one should select
> Out of the crowd a mistress or a friend,
> And all the rest, though fair and wise, commend
> To cold oblivion, though it is in the code
> Of modern morals, and the beaten road
> Which those poor slaves with weary footsteps tread,
> Who travel to their home among the dead
> By the broad highway of the world, and so
> With one chained friend, perhaps a jealous foe,
> The dreariest and the longest journey go.

There can be no doubt that to close one's mind on marriage against all the approaches of love from elsewhere is to diminish receptivity and sympathy and the opportunities of valuable human contacts. It is to do violence to something which, from the most idealistic standpoint, is in itself desirable. And like every kind of restrictive morality it tends to promote what one may call a policeman's outlook upon the whole of human life—the outlook, that is to say, which is always looking for an opportunity to forbid something.[15]

Russell practiced what he preached: He had three marriages and two long-term mistresses over the years.

What Russell and the O'Neills are saying, it seems, is that a marriage of two decades or so should be strong enough to withstand or even encourage lapses in blind fidelity—and if it isn't, then perhaps it should be dissolved; it's a risk one has to take.

Intellectually, the argument has tremendous appeal, especially to the adulterer. But many of the psychiatrists, psychologists, clergymen, and other professionals whom I interviewed for this book say such theories raise almost as many questions as they try to answer. What about the odd man (or woman) out? What about the very real danger that what starts out as a dalliance will turn into something more serious and the wife or husband will end up in the trash can, so to speak? What happens to the pride of the errant, aging Romeo if his lady love—especially if she's younger—jilts him for a younger man? The variations are seemingly unlimited, and the professional helpers see them all.

Dr. Eric Riss, a Manhattan psychotherapist who has been counseling troubled married couples for more than two decades, considers the O'Neills' book nonsense—dangerous nonsense.

"I'm in favor of writing the popular book that explains to the layman psychological concepts that have been painstakingly arrived at through clinical work, but I get very upset by seemingly simple solutions such as this because people take them seriously— and then get very disappointed when they don't work," he tells me.

Riss says that for one thing, there's nothing new about such marriage styles. They've all been tried before, most notably during the moral decline of ancient Greece and Rome. To quote Martial, a second-century Roman poet:

> In many a house, when the marriage bonds were growing feeble and beginning to give way, and were almost severed, an adulterer has set all matters right.

Riss contends that for all its faults, the only form of marriage that has stood the test of time is one in which each party, "can at least hope for permanence, hope for stability, hope for trust."

Riss sees the extramarital affair as a symptom of "something going on in the marriage that the couple hasn't been able to deal with. The problem hasn't been talked about; it hasn't been resolved. When the degree of tension gets high enough, then one's love feelings go down. Then the fantasies start about an ideal love. The desire for extramarital sex is invariably the result of a high level of hostility.

"When your friend Charlie says he's 'bored' with Jane, it just isn't so. There has to be tension there—anger or rage—tension that he might not even be aware of. But this sort of thing *can* be dealt with if people are willing to work at it. So to say that extramarital affairs are desirable is to be completely oblivious to the complexities of marriage."

Many agree with Riss. "Few psychiatrists condone it [adultery] in spite of the popular mythology that psychiatry encourages sexual activity because the frustration and inhibition of sexual needs may produce mental illness," says psychiatrist Leon Salzman in an article in *The Psychodynamics of Work and Marriage*, edited by Jules Masserman:

> The concept of sexual etiology [origin] of mental disorder is often misrepresented by a greater emphasis on the adequate fulfillment of sexual needs than on the value of mature, loving relationship, both sexual and nonsexual. Some psychiatrists as well as patients who follow this notion presume that adequate treatment will free a person for a full, unrestrained, and uninhibited sexual life and justify infidelity. . . . Whether man is essentially monogamous or polygamous, there is sufficient evidence to bear out the contention that a direct relationship exists between love and the degree of fidelity in a relationship. Its [adultery's] presence, therefore, is always indicative of some degree of non-involvement, or failure of commitment.[16]

I asked psychologist Sallie S. Schumacher, director of the Human Sexuality Program at Long Island Jewish Medical Center in New Hyde Park, New York, about all this. She finds that few of us are emotionally equipped to "swing." Even when marriage partners grant one another consent to have affairs, jealousy, envy, possessiveness, and deeper psychological difficulties invariably emerge to make life miserable for all concerned.

Priests, rabbis, and ministers see the same problems as the psychiatrists and sexual therapists. Monsignor James T. McHugh, family life director of the U.S. Catholic Conference in Washington, D.C., believes, however, that psychiatrists tend to develop a negative view of marriage because they deal primarily with men and women whose marriages are in trouble.

"Like all the rest of us, the middle-aged man needs constant reassurance," says McHugh, "and this, combined with the pressures of corporate and family life, often render the man susceptible to the pretty young thing who—miracle of miracles—finds him wildly attractive."

But, the monsignor insists, the man who has worked to keep his marriage a "continually developing, open-ended relationship, one which is mutually sustaining," will find such temptation less than compelling. And the man who does yield to temptation invariably adds a heavy sense of guilt to his already full bag of tensions.

Rabbi Mordecai Brill, chairman of the National Commission on Marriage and the Family of the Synagogue Council of America, believes that the middle-aged Jewish man may have a healthier, more open approach to sex and marriage than some of his more puritanical brethren of other faiths.

"Jews are family centered, uniquely so," he says. "Even so, we do young people a real disservice when we talk of living happily ever after. Marriage is a seven-day, seven-night-a-week relationship. For it to stay bright and alive, both partners must continue to grow emotionally, spiritually, and intellectually. And there is no perfect marriage. We must all learn to live with frustrations."

Brill observes that the middle-aged man who frolics with his extramarital lady love often does irreparable damage to his marriage. "Sometimes, however, the ensuing crisis saves the marriage because it forces both partners to face and resolve problems that they had avoided before," he says.

Dr. Bernice Neugarten, professor of human development at the University of Chicago, has been studying the problems of middle-aged women—and to a somewhat lesser extent, middle-aged men—for twenty years or more. I asked her views on extramarital excursions.

"Sure, who in the world hasn't been bored with one's mate at one time or another?" she says. "But other things grow up in the course of time—call it sympathy, call it affection, call it old-fashioned love—and we're all leery of losing this. I don't think people are going to give up the need that we all have for long-term, intimate relationships. This is an enormous need, at all ages.

"Intimacy can be quickly attained, but it somehow doesn't suffice if it is without length. A truly liberated, educated man of middle age doesn't expect all possible virtues to be embodied in his mate. In an overly crude way, what I'm saying is this: You can go to bed with someone, but that somehow doesn't dismiss the need for the long-standing relationship; you *still* want to go home to someone who has known you for twenty-five years."

Norman Sheresky, an authority on divorce law, numbers himself among those who vigorously oppose the open marriage concept. He says that his experience with thousands of New York divorce cases has taught him that honesty is usually the worst policy in such matters.

"The O'Neills' theory runs contrary to practical, almost immutable laws of human nature," said Sheresky one day in his Manhattan office. "Men are possessive characters. They like to conquer, win, acquire, and possess. It is simply not acceptable to a man to share his possessions. He will do anything to get rid of a paramour. If he finds out his wife is having an affair, here's what he usually says: 'That slut!' And if I ask: 'You've never fooled around?' He says, 'That's different!' It's always different."

With writer Marya Mannes, Sheresky authored a book on divorce, *Uncoupling: The Art of Coming Apart,* in which he does draw a line between the fling or one-night stand, and the more extended affair, suggesting that flings *can* provide escape valves if discreetly conducted. But he considers longer-range affairs "serious risks." And Sheresky writes that if a man confesses, "his wife may forgive, but she'll never forget."[17]

"To most mature and loving husbands and wives, the thought of the other in another's arms is a stab of pain and fear," he writes. "Right or wrong, this sense of exclusive possession is still a deep human need," and restraint from indulging in affairs is "the main pillar of their union."[18]

Carle C. Zimmerman, author of a major history of the family entitled *Family and Civilization,* took an apocalyptic view of American society three decades ago, seeing in adultery, easy divorce, and other such things, clear historical parallels to societies in moral decay.

"The most prevalent idea is that the family has merely to achieve the freeing of the individual to arrive at its ideal. The attitude is somewhat ambivalent: We want to retain the family but it must not interfere with our love affairs."[19]

When professionals disagree so markedly, where does a man turn for advice in coping with an extramarital affair? I put this problem to psychiatrist Herbert Klemme and he came up with a reasonable answer to the question of whether one should play the "your place or mine?" game in the first place.

Now in his early fifties, Klemme for years conducted continuing education seminars for business executives at the Menninger Foundation and is now in private psychiatric practice in Minnesota. As a result of his own stocktaking about ten years ago, Klemme gave up the practice of general medicine to become a psychiatrist. At the time, he tells me, he had never heard the term "middle age crisis," and he thought, at first, that his own inward searching was unique. Since then, he has been a close observer of the midlife crisis. Says Klemme:

"If a man and woman have been successful in development tasks of an evolving, growing personality, and have learned to be introspective and know themselves pretty well, they will develop the capability of becoming closer to one another. If his or her partner hasn't experienced similar growth, the gap between them will grow wider. The person who is seeking intimacy—let's say it's the man—will approach the person who hasn't grown and developed and will be rebuffed, pushed back, with: 'You're getting too close,' or 'What more do you want from me?'

"The man who did the approaching will feel rejected and hurt and think there must be something wrong with him. Then— often under the illusion of intimacy that alcohol provides—a pretty young thing becomes available. I think that situation is one of the main things that motivates a man to try and see if he can find a new kind of intimacy that will be more satisfying— the kind of intimacy which may still be possible with his wife if the two of them did some work on it.

"But married people get locked into ritual and routine and lack of communication and lack of marriage cultivation which leads to a kind of parallel existence. He does his thing and she does hers, and they just don't develop an adeptness at real communication. They get locked into habit patterns established at age twenty-five, say, which are no longer necessary, which are archaic, and not very gratifying to either one of them.

"But often it's the woman who is seeking greater intimacy and the man who hasn't grown. In the kind of cultural values we've incorporated in ourselves, to be a man today is to be independent, unneedful, to stand on your own two feet. This Horatio Alger kind of ethic also leads us to assume that we shouldn't need somebody to love us—we shouldn't be needful of an interdependent relationship.

"I know a man who developed an illness, diagnosed as a possible malignancy. It took them months to find out that it wasn't but he never told his wife. That's the kind of independence I'm talking about; the hyperindependent man. But it's also a characteristic of the 'successful' man. At a time when he needed support and love and attention—to accept a dependent role with his wife—he couldn't. He denied himself. He also denied something the wife needed to give very much, and you can imagine what the relationship was between that couple. And that's not an unusual case. A man will have a heart pain—he won't tell anybody—and he'll just go on."

Klemme applies the continuum concept to the matter of extramarital affairs. "Let's take all men. At one end of the continuum, you have those men who freely have affairs and feel very little guilt—some of their wives know about it, some of them don't; some of the wives accept it, some of them don't. In the middle, you might have the man who has had one affair that made him feel so guilty that he never had another one. And at the other end of the continuum, you have the man who might have fantasies about having an affair but will allow himself only a quick glance.

"So what's normal? I can't take an 'either/or' position. If a man doesn't feel guilty, if he doesn't feel there is anything wrong with what he's doing, then he views that as normal behavior. The man who feels guilty, wouldn't feel guilty if he thought what he was doing was right. If you do feel guilty, then you'll feel badly, and it will do psychological harm.

"One of the things every one of us has to learn is what we can do and what we cannot do, within the limits of our own internal value system. My internal value system limits what I can do; it labels what I do, 'right' and 'wrong,' and if I get too far out of line, it will punish the hell out of me.

"I can't conceptualize 'open marriage.' But if you have two people who love each other, and they don't feel guilty, then that's normal for them.

"What I'm going to say will sound hackneyed. But it's what philosophers have been telling us for thousands of years: 'Know thyself.' Everyone has to come to grips with this—yet they so rarely do."

6 *"The Problem Is Provoked by Having Teen-aged Sons"*

DEFIANCE of one's father is part of growing up, we're told. The late Haim Ginott, a clinical psychologist, spoke of the teen-aged boy's "inner radar," which unerringly detects the actions that will most annoy his father. Mostly they are little things—on the surface at least.

The boy mindlessly slaps a dirty bare foot on the kitchen linoleum during supper.

Angry growl from the old man.

The kid borrows the car without asking permission.

Angry bellow from the old man.

The kid flips the stereo to full blast while his father is snoozing.

Angry roar from the old man.

The boy walks about in a fogbank of his own creation. Everything "bores" him. He is flunking two subjects, though the school reports that his IQ is high. He is an "underachiever." Mostly, though, it's the boy's hostility that gets to old Dad.

Why should there be this defiance? And what else is going on between father and son? A great deal is going on, say psychiatrists.

There are few relationships that can be more sensitive than that of a fortyish father and his teen-age son. Each harbors conscious and unconscious feelings of love and hate for the other. The son is emerging from childhood into young adulthood, the father is emerging from young adulthood into middle age. If either fails to make a natural transition, relations between the two can become seriously strained.

Having forgotten and unconsciously rejected his own adolescence, a man has little patience with a son who often comes through to him as an ungrateful whelp. Yet bizarre behavior by a teen-age boy is not unusual.

Says Anna Freud in the multi-volume *The Psychoanalytic Study of the Child:*

> It is normal for an adolescent to behave in an inconsistent and unpredictable manner, to fight his impulses, and to accept them; to love his parents and to hate them; to be deeply ashamed to acknowledge his mother before others, and unexpectedly to desire heart-to-heart talks with her; to thrive on imitation and identify with others, while searching unceasingly for his own identity; to be more idealistic, artistic, generous, and unselfish than he ever will be again, but also the opposite: self-centered, egoistic, calculating. Such fluctuations between extreme opposites would be deemed highly abnormal at any other time of life. At this time, they may signify no more than that an adult structure of personality takes a long time to emerge, that the ego of the individual in question does not cease to experiment, and is in no hurry to close down on possibilities.[1]

In Shakespeare's *The Winter's Tale,* an old shepherd says:

> I would there were no age between ten and three-and-twenty, or that youth would sleep out the rest; for there is nothing in the between but getting wenches with child, wronging the ancientry, stealing, fighting.

At a time when a man has his own share of problems, he's expected to deal Solomonlike with a son whom the Lord has apparently put on this Earth to agitate him.

Father and son has proven a mighty theme in literature. Sigmund Freud noted that parricide was the theme of three of the greatest masterpieces: Sophocles' *Oedipus Rex,* Shakespeare's *Hamlet,* and Dostoevsky's *The Brothers Karamazov.*

Freud believed that we all have an unconscious wish to kill our fathers. He saw parricide as "the principal and primal crime of humanity as well as of the individual." Morever, he continued: "The beginnings of religion, morals, society, and art converge on the Oedipus complex. This is in complete agreement with the psychoanalytic finding that the same complex constitutes the nucleus of all neuroses."[2]

The relationship of a boy to his father is highly ambivalent.

"In addition to the hate which seeks to get rid of the father as a rival, a measure of tenderness for him is also habitually present," said Freud. "The two attitudes of mind combine to produce identification with the father; the boy wants to be in his father's place because he admires him, and wants to be like him, and also because he wants to put him out of the way."[3]

Freud no longer totally dominates psychiatric thought, of course, but his followers remain legion.

"There is no question that in many instances in my clinical practice the Oedipus complex is a completely accurate description of the problem," says Robert Butler. "In the classic formulation, the child of two or three wants his mother completely to himself and wants to wipe out the old man. Between ages four and six he works this through. But there are usually some residual things, and it's as though in the years fourteen to seventeen a second edition of the paper comes out, and the boy again works through his feelings toward his mother and his father.

"If handled with subtlety and decency, it's a positive thing— positive in the sense that this is the first chance a boy has to work out something with a member of the opposite sex. Presumably, a happy resolution of the Oedipus complex also will lead to a more successful marriage."

Failure to resolve oedipal conflicts can contribute to such middle-age problems as success depression. This occurs when a man who had an unfairly authoritarian father subsequently exceeds his father's accomplishments, thus symbolically destroying him.

Yet the authoritarian father who is also even-handed and just is generally revered by sons who feel no depression whatever if they manage to outstrip him in life's battles. The late Senator Robert F. Kennedy said of his father, Joseph P. Kennedy:

"He has called on the best that was in us. There was no such thing as half-trying. Whether it was running a race or catching a football, competing in school—we were to try. And we were to try harder than anyone else. 'After you have done the best you can,' he used to say, 'to hell with it.' "[4]

Dr. Gerald H. J. Pearson says in his book *Adolescence and the Conflict of Generations* that the teen-age boy "still feels unconsciously toward his father the hatred, fear, and love he felt during the oedipal period. Consciously, he tends to regard him with more or less respect, often with considerable deprecation; and he tends to stay away from him as much as possible. This defense of spatial distance is frequently reinforced by a certain dimming of perception so that he does not hear or perceive what his father is saying, and by a tendency to make monosyllabic replies when questioned."[5]

What of the father? For years the ills of male youth have been laid at Mom's feet. Now Dad is catching some of the fire.

Gerald Pearson believes every father unconsciously envies his son's youth, vigor, sexual prowess, and seemingly limitless horizon. The father resents growing old—especially in a youth-happy culture—and so, to forestall his own decline, he tries to hold his adolescent son back.

The father sees the son as an extension to himself and wants the boy to reflect the better side of his personality. Moreover, realizing that certain of life's goals are now beyond his reach, the father sets out to achieve them vicariously through his son.

"Unconsciously the middle-aged parent has these feelings toward his own children," says Pearson. "The feelings may be conscious, but what usually appears are defenses against them—overprotection, overconcern, permissiveness—or direct expressions of them: overrestrictive actions; neglect of the adolescent's interests; derogatory attitudes toward the adolescent's views; impertinent demands for complete knowledge of the adolescent's thoughts and actions. The reason for these actions is that they are all done 'for the good of the child.' "[6]

Wilhelm Reich, a Freud follower who later went a separate path, believed passionately that the family, the church, and other social institutions conspired to repress the teen-ager's sexuality, thus causing his neuroses.

"All the phenomena of the conflict of puberty and the neurosis of puberty derive from one fact," says Reich in *The Sexual Revolution*. "This is the conflict between the fact that an adolescent at about the age of fifteen reaches sexual maturity, i.e., experiences the physiological necessity of sexual intercourse and the capacity to procreate or bear children, and the other fact of being economically and structurally incapable of creating the legal framework demanded by society for sexual intercourse, i.e., marriage."[7]

Reich's ideas are still unsettling Europeans. In 1973, Dr. Jean Carpentier, a follower of Reich, wrote a pamphlet entitled "Let Us Learn to Make Love" that was widely distributed in French high schools. The pamphlet urged adolescents to engage in sexual intercourse or homosexual acts—and if this was not feasible, masturbation—in defiance of what he termed "hypocritical moral authority."

"The crisis of separation and identification in the adolescent boy often coincides with the father's midlife crisis," says a National Institute of Mental Health study of troubled adolescent boys described in *Psychiatry* magazine by Drs. L. David Levi, Helm Stierlin, and Robert J. Savard. "We noted a recurring pattern of pathologic separation. In their own crisis of integrity, middle-aged fathers seemed to suffer in a state of masked depression and consequently resigned from conflict with their sons, or sought to annihilate their sons' self-esteem."[8]

The authors use the term "loving fight" to describe the father-son conflict that is seen as "a mutually growth-producing alternative."

"An adolescent with seemingly open choices in work and love objects forces the middle-aged father to complete his grieving over lost alternatives and reaffirm his own life choices," conclude the authors. "If the father cannot do this, he may envy and disparage his son or, alternatively, overidentify with him in trying to relive through him what he feels he has missed."[9]

Many fathers reach such conclusions instinctively, and express themselves more pithily. Says Karl Harr, a former Rhodes Scholar, Princeton football star, and now an aerospace executive: "If your kids don't shoot you in the head they don't emerge as individuals. But you owe them something to fight against. I think the whole thing's great. The minute my thinking gets fuzzy, my two sons jump me. They've got to conquer the ghost that is their father. Great experience. Hell, there's my immortality."

Speaking of the midlife crisis, Roy Menninger tells me he has found, too, that for many men "this problem is provoked by having teen-aged sons. You see the men lived through the problem of developing their own identities when they were one, two, three, four, and five. Then they got kind of settled until they were teen-agers and then the advent of sexuality brought up all those old issues: 'Who am I?' and 'How good am I?' and 'Am I a real man?' Entry into the adult world in the early twenties brings again the questions of adequacy and questions like: 'How well do I like myself?'

"And becoming a parent for the first time *again* stimulates these same old questions that you thought were settled and resolved. Whammo! There they are again. Having adolescent children and, for a man, particularly, having adolescent sons, causes one to literally reexperience all the anxieties of his own adolescence. Some men have told me with amazement that issues that used to go around in their heads and keep them awake all night as teen-agers were doing the same thing again at forty or forty-five.

"It usually turned out that these men felt quite unable to deal effectively with their sons. They couldn't decide whether to play the heavy or whether to try to be a buddy, and neither system worked, or if it worked, not for very long. Their sons showed many aspects of behavior that their fathers immediately disliked, and then the fathers recognized that these were aspects of their own personalities that they had not liked. And they found that they couldn't get their sons to apply themselves to anything and hang in there and work at it, that their sons had a rather lackadaisical attitude and the presumption that God would provide.

"It's hard for most of us not to take it personally, as an indictment of us as people. This thing ignites the sleeping fuse that goes back into our own pasts. Suddenly we find ourselves reexperiencing the anxieties of days gone by. This gets transferred into the job situation, and one begins to experience these issues in relation to one's superiors and subordinates. And what was already a problem is now a twofold or threefold problem.

"One deals with one's son out of a feeling of loyalty and commitment. Then he does something which seems to violate all the commitments—something stupid, or thoughtless, or destructive. And you feel betrayed. This then, is not unlike situations in which you've put trust in a subordinate and have expected great things from him and then he appears to have violated his personal commitment to you. Or, put otherwise, it could be that a man who is involved with working out his relationship to his son at that time may be hypersensitive to perfectly ordinary office situations and simply manage to misperceive them as issues of loyalty and gratitude which they aren't at all.

"When they see their son having considerable difficulties which they seem to be unable to help him manage, then fathers very often begin to think: 'What did I do wrong?' or 'I wasn't a good father,' and this then ignites a whole set of self-doubts turning on the issue of 'How good am I anyway? I'm no good as a father, and I've been divorced, and I haven't achieved the sales record this year that I achieved last—I'm running 50 percent behind— and maybe I really am *not* any good.'

"It's a sort of selective perception, picking all sorts of things out and wrapping them into one bundle with a little ribbon around it which is labeled: 'I'm no damned good.'"

Representative James Symington, Democrat of Missouri, says that he is now very close to his father, former Senator Stuart Symington, but that he never really got to know him until 1952 when his father gave up a highly successful business career to run for the Senate against enormous odds. Young Symington campaigned with his father throughout the state and discovered for the first time that the elder Symington was capable of making mistakes, saying the wrong thing, becoming grim.

"He suddenly came into focus for me as a natural man," says Congressman Symington, "Not an ordinary man, to be sure, but a mortal one."

And this brings up a point that Dan Levinson likes to emphasize. "It's hard for many fathers to give up their anonymity, but as our kids grow older, it's vital that we do," says Levinson. "Preadolescent kids can hardly know us as persons; it's too complicated. But what mostly disappoints adolescents is that we won't let ourselves be known; that we continue to wear a mask, or be phony. As my kids have grown older, and we are on more equal terms, we have more of a friendship; I am more ready to respond. It's valuable to me that they can know my faults and limitations and still care for me."

In *The Conquest of Happiness*, Bertrand Russell says that to succeed as a father requires "a certain reverence for another personality, an intimate blend of power and tenderness."[10] And for rambunctious adolescents, he has this reminder:

"The value of parental affection lies largely in the fact that it is more reliable than any other affection. One's friends like one for one's merits; one's lovers for one's charms. If the merits or the charms diminish, the friends and lovers may vanish. But it is in times of misfortune that parents are most to be relied upon; in illness; and even in disgrace, if the parents are the right sort. Our parents love us because we are their children, and this is unalterable fact."[11]

7 "We Know of No Intrinsic Limits to the Lifespan. . . ."

ON THE EVE of his fortieth birthday, writer Cyril Connolly saw himself in a dream. "Gin, whisky, sloth, fear, guilt, tobacco had made themselves my inquilines; alcohol sloshed about within, while the tendrils of melon and vine grew out of ears and nostrils; my mind was a worn gramophone record, my true self was such a ruin as to seem non-existent." Next morning, Connolly concluded that the dream had been close to the mark. Even in the full light of day he saw himself as "a ham actor, moth-eaten with self-pity. . . . Approaching forty, I am about to heave my carcass of vanity, boredom, and guilt into the next decade."[1]

A young man lives through his body, as the saying goes; an old man lives against it. Physical strength increases until the mid-twenties, then begins to ebb. Loss of energy and the other many insults of aging come upon us with silent tread. We reject them as long as we can. When rejection is no longer possible, we tend to react like the typical combat soldier the first time under fire: "My God! They're shooting at *me!*"

Gerontology is the study of the silent, gradual, cumulative changes that take place within cells, tissues, organs, and organ systems over time. Study of the aging process draws upon an array of disciplines including biology, genetics, biochemistry, psychology, medicine, and the social sciences. The gerontologist is as interested in the first week of man's life as the last. Indeed, in his attempt to penetrate the impenetrable, the gerontologist has recently found himself unwittingly involved with religion, mysticism, call it what you will. Recent speculation by a handful of reputable scientists and science writers that immortality for humans may be achievable has added a whiff of stardust to a field becalmed from its inception in the backwaters of funding neglect, medical profession disinterest, and public distaste for the subject matter.

Pasteur was one of the early scientist-mystics. He wrote:

"What is beyond? The human actuated by an invisible force, will never cease to ask itself: What is beyond? It is of no use to answer: Beyond is limitless space, limitless time, or limitless grandeur; no one understands those words. He who proclaims the existence of the Infinite—and none can avoid it—accumulates in that affirmation more of the supernatural than is to be found in all the miracles of all the religions; for the notion of the Infinite presents that double character that it forces itself upon us, yet is incomprehensible. . . ."[2]

The thrust of gerontological research has been shifting in the last five to ten years from identification and description of biological changes in the aging body, to more concentrated investigation of cellular and molecular mechanisms of aging. Encouraging advances have recently been made in formulating biological theories of aging, many of which have been confirmed by experiments with laboratory animals. These have led to predictions in a few quarters that by the year 2000, scientists will be able to slow down the aging process and increase life span anywhere from fifteen to 150 years or more. Until very recently, such forecasts were generally issued by quacks. This is no longer the case.

Some leading gerontologists believe these recent forecasts to be nonsense, though they are generally careful to express respect for the forecasters' credentials as scientists. These skeptics say the most we can hope for is a continuation of the very gradual upward drift in the average age of death in recent decades. They also expect that today's promising lines of research will result in fewer debilities and discomforts for the increasing numbers of men and women who are now living beyond the age of sixty-five. These people number about 22,000,000, or one-tenth of the population, and their percentage will continue to grow. Their slowly gathering influence has given impetus to government support of research in gerontology and in geriatrics, the branch of medicine concerned more narrowly with prevention and treatment of diseases that afflict the aged.

Along with geriatrics, gerontology is still in its infancy, tracing its origins in this country to the 1930s when medical men and others interested in the aging process started meeting together in informal groups around the country. Not until 1945 was the Gerontological Society formed.

Dean of American gerontologists—and a leader of those who think that predictions of immortality are without strong foundation—is Dr. Nathan W. Shock, a physiologist, and director of the Gerontology Research Center of the National Institute on Aging, in Baltimore. Shock came to Baltimore in 1941 to inaugurate the U.S. government's gerontology research program, after nearly a decade at the University of California at Berkeley studying the growth and development of children through the period of adolescence.

Shock is an Indianan, a wise, soft-spoken individual nearing the promised biblical span; bespectacled, a pipe smoker, he's given to wearing comfortable old sweaters to work. In his off-hours, he raises African violets indoors, and roses outdoors, and has never had a seriously sick day in his life.

Shock was in his mid-thirties when he started his pioneering work on the bleak, treeless grounds of Baltimore City Hospitals overlooking a smoky, industrial part of town. His staff consisted of one assistant; his budget was low; and he was one of about one hundred scientists in the entire United States involved directly in gerontological research at that time.

Today, Shock directs the largest gerontology research center in this country, with a staff of 150 scientists and technicians. Though there are still probably only a few thousand scientists directly involved in gerontological research in America, the field has become increasingly attractive to young scientists, and is now steadily growing.

Shock believes gerontology was held back for a long time by the feeling that little could be done about aging and that research would prove useless. All too many medical doctors still hold this view, and Shock is still fighting against that attitude. Little funding was available in the early days, and as research was costly, often tedious, and almost always undramatic, ambitious young men went elsewhere, leaving the field to a few dedicated scientists like Shock, some people who didn't fit in anywhere else, and a sprinkling of charlatans.

Men such as Shock are rather like oceanographers, patiently tossing little sample bottles into the sea, drawing them up, studying their contents in the quiet of their laboratories, then tossing them again into deeper depths. Such basic research only rarely provides exciting reading matter for the general public. Moreover, editors have long operated on the assumption, gained from experience, that articles involving death and aging were not circulation builders. Death has only recently become downright trendy, and editors—even the editors of women's magazines—are now beginning to treat the subject of aging less gingerly. By the same token, magazines and newspapers have traditionally been all too happy to publish the predictions of this or that scientist that eternal youth was at hand, or descriptions of the latest Alpine "rejuvenation" clinic where cell tissues of fetal lambs or whatnot were reportedly being injected into the veins of popes, prime ministers, and playboys.

Shock says there have been many charlatans in the field who have had no interest in doing real research, but who have been "chasing the Holy Grail."

He says that so little was known about the aging process three or four decades ago that the basic questions had to be asked first. There is something, for example, that renders older people and older animals more susceptible to disease—but what is it? The basic physiology of aging had to be learned.

The study of the physiology of aging has posed the same problems as long-term psychological studies. There's the finiteness of the experimenter's own life, for one thing, though he can obviously employ understudies. Then there's the very real problem of finding subjects from the community at large who are dedicated enough to inconvenience themselves even a few days a year for the duration of their lives without financial remuneration.

From the outset, Shock has concentrated his research upon men. At first, he had to rely for subjects upon male residents of an indigent old people's home on the hospital grounds, and upon such medical students as he could find. This proved unsatisfactory on a number of counts. Most of the institutionalized aged were so afflicted with chronic diseases that their normal aging processes were effectively masked. Then again, there was an uncovered gap of three or four decades between his two age groups. Shock needed hundreds of men from age twenty onward whom he could study for the rest of their lives.

In 1958 his problem was solved by chance. A retired medical missionary, Dr. William W. Peter, drove into Baltimore one day and offered to will his body to a hospital for research. The hospital politely turned down the offer, but Shock heard about it, and asked Dr. Peter if he might study his body *before* he died.

The physician cheerfully agreed. Moreover, Dr. Peter returned to his home on Chesapeake Bay—a little community known informally as "Scientists' Cliffs"—and recruited sixty more volunteers for Shock from among the scientists, doctors, college administrators, and U.S. civil servants who lived there. Motivated by Dr. Peter's enthusiasm, and by their own curiosity, the men agreed to come to Shock's laboratory once every 18 months to undergo a battery of seventy tests stretching over two and a half days. Men over seventy were to come in once every 12 months.

The volunteers are housed in a wing of Baltimore City Hospitals and dine in the hospital cafeteria, though some of them slip over to Haussner's, a celebrated local restaurant, at their own expense. They've been dubbed "the nation's most distinguished guinea pigs," and that they certainly must be.

The ranks have gradually grown to the current limit of 650 men ranging in age from twenty into the nineties, and Shock has a long list of volunteers waiting to become subjects. Shock's guinea pigs call themselves the "Select Society of Seeking Scientists, Saints, and Sinners," and their loyalty to the program has been remarkable, their dropout rate negligible. Most leave the program only when they die.

The men spend a strenuous two and a half days. They trudge on treadmills to test the force of their heartbeat; squeeze grip-measuring devices to reveal aspects of muscle function; submit to pituitary hormone injections to measure the responsiveness of their endocrine glands. . . .

Aging involves breakdowns in the complicated control systems of the body's cardiovascular, renal, pulmonary, endocrine, and nervous systems, which must work together for total performance. Shock has devised experiments to measure the efficiency of organ system coordination, and a man's capacity for work and exercise.

In one experiment, the subject lies on his back and turns a crank while measurements are taken of his blood pressure, heart rate, and the amount of oxygen required for the work. A mask over the subject's face captures respiratory gases so that measurements can be taken of his oxygen consumption and carbon dioxide production.

Measurements are taken before, during, and after the cranking exercise to determine the subject's norms, and the speed with which his bodily functions such as blood pressure, heart rate, and oxygen consumption, recover. The experimenters try to determine the maximum amount of cranking a man can carry out and still have his heart return to normal within two minutes.

Shock has written in a report on his research that between the ages of thirty-five and eighty, the maximum work rates for short bursts of cranking falls nearly 60 percent:

> Physical performance, of course, reflects the combined capacity of the different organ systems of the body working together. The ability to work depends on the strength of the muscles, the coordination of movement by the nervous system, the effectiveness of the heart in propelling blood from the lungs to the working muscles, the rate at which air moves in and out of the lungs, the efficiency of the lung in its gas exchange function, the response of the kidneys to the task of removing excess waste materials from the blood, the synchronization of metabolic processes by the endocrine glands, and, finally, the constancy with which the buffer systems in the blood maintain the chemical environment in the body. In order to determine the causes of the decline in overall capacity, it is necessary to assess the effects of aging on each of the organ systems.[3]

Organ system coordination can go awry in a number of ways, said Shock one day, discussing this research with me. He said that when blood-sugar levels rise in a young man, for example, the endocrine gland we know as the pancreas gets the message right away and releases appropriate amounts of insulin hormone to regulate the amount of sugar available to the cells for production of heat and energy. "But the pancreas of an older man might sit there and not recognize the signals telling it to get to work," said Shock with a smile. "You have to bang the pancreas on the head, so to speak."

Similarly, there's a mechanism that tells the heart to beat more slowly when blood pressure rises. This mechanism, too, can prove sluggish in an older person.

No one knows why one organ system ages more rapidly than another, why some show wear and tear with time while others remain relatively unaffected. Shock says that breathing capacity and cardiac output, for example, decline markedly with time, while conduction of nerve impulses does not. So when you're talking about bodily functions involved in sustained physical exertion, the body demonstrates considerable impairment.

Another mystery is why some men age rapidly, some slowly. A number of Shock's seventy-year-old subjects sail through his tests with far better results than men ten or fifteen years younger.

The principal theories of aging resolve themselves into the heredity versus environment conundrum: Is aging contained in the cell's genetic material? Or is aging the result of the cumulative "insults" a body receives over the years?

One thing is certain: There is no single, denotable biological decrement that sets midlife apart as a stage in the male life cycle, nothing to compare remotely to the shutting down of ovarian function in the female during menopause. Production of male reproductive hormones starts declining before age twenty, and continues declining very gradually in the vast majority of cases into extreme old age.

Psychiatrist Jack Weinberg often speaks of aging as "a crisis in slow motion." Shock agrees.

"All of this is more psychological than physiological," explains Shock. "What's happening here is that you lose your reserve capacity. This is the essence of aging, I think. We all die a little every day. This decline in capacity and function over the years correlates directly with the progressive loss of body tissues. The loss of tissue has been associated with the disappearance of cells from muscles, the nervous system, the brain, and other vital organs. So you find, say, that you can't play as fast a game of handball as you used to, and the time comes when you must face up to it.

"On the other hand, it's a mistake to face up to it too much, to give in to it, and stop playing handball if you enjoy it, and have been playing steadily.

"The big factor in aging is the time required to do something— and this goes across the board, whether it's reaction time in the psychological sense, or the speed with which you readjust your blood level after you've been given a dose of sugar. If you engage in strenuous exercise, the older you are, the longer it takes you to get your pulse back to its normal condition."

Only when scientists discover the causes of the cell's deterioration and death will they understand the aging process. Biochemist F. Marrott Sinex of Boston University says: "Aging is one of the major things that man has wondered about since we first meet him in his written record. His mythology, his religion, and now you might say the religious side of his technology, is directed to finding the meaning of the mortality of man. Now there's a meaning to the mortality of man which is rooted in biochemistry and molecular biology. I think it would be fun to find out what that meaning is."[4]

Our bodies consist of some 60 trillion cells, miraculous blobs of jellylike protoplasm. Enclosed within a membrane .0000001-millimeter thick which transports nutrients in and waste materials out, each cell contains a nucleus surrounded by cytoplasm. Within the nucleus are 46 chromosomes or threadlike linkages of genes numbering in the millions, and tightly coiled within the chromosomes is the genetic material, deoxyribonucleic acid, or DNA. Included in the cytoplasm is ribonucleic acid, or RNA.

DNA determines the nature of all life, of the more than two million species of living things. In the words of biologist Jacob Bronowski, DNA's function is "to spell out the message of inheritance in every creature we know, from bacterium to elephant, from a virus to a rose."[5]

Biologist Edward Frankel also puts it vividly: "All the DNA in a human egg cell weighs about a ten-trillionth of an ounce, and measures in the hundred-millionths of an inch. Nevertheless, the DNA in a single cell holds all the hereditary information necessary to guide its development into a full-grown man or woman.

Although DNA is unbelievably small, it contains an incredible amount of genetic information, enough to fill a thousand-volume encyclopedia."[6]

DNA also stores instructions for the formation of molecules of protein, especially enzymes, which are essential for the chemical working of the cell. This information is transmitted from the DNA molecule to the place where the proteins are formed in the cell, by RNA which "reads" only that part of the DNA molecule required to form a specific protein or enzyme.

DNA may have yet another function, says Dr. Leonard Hayflick, professor of microbiology at Stanford University School of Medicine. "There may be a specific gene carrying a specific program of aging," says Hayflick. "Or a sequence of genes at the end of the DNA strain that says, in effect, 'That's enough. Let's start closing things down.' "[7]

In 1969 a DNA molecule—magnified more than seven million times—was seen for the first time with the aid of an electron microscope, one of a number of wondrous tools recently developed for cellular biology.

Human cells come in about 100 varieties, and in many different shapes including rods, discs, and spheres. They have myriad specialized tasks. White blood cells roam the body destroying invading bacteria; cells that form bone collect calcium salts; other cells manufacture digestive enzymes and hormones. . . .

Cells reproduce themselves by a dividing or doubling process known as mitosis. Certain types of cells, however, do not reproduce, including those of the brain, muscles, and nerves. Once gone, they're gone forever.

An adult has something like 30 billion neurons or brain cells and perhaps as many as ten times that number of glial cells, a more than ample supply for our present lifespan. By age thirty-five, some 1,000 neurons die every day, but they're not missed. Brain cell attrition is reflected in the decrease in average brain weight from 3.03 pounds at age 30, to 2.72 pounds at age ninety.

There is evidence that certain types of human and animal cells are programmed to divide and reproduce themselves a fixed number of times, the cells of long-lived animals doubling more times than those of the short-lived.

Leonard Hayflick discovered that cells taken from the lung tissue of human embryos underwent 50 divisions in their laboratory culture before dying. Similar cells taken from a man of twenty divided about 30 times; from an old man, about 20 times.

Hayflick found something else that strengthens the genetic clock thesis. He submitted batches of cells from individuals of varying ages to a temperature of 190 degrees below zero. When he thawed them out a few years later, they resumed their doubling where they had left off. In other words, they "remembered" where they had been in the doubling cycle.

Long before a man reaches old age, his cells begin to double more slowly and deteriorate in other ways, and it is to this problem that Hayflick has been devoting his research in recent years.

There is ample evidence that nature loses interest in an animal once it has mated and reproduced itself, thus guaranteeing survival of the species. In line with this, some scientists theorize that the genetic program simply runs out of instructions with time, leaving the body's cells in a state of figurative demoralization and breakdown.

To carry out DNA's coded instructions to produce proteins, RNA must read them correctly, or literally, if you will. There is no room for ambiguity in this part of nature's system. Some theorists believe that errors occur from time to time during the repeated readings over the years. These errors—they've been likened to nicks that scar a favorite old phonograph record—may accumulate and result in destruction of a cell. This is known as the "error theory."

"Free radicals" are another prime suspect in the death of cells. Free radicals are highly reactive fragments of molecules, often containing oxygen, that result from faulty cell metabolism. These troublemakers rove through our bodies seeking other molecules with which to combine, often touching off harmful chemical reactions that, for example, damage cell membranes.

British gerontologist Alex Comfort—best known to the American public as the author of *The Joy of Sex* and its sequel—has likened free radicals to male convention delegates ready to react with just about anything in skirts.

Free radical oxidants are a factor in causing butter to turn rancid, oily rags to erupt in spontaneous combustion, and other such phenomena. Scientists have discovered that if they include certain antioxidant chemicals in the diet of laboratory mice, some live longer than normally.

Free radicals are responsible for some of the cross-linkage or fusing of protein molecules known as collagen. "Collagen, which is the primary constituent of connective tissue, represents a supporting framework for many tissues and organs of the body," says Shock. "In a young animal, collagen fibre acts more or less like springs which impart elastic properties for organs. With increasing age, the elasticity is lost primarily because cross-links form between cell fibres or within the collagen molecules themselves."

Another major research area for gerontologists concerns the malfunction and breakdown of parts of our immensely powerful and complicated immune system.

The body's first line of defense against disease are the skin and mucous membranes; the second line are the lymphocytes or lymph cells which are manufactured in bone marrow. The apparent task of the lymphocytes is to spot bacteria, viruses, poisons, foreign tissue and other invading enemy agents and sound the alarm, triggering the immune response.

There are a number of theories about how the immune system becomes deranged. One theory is that the thymus gland ages early, and presumably processes a decreasing number of lymphocytes. It's known that after about age twenty-five, a man's thymus produces decreasing amounts of the hormone thymocin, which is a stimulant to the immune system. Thymocin production ceases entirely by the time a man reaches about age fifty. Mice injected with thymocin have demonstrated increased immunity and resistance to disease, but as with most of these theories, it's not known whether this would hold true for men.

Second, our aging "killer" cells sometimes either fail to recognize the enemy, or else produce antibodies which become confused and attack the host or friendly cells. In any event, we produce fewer antibodies as the years go by.

The brain has been called the most complicated piece of matter in the universe. A computer capable of duplicating the work of this three-pound mass of gray-and-white tissue packed inside our skulls would be of a size to cover the face of the Earth, we're told. So it's not surprising that the brain—specifically that part of it called the hypothalamus—is suspected of playing an important role in the aging process.

Though the hypothalamus accounts for only 3 percent of the brain's total weight, and is answerable to higher authority in the person of the cerebrum, it is an important middle-manager, so to speak. Located near the brain's underside, the hypothalamus is connected by nerve routes to the cerebral cortex at one end, and at the other to the pituitary gland, which controls the endocrine system. Hence the hypothalamus has been likened to a switchboard helping to keep the body in equilibrium.

The hypothalamus is involved in many of the body's most fundamental activities, including sexual drive, appetite, sleep, and body temperature. It's in its capacity as an overseer, through the pituitary, of the endocrine system, that the hypothalamus is believed to influence aging, most dramatically in the female.

At puberty, for example, the ovaries step up production of estrogen, the principal female hormone, and progesterone. At menopause, the hypothalamus changes its signals, and the ovaries stop producing eggs, and also stop, or greatly diminish, the output of estrogen.

Experiments and theories such as these are what have given new life to the study of aging. They're part of the silent explosion of knowledge in cellular biology typified by the discovery of DNA's structure in 1953 by Drs. James D. Watson and Francis H. C. Crick, one of the most important biological discoveries of all time. Consequently, a "fountain of youth" school of gerontology has emerged, numbering Alex Comfort and Bernard Strehler among its members.

Comfort has predicted that by the year 2000, science will have the means at hand to extend life by 20 percent or fifteen years, and that the psychological effect of this will be enormous.

"Bearing in mind the rate of growth in biology and the intensification of the research effort that would surely follow the first and minimal demonstration, one bonus could lead to others," says Comfort. "What is clear is that even a slight breach in the primeval human certainty that we will die between the ages of seventy and ninety, will produce vast changes in our self-estimate. Show once that aging can be pushed back and, like the generation that has lived with the pill, we shall never be able to go back to the old attitudes."[8]

Strehler has said "the aging puzzle will be essentially solved by the year 2000, perhaps sooner. We will then have the tools to considerably lengthen man's life span." Someday, he says, "we may live indefinitely."[9]

Biophysicist Robert Sinsheimer of the California Institute of Technology says: "Even the timeless patterns of growth and maturity and aging will be subject to our design. We know of no intrinsic limits to the life span. How long would you like to live?"[10]

Science writers Isaac Asimov and Arthur Clarke are members of this school. "If we come to understand the biochemical and biophysical changes involved in aging, and if we can learn to delay or even reverse the process by the year 2000, we may face a future society in which men and women will routinely live to over 100,"[11] says Asimov. Clarke predicts that immortality will be achieved by the year 2100.

If scientists do succeed in extending life to any substantial degree, Comfort is undoubtedly correct: The implications will be positively staggering. The thinking of theologians, economists, medical men, philosophers—everyone—will be turned upside down.

Will life continue to have meaning if death has been indefinitely postponed? What precious metal will symbolize one's 200th wedding anniversary? Are we talking about Nirvana, or an eternity of office politics at Amalgamated Widget? Will we stop having children?

Unless great progress is made in eliminating the economic and social ills that afflict so many of today's aged, the extension of life span to even 150 years could be calamitous. The problem calls to mind the story of Tithonus, the lover of Aurora, the Goddess of Dawn, in Greek mythology.

Aurora persuaded Jupiter to make Tithonus immortal, but neglected to stipulate that her lover also be endowed with eternal youth. Tithonus grew old, his hair turned gray, his limbs grew rickety. When he could no longer walk, Aurora locked him in a room whence came his pathetic cries. Finally, Aurora wearied of him and turned him into a grasshopper.

Are we really on the threshold of eliminating today's killer diseases, of dramatically increased life span, even immortality? Many scientists think not.

Dr. Bernard Davis, a professor of bacterial physiology at Harvard Medical School, says: "My general view is that our success in conquering most infectious diseases, and in developing elaborate means for improving health in many other diseases, combined with our fantastic rate of advance in understanding molecular and cellular biology, have given rise to a most unrealistic set of extrapolations in the medical area. I have very serious doubts that research will lead to dramatic changes in so deep-seated a product of evolution as the aging process."[12] Dr. Lewis Thomas, president of the Memorial Sloan-Kettering Cancer Center in Manhattan, echoes this view in his best-selling *The Lives of a Cell.*

I asked Dr. George Maddox, director of Duke University's Center for the Study of Aging and Human Development, about the prospects of immortality for today's middle-aged man. Maddox replied that he and his staff find the predictions of the Fountain of Youth school of gerontologists "downright mind boggling."

"If you ask whether some measure of chemical control of aging will one day be feasible, the answer has to be 'yes,'" said Maddox. "But if you ask us whether we'd invest in a company working on the problem, we'd say, 'No!'"

Finally, I asked Nathan Shock about this, and he replied: "I don't think there's going to be a sudden breakthrough that's going to double or triple the life span simply because in order to do that, you'll have to engage in genetic engineering. Obviously, there's a genetic pattern that determines the average age of men and animals. But so far, nobody has been able to find a specific gene or chromosome that codes for life span. To alter the genetic code, you've got to have an identifiable locus to work with. That's a long way off in my opinion."

Shock does not believe that increase in life span should even be the goal of gerontology at this time. "In my opinion, the ultimate goal of cell research on aging is to improve the performance and well-being of older people. The goal is to improve the quality of life in the later years by reducing the incidence of disabilities which afflict many elderly.

"None of us reaches our full potential life span as determined genetically. Some disease or combination of diseases shortens our life. It is here that I think we're going to improve. It is here that we can learn to relieve disability and improve health so later years are not so related to long-term illness."

Meanwhile, we must live with cold, statistical facts of life and death. The maximum length of man's life hasn't changed markedly for centuries. The days of our years remain three-score and ten. What has increased dramatically is life expectancy at birth.

In 1900 the life expectancy at birth of white American males was about forty-six years. It's now about sixty-eight years, an increase of more than twenty-two years. This increase was brought about by a lowering of the rate of infant mortality; containment of such previous killers as pneumonia, influenza, tuberculosis, typhoid fever; improvements in nutrition. More of today's male infants are living to late adulthood, in other words, than those born in 1900.

However, life expectancy once a man has reached age sixty-five, has changed very little. At the turn of the century, a man of sixty-five could expect to reach about seventy-six. Today his life expectancy is about seventy-eight—a two-year increase in three-quarters of a century.

Twenty-five years ago, the life-expectancy-at-birth curve that had been going up so splendidly, flattened out, and has since been inching upward at the rate of only a few months per year. It's this modest increase in life expectancy that Shock expects to continue. Nothing more.

Shock says that after age thirty, "mortality increases rapidly—in precise logarithmic ratio to age in the population as a whole—because the elderly become more susceptible to diseases that kill, such as cancer and cardiovascular ailments. The mortality curve goes up just as smooth as silk. If a heart attack doesn't get you, something else will. That's about the size of it."

The National Center for Health Statistics says that between the ages of thirty and fifty, deaths per 100,000 men rise from 230 to 1,180, a fivefold increase; between fifty and seventy, the rise is from 950 to 4,700, another fivefold increase, and so on.

It's generally realized that women have all the best of it in the actuarial tables—and they keep increasing their lead. Life expectancy at birth for white American women in 1900 was forty-eight, two years longer than men; today it is seventy-five, seven years longer than men. Life expectancy for women at age sixty-five in 1900 was sixty-seven; today it is eighty-two, four years longer than men.

The biological superiority of women holds true in every mammalian species studied, and in nearly all other species as well. Dr. Estelle Ramey, a geneticist in Georgetown University Hospital's Department of Physiology and Biophysics, has written that the x-y chromosomes which determine maleness have fewer "safety factors" than the x-x chromosomes which determine femaleness. Consequently, says Dr. Ramey, "the male fetus has a 12 percent greater abortion rate in all mammalian species. More boys die during pregnancy. Also, in the first week of life in humans, 34 percent more boy babies die than girl babies."[13]

Dr. Ramey says that the death rate during the first week of life is generally due to congenital "irregularities," such as gastro-intestinal and cardiovascular problems. Male babies have less resistance than female babies to infection, another cause of death.

Between the ages of thirty-five and fifty-five, the death rate of men from cardiovascular disease is three times that of women. Dr. Ramey believes the male hormonal system may be the culprit, in combination with social pressures that subject the male to far more stress than females. In a stressful situation, she notes, blood vessels constrict and blood pressure goes up. After the period of stress has passed, testosterone has the effect of maintaining the constriction of the blood vessels, and when this persists, high blood pressure is the result.

Before menopause, a woman's female hormones appear to protect her from cardiovascular disease by counteracting the effects of the testosterone that she, too, has in her system. "In women after menopause, the incidence of cardiovascular disease rises very significantly. Even then, in the group that lives between 85 and 100 years, they tend to outlive men.... This is a long-term effect on blood vessels, so women start later to develop atherosclerosis and related diseases."[14]

Dr. Ramey has successfully combined career and marriage. She believes that once men open up career opportunities to women, men themselves will be the biggest gainers. In an interview recently she put it this way:

"The irony is that men have designed a society which is calculated to make it difficult for them to live to a ripe old age. They insist on subjecting themselves, without any help at all from their natural partners, to the severe stress of running a society. They don't even allow themselves a good cry—so they bleed internally instead. Obviously something needs to be done about sharing the stresses, and in finding ways of protecting this fragile sex, which is male, in a physiologic way.

"I haven't seen anything in my lifetime more useful to men than the women's liberation movement in terms, ultimately, it seems to me, of their well-being and survival. Women, by insisting on taking over some of the responsibility, are essentially forcing men to live better lives."

(With the attractive Dr. Ramey, however, it may be a question of, "physician heal thyself." She confessed to me a while back that she had been working so hard she had collapsed from exhaustion while lecturing—and her husband had insisted upon taking her on a vacation.)

Nathan Shock says there are a number of things a man in midlife can do to improve his health, and possibly increase his life span. They are all simple, common-sense things that have been in the public domain for a long time, the staple advice of general practitioners the country over: weight control, elimination of cigarette smoking, exercise, and reduction of animal fats in the diet to keep blood cholesterol levels down.

"The fat population by any measure doesn't live as long," he declares. "They develop diseases, from arteriosclerosis to high blood pressure to diabetes to joint and back problems.

"The other big thing is cigarette smoking. If we could wipe out obesity and cigarette smoking, it might have a bigger impact than anything we've got yet in the research labs. The nub of the problem is that we haven't found out yet how to change human customs."

There is a preventive medicine organization, the Life Extension Institute, which *has* found a way to change, or at least alter some human customs; to motivate men to take better care of their health. The institute's behavior modifier combines fear with reassurance.

 **"To Us, Jogging Is Murder...."**

DEGENERATIVE DISEASES of the heart and blood vessels, and a handful of malignant neoplasms or cancer, account for most deaths of middle-aged men. Their onset can be silent and of many years' duration; some are importantly affected by one's living habits; some can be detected early and contained or cured. Sometimes these diseases strike out of the blue, no matter how sensibly we live, how religious we are about having medical checkups. In this situation, the Life Extension Institute makes a convincing argument for prudence.

"The resources that you have in your various body systems are so great that you can abuse them for forty or fifty years and never really cause much of a deterioration in the way you feel," says Dr. John McCann. "Alcohol is a prime example; it can take twenty years to make inroads on the liver. The same with tobacco's effects on the heart and lungs. But when things do start coming apart, 'That's all she wrote,' in all too many cases."

McCann, a big man in his early fifties, is dedicated to the principles of preventive medicine. A B-17 bomber pilot in World War II, his field was aerospace medicine as a career Air Force man, and with contractors such as General Dynamics after his mid-1960s retirement as colonel. McCann was named medical director of Life Extension in 1971.

Clear evidence that heart disease can get started early has been reflected in autopsies of young Americans killed in action during the Korean and Vietnam wars showing that 80 percent already had arteriosclerotic lesions of the blood vessels of the heart.

"Fifteen percent of those from the Korean conflict had lesions far enough advanced to occlude 50 percent or more of the lumen or passageways in a number of coronary arteries," says McCann. "Similar assays of Vietnam casualties indicated the incidence had risen to 25 percent. The change in incidence over a relatively short time span implies that the disease process is now affecting more individuals."

Based upon the condition of a man's blood vessels, medicine now feels confident that it can identify far in advance whether or not he's a likely candidate for coronary crisis. But such discussion has little positive effect upon grown men, says McCann, echoing the experience of other doctors—many of whom don't follow their own advice and warnings. It's hackneyed to say that it takes a heart attack to motivate a man to modify harmful lifelong habits of work, eating, drinking, smoking, sedentariness, or whatever—but such is too often the case.

Dr. William Barclay, chairman of the American Medical Association's Committee on Hypertension, says: "The maintenance of health has a very low priority in this country. It's only when you get sick that you put a high priority on health, on getting well. If we could change people's habits, we'd have a tremendous impact."[1]

Barclay is concerned because an estimated 60,000 Americans die annually as a direct result of hypertension, or high blood pressure, while 1,500,000 more suffer coronary occlusions with myocardial infarction, or heart attacks, and cerebrovascular accidents, or strokes, resulting in part from hypertension.

Barclay's education program is aimed at doctors as well as the general public, because many of them still cling to the mistaken belief that high blood pressure is a normal part of the aging process, and not necessarily harmful.

If it's true, as Barclay contends, that health maintenance has a low priority in the United States, then the medical profession must share some of the blame, for it has traditionally looked upon preventive medicine as of secondary importance. As John McCann says, "There's no way a young physician can become a Ben Casey in this field."

The concept of the annual physical examination is a relatively recent one. Though a number of prominent men including Teddy Roosevelt, William Howard Taft, and Irving Fisher, a Yale University economics professor, are associated with its origins, the credit for the idea must go to a man named Harold Ley.

As a teen-age boy before the turn of the century, Ley worked as a clerk in the actuarial department of the Massachusetts Mutual Life Insurance Company. The actuarial tables he worked with disturbed him, for they revealed that great numbers of American men died prematurely. In time, Ley left the insurance company and became a successful contractor in Manhattan. When he'd established himself financially, Ley returned to the problem of mortality. He came up with the idea of periodic medical examinations: If a man could be encouraged to have such examinations, he reasoned, then doctors might diagnose diseases in the early stages, and the man would be healthier and live longer.

John McCann says Ley then reasoned that if he "could go to the insurance companies and convince them that if they participate, and perhaps underwrite the cost of such examinations, they would gain business; the man would live longer, pay more premiums; the insurance companies' actuarial tables would look better—and everyone would benefit."

Ley succeeded brilliantly, and Life Extension Institute, founded in 1913, was the result. Former President William Howard Taft served as the organization's first chairman of the board, and Metropolitan Life Insurance Company was its principal sponsor and client. Soon other insurance companies joined Metropolitan in sending their policy applicants to the institute for medical examinations.

The nation's health had improved vastly by the end of World War II, and the insurance companies began to phase out of Life Extension. Their places were taken by big industrial firms who were concerned with maintaining the health of key executives in whom they had heavy investments. Now an affiliate of Dun & Bradstreet, the institute provides annual health examinations for executives of more than 1,500 companies, and untold other individuals. In recent years, labor unions have begun to bargain for health examinations as part of their fringe benefits.

The scope of these examinations has increased considerably

since 1913. "During the first two decades of this century, 75 percent of all deaths were the result of infectious disease," says Life Extension's Dr. Harry J. Johnson. "Then man was destroyed by agents outside the human body that entered via the mouth, nose, and throat. Today man is destroyed from within by a breakdown of the internal organs, especially the heart and circulatory system. Consequently, the scope of our health examinations has become much more sophisticated, and our major emphasis is now upon detection of degenerative disease."

There is emphasis, too, upon disease-prevention, and disease-deferment.

"The remarkable increase in life expectancy recorded during the first half of this century was made possible by preventing disease, not by treating it," says Johnson. "Infectious diseases were brought under control by immunization and better sanitation. Further increase in life expectancy will reflect ability to prevent or defer cardiovascular disease. Such deferment will of necessity depend to a large degree upon how successful we are in convincing people to modify their habits of living. The health examination provides an ideal opportunity to do a selling job."

An important part of Life Extension's selling job is its "Health Hazard Appraisal," which attempts to compute your chances of being alive ten years hence. If you don't like your odds, Life Extension outlines the steps that you should take to improve them.

First, you fill out a forty-page health hazard appraisal form that reveals in detail your medical history and living habits. Then you undergo a stem-to-stern medical examination. This can be done at the institute's medical center in Manhattan, at its affiliates in Los Angeles, San Francisco, San Diego, or by one of the 800 private physicians in major U.S. cities who perform examinations along the institute's prescribed lines.

The results of your medical examination and medical history are fed into a computer operated by the institute's San Diego affiliate, Inter Health. There they are played against a bank of actuarial data on other Americans of your age, race, and sex. In this manner, it's determined where you stand compared with the statistically average person in your life situation.

"What we have here is a beautiful communications device to

impel a person to take better care of himself," says John McCann. "At any point in life, there are anywhere from a dozen to fifteen conditions which comprise the major part—about 70 percent— of the risk we face. Thousands of conditions—such as being struck by lightning—make up the remaining 30 percent. What we do is identify and quantify the major hazards and identify the specific threats to each individual."

As an institute client, you receive a computer printout that flags the serious hazards you face, estimates your chances of dying of these causes in the next decade, and tells you what you can do to lessen your chances of leaving this world soon.

You are assigned an "appraisal age" and a "compliance age." Your chronological age may be forty, for example, but let's say the computer appraises your health profile as that of a man of fifty-three. The compliance age is the new appraisal age you can achieve if you change your living habits and have health defects, if any, corrected.

It takes about ten days to two weeks for the results of your examination and computer analysis to come in. A consultation with an institute doctor follows, and you take the results of your health hazard appraisal and medical examination home to your regular doctor. Twelve months later, you repeat the process.

Admittedly, it's a psychological device to toss a bit of a scare into an individual. But the appraisal is founded on solid actuarial fact: data on the causes of death gathered from studies by the U.S. Public Health Service, medical schools, university research projects, and insurance companies.

Dr. Lewis Robbins, a former public health service physician who won the 1972 Lambert Award for his pioneering work in developing such death-risk appraisals, worked with Dr. Charles Ross of Inter Health and the institute in preparing the computer bank.

Let's look for a moment at the white male, aged fifty to fifty-four. The major threats to his life, in order of seriousness, are: coronary, or arteriosclerotic heart disease; cancer of the lung; stroke; cirrhosis of the liver; motor vehicle accident; suicide; bronchitis and emphysema; cancer of the intestines and rectum; pneumonia; and rheumatic heart disease.

A fifty-year-old Florida businessman who recently took the examination and health hazard appraisal, received this covering letter from McCann:

"Your appraisal indicates that your current risks are somewhat above average. A significant contributing factor to this is your elevated blood pressure, cholesterol, and weight. . . . I would also caution you to watch your alcoholic consumption, and, in particular, don't mix it with driving."

The Floridian learned, doubtless to his chagrin, that while his chronological age was fifty, he had the body of a man of sixty-two. He found, too, that he was a prime candidate for heart trouble.

Of every 100,000 white males aged fifty, the institute's actuarial tables show that 5,874 will die within ten years of heart disease. (*Arteriosclerosis* is a general term covering the various conditions that bring about the thickening and hardening of artery walls and loss of their elasticity. *Atherosclerosis* is a form of arteriosclerosis characterized by a thickening of the inner layer of the artery wall by lipids, or fatty deposits, decreasing the inner diameter of the artery.) Because of the Florida man's physical condition and living habits, he is in the age-sixty-two category where 13,759 will die of heart disease.

The man's blood pressure is 150 over 108, which means that he is 3.4 times more likely than the average man to succumb to heart disease. By bringing his blood pressure down to a moderate 120 over 80 or less, his risk will be only 1.3 times more than the average. He will remain more than the average risk because it is assumed that his high blood pressure has already caused harm.

His cholesterol count was high, too: it registered 288. The computer said this figure must be reduced to 180 or less.

Our man is also 32 percent overweight, another risk factor in heart disease. The computer ordered him to take the weight off.

Finally, the Floridian had confessed on his medical history that he consumed from 7 to 24 drinks per week. (If he's like most of us, he underestimated his consumption.) This rate of drinking, combined with his other failings, renders him twice as likely as the average man of fifty to contract cirrhosis of the liver, the No.

4 killer of his age and sex and race group. It also sets him up for increased exposure to a fatal automobile accident.

Said the computer mercilessly: "Stop drinking."

The Florida man can choose to ignore the data, or he can decide to shape up. He'll shape up, says McCann confidently.

Many of the men who return year after year to Life Extension become vitally interested in and knowledgeable about their health. In this regard, they're like Nathan Shock's subjects in Baltimore who exhibit a far higher degree of health consciousness than the general run of men, and who, incidentally, enjoy a significantly lower death rate as well.

Life Extension's most comprehensive examination for men over thirty-five—the cost is comparable to that of an examination by your general practitioner—lasts more than three hours. But the institute has managed to make things as pleasant as possible. The Manhattan facility, for example, occupies an entire floor high in a midtown skyscraper. After changing into a white cotton pajama-like suit, you and the other clients pad from consulting room to laboratory to consulting room over deep, comfortable carpet. Modern paintings adorn the brightly colored walls. Soft music drifts from the ceiling. Lovely nurses slip back and forth.

You're examined by half a dozen specialists, most of whom are carrying on important research in their fields. They have the latest in diagnostic equipment, and laboratory tests are carried out in real time. A "Sequential Multiple Analyzer plus Computer," for example, records your twenty critical blood chemistries—including cholesterol level—in sixty seconds.

Your first examination consists of a probe of the prostate gland, and of the rectum and sigmoid colon.

Prostate disorders don't generally crop up until age fifty; thereafter, they're so commonplace they've come to be known as "male trouble" now that they've become accepted as a topic of conversation even in mixed company. Nearly two-thirds of American men over age sixty experience enlargement of the prostate, and the percentage continues to increase with age. Enlargement per se is not always painful or harmful, though it frequently is.

"Cancer originating in this gland is the third commonest malignancy among North American males, and the third-ranking cause of cancer deaths among men," notes science writer Gilbert Cant. "No fewer than 60,000 men in the United States will have prostate cancer diagnosed this year, and 20,000 will die from the spread of the disease."[2]

The principal task of the prostate gland—actually a group of lobes located at the neck of the bladder—is to store most of the seminal fluid that dilutes and carries the spermatozoa on their journey through the urethra, or urine tube. (The balance of the seminal fluid comes from the two seminal vesicles nearby.)

For reasons not clearly understood, the prostate gland tends to enlarge, even though a man's production of sex hormones diminishes with time. "Simple or benign enlargement may produce no symptoms, but inflammation of the gland—prostatitis— is almost certain to do so in painful and embarrassing ways," says Cant. "If an active infection can be diagnosed and its bacterial cause identified, this form of prostatitis can usually be controlled, if not cured, by modern 'wonder' drugs. But in many cases, with equal distress, no infection can be demonstrated, and the diagnosis becomes non-infectious prostatitis.

"By whatever name, any disorder of the prostate is likely to cause painful, difficult, and too frequent or incomplete urination. This is because the urethra, as it leaves the bladder, passes almost immediately into a sort of tunnel through the prostate, where it can be squeezed by enlarged or inflamed tissue. . . . All prostatologists agree that far too few men over the age of forty have an annual physical in which the prostate is palpated. And for men over sixty, or even fifty, perhaps that should be a semiannual examination," says Cant.[3]

While the prostate examination is quickly over and only momentarily uncomfortable, the proctosigmoidoscopy can be painful. Life Extension proctologist Paul Morton puts the apprehensive client at ease by first explaining why and when to expect discomfort. The pain results when the rigid ten-inch metal sigmoidoscope tube that he employs to search for polyps, or growths, begins to stretch the blood vessels in the flexible tube that is the colon.

If Morton spots anything with the sigmoidoscope's light source that leads him to suspect disorders farther along in the colon, he's equipped to carry out a more extended examination.

For years, Americans have heard alarming and often conflicting statistics about the coronary heart disease death rate. During the 1940s and 1950s, the death rate did rise steadily and unequivocally, subject to swings every three years or so when respiratory disease epidemics carried off extra numbers of men and women with weak hearts. Since the mid-1960s—when, it now appears, the death rate began to stabilize—the situation has become less clear. Cardiologists themselves are not certain whether the death rate has stabilized, or has actually started to decline.

A number of factors have clouded the issue. In 1968 the World Health Organization changed the classification of coronary heart disease—which it now calls ischemic heart disease—making it more complicated to compare death rates since that time with those of earlier years. There was a respiratory disease epidemic in 1968, but there has not been one since, and some authorities think that the decline in coronary heart disease death rate since that time may be in large measure a reflection of the absence of another such epidemic.

In the years 1968 through 1972, the death rate of white American males between the ages of 35 and 44 dropped from 87.5 per 100,000 to 75.4, an 11.5 percent decline. In the 45-to-54 age group, the drop was from 348.2 to 312.9, or 7.7 percent; and in the 55-to-64 age group, the decline was from 953.7 to 867, or 6.6 percent.

Statisticians Tavia Gordon and Thomas Thom, of the National Heart and Lung Institute, writing in the June 1975 issue of *Preventive Medicine*, reflect the government's cautious belief that the coronary heart disease death rate has flattened out:

"Since 1968, a slight but non-trivial decrease in coronary heart disease mortality has occurred. This decline is probably real. . . . Most of the decrease in coronary heart disease mortality may be due to epidemic fluctuations in the incidence of respiratory disease. We would infer from this that mortality from coronary heart disease which had stabilized in this country by the latter half of the 1960s, remained stabilized in the early 1970s."[4]

There is, however, no ambiguity about the fact that whether the death rate of coronary heart disease has stabilized or started downward, it still remains the principal killer of American men and women. In 1972 there were 1,800,000 deaths from all causes, including accidents and suicides. Coronary heart disease accounted for 684,000 deaths. Deaths from hypertension, stroke, and rheumatic heart disease—all of which have been declining for some time—came to more than 200,000.

Some of the medical men who believe that the coronary death rate has turned downward, attribute it to a number of factors, including the decrease in cigarette smoking, and an increasing awareness on the general public's part that diet, exercise, weight, blood pressure, and the stress and pace of life all affect their hearts and vascular systems. These doctors cite as an additional factor the inception of special coronary care units in hospitals during the 1960s.

In most annual medical checkups, an electrocardiogram or EKG—a graphic record of the electrical currents produced by the heart muscle—is taken with the subject in a resting condition. At Life Extension, the resting EKG, and resting blood pressure, are supplemented by a stress test in which the subject trudges on a treadmill at a gradually increasing speed and angle while his heart rate and blood pressure are monitored on an oscilloscope by cardiologist John T. Finkenstaedt, with a nurse standing by.

Before you reach Finkenstaedt's laboratory, which is the last stop of your medical examination, he already has a pretty good line on you. He has read your medical history; he has your resting EKG taken earlier by a technician; and he has your "lipid profile," consisting of measurements of your cholesterol, triglyceride, and lipoprotein levels, which when high are associated with the risk of coronary atherosclerosis.

After your lung capacity has been tested on a pulmonary screener, a number of electrodes are attached to your upper body. The "Sub-maximal Exercise Tolerance Test on Treadmill" progresses through a maximum of six stages—few men or women complete the course—totaling 18 minutes. The test starts with the treadmill running at 1.7 miles per hour at an angle of 10 degrees for three minutes, continuing through 6-, 9-, 12-, 15-, and 18-minute stages, the final one at 5.5 m.p.h. and 20 degrees.

The stress test was designed to detect diseases and abnormalities of the heart and blood vessels earlier than previously possible. Dr. Finkenstaedt has put more than 5,000 men and women through stress-testing in recent years, and he's been able to spot far more problems than he did when relying upon resting EKGs.

The stress test also has an invaluable psychological function: it motivates many men to get in shape. For any illusions you may have harbored about your physical condition evaporate with embarrassing rapidity on the treadmill as its speed and angle increase. You start out easily enough but before many minutes have passed, you're perspiring and panting while linear blips fly across the oscilloscope screen putting it all in a squiggly record.

When the blips tell Finkenstaedt that you've had enough, he turns off the treadmill. Now he determines how long it takes your heart to return to normal.

Armed with EKG graphs and other data, Finkenstaedt takes you back to his office for a Dutch uncle talk, with emphasis upon the importance of an exercise program. His discussion is low key, for he's discovered that the EKGs, blood pressure levels, and the treadmill experience have already done the selling job.

"I had a guy fifty-one years old in here this morning," he said recently while I sat in his office recovering from a brief walk on his machine. "He was way overweight; his lipids were abnormally high. He's a two-pack-a-day man. His pulmonary screening revealed early obstructive lung disease. He was so out of breath at the beginning of the third stage of stress testing that I had to stop him. He went out of here scared to death but determined to do something about it. I bet he will, too. If these fellahs will listen to you, it's amazing the change that can take place in just six months."

Finkenstaedt has to caution such men not to plunge into a sudden program of vigorous exercise, lest they jog or bicycle to their deaths, as so many middle-aged men have been doing in recent years. "To us, jogging is murder," agrees Dr. Meyer Friedman, a prominent West Coast cardiologist, who says that no one over age thirty-five should suddenly start jogging without first having an EKG, and consultation with a doctor.

While most cardiologists probably agree with Finkenstaedt

about the impact upon the heart of smoking, obesity, and so forth, a number of authorities contend that the evidence is not conclusive. Finkenstaedt's answer is a convincing one, which he demonstrates with before-and-after EKGs of out-of-shape, overweight, high-lipid, smokers who mend their ways over a six-month period. The improvement in their pulmonary capacity, their treadmill endurance, and the strength and health of their heart is unarguable.

"You *can't* argue with an EKG," says Finkenstaedt with finality.

For most of the men who've taken Life Extension examinations over the years, says John McCann, the major benefit has been reassurance. The reassurance comes from increased knowledge about themselves, and the realization that "without question, the greatest untapped resource of health care in this country is the individual himself; the potential capability that is available in each of us to properly control and alter our living habits. The evidence is in: Whether you live or die is often squarely in your own hands."

9 "Impotence Is Nearly Always Psychogenic...."

WRITER Martha Weinman Lear has wittily summarized the plight of middle-aged man. "The hormone-producing levels are dropping, the sexual vigor is diminishing...the children are leaving, the parents are dying, the job horizons are narrowing, the friends are having the first heart attacks; the past floods by in a fog of hopes unrealized, opportunities not grasped, women not bedded, potential not fulfilled, and the future is a confrontation with one's own mortality."[1]

Though most of these problems are psychological, there's no place that I know of where a man can go for an annual emotional checkup, something akin to Life Extension's medical examination. Psychiatrists say that such a checkup could be developed, but that most men refuse to admit to themselves that their problems might be psychological.

Psychiatrist Herbert Klemme tells me he has found that there's "'a great American collusion' whereby everybody works very hard to help everybody else avoid acknowledging that psychological or emotional problems are at the root of their midlife difficulties. For example, if a man is in a state of depression, and he complains of being exhausted, of not being able to sleep very well, somebody's going to tell him that he's coming down with flu, or that he's working too hard, or that it's the noisy neighbors. The man's doctor is in a bind because the man will come in and say, in effect: 'You *will* find something physically wrong with me.' If the doctor tells him his problem is psychological, he must be very tactful or the guy will walk out and never come back. Impotence is a very common symptom of depression in a man. But how many men know that? They come to the doctor and ask for a testosterone shot."

Dr. Harold Lear, director of the Human Sexuality Program at Mount Sinai Hospital in Manhattan, confirms that impotence is nearly always psychogenic, and like the midlife crisis itself, in a larger sense, the result of a constellation of psychological, physiological, and cultural stress factors such as those described above by his wife, writer Martha Lear.

"I see a triad of things converging in middle life, and they're all stress factors," says Dr. Lear. "The critical thing is: How does one cope? Here we bring in the question of coping mechanisms. If you have a man who is comfortable adapting to stress, and has been adapting in a mature way throughout his life, he adapts the same way at midlife, and isn't as likely to develop the compilation of behavioral and emotional changes that we lump together in the middle-aged syndrome."

Everyone knows what stress is in a general way, though its scientific meaning isn't always clearly understood. Stress is the spice of life and we couldn't avoid it if we would; harmful stress, or "distress" is something else again. Dr. Hans Selye, the Austrian-born biochemist who fathered the concept of biologic stress in the mid-1930s, believes that if stress were better understood, men could pattern their lives more happily, that "the rules which act so efficiently at the levels of the cells and organs could also be the source of a natural philosophy of life, leading to a code of behavior based on scientific principles. This code is quite compatible with and independent of any religion, political system, or philosophy. It deals only with a strategy for optimal life after birth, irrespective of how one came into being."[2]

Selye defines stress as "the non-specific response of the body to any demand made upon it"—a non-specific definition, to be sure, but we all know what he means, I think. The man who leaps from the path of an onrushing car, the surgeon racing against time to save a patient's life, the maitre d' of a restaurant trying to assuage impatient customers—they all feel the effects of stress.

While the nature of the difficulties each man faces is different, their bodies all undergo a similar three-stage "biologic stress reaction" which Selye also calls the "general adaptation syndrome." Selye's theory:

Alarm marks the first stage when the body's resources rally to battle the stressor, to prepare for the familiar "fight or flight" response that he inherited from his primitive ancestors, and that he shares with the animals. Everyone has experienced it: the butterflies in the stomach, the quickened pulse, the tingling of adrenalin pulsing into the bloodstream. . . .

Resistance marks the second stage, when the body does battle with the stressor, be it a virus, a bus bearing down at high speed, a dreaded summons to the office of a hated boss. . . .

Exhaustion marks the third stage if equilibrium does not return; if the stress can find no outlet in physical activity, or an emotional letting off of steam. Bottled-up anger, fear, or frustration will find expression on its own in emotional or physical illness.

A typical case of a man experiencing fear, anger, and frustration simultaneously is the poor wretch burdened with an unpleasant boss. The unhappy man, says writer Anthony Storr, "is frightened of losing his job, and probably frightened of the boss himself. At the same time, he is resentful of being pushed around, and may also resent living in a society where unemployment means that the possibility of changing his job is minimal."[3]

"I'm fifty-four years old," a man told Martha Lear one day. "Fifteen years ago, if they had told me, 'Listen, we can't give you a raise,' I might have said, 'The hell with you guys. You can take this job and shove it,' and I would have gone somewhere else. But when it happened now, where could I go? Who is hiring fifty-four-year-old men these days? I was terribly depressed. It created a whole bunch of complexes I never knew I had. It knocked the hell out of my sex life and everything else."[4]

Such a man has been forced to put a clamp on the nervous and chemical reactions rampaging through his system. And this, says Hans Selye, "is like slamming on the brakes of your car—and accelerating at the same time."

Hans Selye believes that man responds to stress with a genetically determined store of vitality or "adaptation energy," and that there is no way to restore it once it has been exhausted.

"It is finite, but he must spend it to complete the mission that he has been built to perform. Insurmountable obstacles lead to complication, frustration, and breakdown. To avoid distress, each individual must first find out his optimum stress level, and then use his adaptation energy in a way that does not conflict with his innate qualifications and preferences.

"Many common diseases—peptic ulcers, nervous breakdowns, high blood pressure—are caused by attempting to endure more stress than we can handle."

As we grow older, of course, it takes us progressively longer to bounce back from stressful experiences.

During the last forty years, ample time has passed for myths to grow up involving stress. Conventional wisdom, for example, has long held that top-level business executives live extremely stressful lives. Numerous surveys, including one by Life Extension in 1958, and another in 1971, indicate that the picture we have of the highly stressed executive may be overdrawn. In the two Life Extension surveys, nearly 90 percent of the thousands of executives queried responded that they did not find their jobs too stressful, a fact that their physical examinations appeared to bear out. Surveys by E. I. duPont de Nemours & Co. reveal that the incidence of stress-related disease increases the *lower* men and women are on the company pyramid. The man running the freight elevator in the back of the plant—dogged by monetary problems, arthritis, or whatever—was invariably found to be more stressed than the executive vice-president.

Man's methods of coping with stress range from martinis to meditation, and appear limited only by his imagination. A Laurentian resort offers "anti-stress vacations" consisting of nude skiing for men and women—a situation that would appear replete with stressful possibilities.

Apart from Hans Selye, few have done more to familiarize the public with the dynamics of stress than cardiologists Meyer Friedman and Ralph Rosenman. In their best-selling *Type A Behavior and Your Heart,* they make a strong case for their theory that stress is the principal cause of the high incidence of coronary heart disease. These heart specialists of Mount Zion Hospital and Medical Center in San Francisco argue that we've created an urban, industrial society where, in Friedman's words, "the stress has become almost unbearable. Everybody is selling his time for money." They contend that our society rewards, hence spawns, hard-driving, impatient, time-conscious men, whose chronically stressful work lives render them more coronary-prone than more reflective, easygoing personalities.

Recently, however, some prominent heart specialists—among them Dr. Richard S. Ross, former president of the American Heart Association, and Dr. Jeremiah Stamler of Northwestern University Medical School—have openly attacked the Friedman-Rosenman thesis as "over-simplistic and distorted."

Many medical men—including Life Extension's Finkenstaedt—take a middle view. They are willing enough to add personality factors and stress to the mix of heart disease causes, the role of emotion in disease having long been accepted.

Of all man's stress-related problems, "testicular insufficiency"—impotence—is perhaps the most embarrassing and devilish. Some psychiatrists report that impotence has been rising alarmingly in recent years, paralleling the rise of women's liberation. Other behavioral scientists believe the apparent increase is simply a reflection of today's more open attitudes toward sexual matters which have encouraged men to come forward for treatment.

Endocrinologists and sexual therapists say that a small percentage of men in late midlife, from about age forty-eight to sixty, suffer "primary testicular insufficiency" which means that their production of the male hormone testosterone has dropped off from purely physiologic causes. This can occur precipitously over the course of a few months, and when it does, a man's symptoms resemble those of women in menopause: nervousness, irritability, indecisiveness, sleeplessness—even hot flashes.

This condition may have given rise to some of the continuing confusion over the term "male menopause." Men have no menses so they obviously can't pause; they have no menstrual cycle so they cannot suffer its cessation, which is part of the female climacteric or termination of ability to reproduce life. So the term "male menopause," as noted earlier, is without scientific foundation—and more than faintly silly.

A few medical men, however, do employ the term "male climacteric" when referring to primary testicular insufficiency, most notably Dr. Herbert S. Kupperman, associate professor of endocrinology at New York University Medical Center. But Kupperman emphasizes that primary testicular insufficiency is the only "pure" male climacteric, and he does not employ the term when referring to secondary testicular insufficiency, which is impotence of psychological origin.

Kupperman says the findings for primary testicular insufficiency are specific: an increase in pituitary gonadotropic hormones—whose function is to stimulate testosterone production by the testes—and a decrease, below certain levels, of testosterone in the blood and urine. Overly simplified, what's happening here is that the pituitary—by sending gonadotropins down the system—is ordering the testes to manufacture sex hormones, but the testes simply cannot comply.

"If a man complains of sexual dysfunction with his wife, but can perform with another woman, or gets an erection in a movie, he is not in the male climacteric," says Kupperman. "The true climacteric is a physiological cessation of testicular function accompanied by vasomotor symptoms, neurological symptoms, and psychosomatic symptoms. If the symptoms are occurring without physiologic expression of diminished testosterone production, and increased gonadotropins, then it is not the male climacteric."[5]

Kupperman prescribes hormone replacement therapy for the male climacteric, and finds that within six weeks, most men start to improve and function again sexually. They must, however, continue the therapy indefinitely. He is able to separate the physiologically induced cases of impotence from the psychologically induced cases by means of placebos.

Like Kupperman, Mount Sinai's Harold Lear is an authority on sexual dysfunction, representing the best of a small but growing number of medical men and women who've been turning to the new specialty of sex therapy that gained impetus in the mid-1960s with the publication by Dr. William H. Masters and Virginia Johnson of their first book, *Human Sexual Response*. Lear's decision to enter the field came as a result of his own midlife stocktaking.

In 1970, at age fifty, Lear says he gave up a successful career as a urologist; he was chief of urology at a Hartford, Connecticut, hospital, and president of the Connecticut State Urological Association. Though happily married, well-to-do, and comfortably established, Lear was unhappy because his career had become routine; he felt that he had seen every possible urological problem at least twice.

During the course of his practice, Lear had noticed that many men and women suffered psychosexually from the implications of disease and disability. Yet few doctors, himself included, were trained to help their patients with such problems. In casting about for a specialty with wider scope, he decided to enter the sex therapy field, even though it meant a considerable cut in income and autonomy.

Lear left Connecticut and took an intensive course in human sexuality, social psychiatry, and community medicine at the University of Pennsylvania's Center for the Study of Sex Education and Medicine in Philadelphia, then moved to Mount Sinai Hospital for more training.

"If a man is impotent or has other sexual problems," says Lear, "he has superimposed anxieties and he brings those into the doctor's office with him. So how he responds to therapy may depend upon many variables.

"He may have magical expectations of a doctor's performance, and the doctor may say: 'I'm going to give you a shot and you're going to be O.K., Joe.' And the doctor gives him a pat on the back, a shot in the ass, and the guy walks out and he's well. What was injected into him may be totally irrevelant to the therapeutic process.

"Contrariwise, you may have the guy who really does have an organic problem. For some reason the flow of juices is such that his testosterone level has been significantly lowered at a relatively young age, say about forty-five. And he comes to the doctor and he's so depressed by what has happened, and he's so defeated, that raising his testosterone level will not affect his depression.

"He'll say: 'I'm over the hill, Doc.' Now that becomes a self-fulfilling prophecy. So that even if you rectify the physiological disability but don't treat the psychological overlay, you're not doing him any good. So you give him the testosterone he needs and he walks out, and he still stays impotent.

"The number of these men with organic problems is very small, and most of them can be cured with a combination of psychotherapy and testosterone. But with most men, sexual problems are in the mind."

When the level of mental stress rises, the level of testosterone goes down as the pituitary gives priority to other hormones. The highly stressed man complaining of impotence is a familiar figure in the general practitioner's waiting room.

When Lear was still in urological practice, a businessman came in one day complaining of urinary frequency. He said his general practitioner had diagnosed his problem as prostatic infection and had treated him but the problem remained.

Lear could find nothing organically wrong with the man, so he sat him down for a talk about his relationship with his wife, and his work. Of the former, the man said matter-of-factly: "I'm impotent." Of the latter, he confessed that he was in deep financial difficulty, so much so that he was holding down two jobs to make ends meet. He conceded that he was chronically worried, exhausted, depressed, and yes, he guessed he was angry with his wife who he felt was responsible in large measure for his having to work so hard.

Lear patiently probed further. The man said that he occasionally stopped by a certain bar, picked up women, and slept with them successfully.

"We sat and talked calmly about all this and he came to understand what was happening to him; and he could articulate his feelings of fear and anger when he went home at night."

Lear urged the man to confront his wife directly with his fears and anger, and see if between them they couldn't change their lives, have more fun together, and lift the economic pressure.

The patient took Lear's advice. Within less than two weeks, the man's urinary problem had disappeared, along with his "impotence."

A man who is impotent for whatever reason has a problem about where to seek help, for the average doctor is not trained to cope with patients' sexual matters. Ten years ago, less than a handful of U.S. medical schools offered any kind of course in human sexuality. Today, a fourth of all medical schools still fail to include such a course.

In Lear's view, the general practitioner shouldn't be expected to help men with sexual dysfunction, any more than they are called upon to conduct neurosurgery, for sexual therapy is a highly specialized field requiring, among other things, a thorough grounding in psychiatry. Even so, he feels that the family doctor can help such a patient by giving him a thorough medical examination—including the blood testosterone test devised in recent years—and reassuring him, if such be the case, that there is nothing organically wrong.

As it stands today, all too many doctors hear a patient's complaint of sexual dysfunction, and say: "What do you expect, Joe: You're forty-seven, for God's sake. You're over the hill." This can cause a tremendous amount of harm.

Even more harm is being done every day by all but about fifty of the estimated 5,000 sexual therapists who've gone into business since about 1970, complains Dr. William H. Masters in a recent article in *Today's Health* warning of sexual therapy quacks. Many of these self-styled therapists falsely advertise that they have been trained by Masters and Johnson, he says, and they have proliferated in the absence of any laws defining legitimate sexual therapy.

When Long Island Jewish Medical Center in New York opened one of the nation's first hospital-based sex therapy clinics in 1971, its director, Dr. Sallie S. Schumacher—who really *did* train at Masters and Johnson's Reproductive Biology Research Foundation in St. Louis—said: "We are now on the threshold of seeing sexual problems handled the same as a headache or a stomach problem."

Lear believes this may hold true with today's young married couples, but that the situation is far more complicated with men and women in middle age.

"Young people today come into the clinic hand in hand, and it's really marvelous," says Lear. "They respond to therapy because they are so malleable. But when you take a couple who've been dealing with each other for twenty years, the battle lines are drawn, the truce areas defined, and the 'free fire zones' clearly delineated. This can be very, very difficult."

Harold Lear is convinced that impotence and other symptoms of the midlife transition would disappear if we managed to create a society which viewed its aging members with pride, and accorded them place. As it stands now, all too many men from age forty onward are rendered caponlike by fear of losing their jobs, knowing they'll probably not get another for a long time, if ever. *Who is hiring fifty-four-year-old men these days?* Still others wonder whether or when they'll be forced into "voluntary" early retirement on a pension that will undoubtedly be too small to live on with any reasonable degree of comfort.

John McCann of Life Extension believes that nothing less than a "restructuring" of our society will reduce the many stress factors that he believes underlie our high coronary disease rate and many other health concerns of middle-aged man.

10 "Now That We All Know How to Spell 'Sex' Backward...."

WE HEAR a great deal from Margaret Mead and other distinguished anthropologists about veneration of the aged among primitive societies. We hear rather less about the primitives who dealt harshly with their ancientry. A number of these societies had imaginative ways of preventing their old people from becoming a burden: They dispatched them to the next world with minimum ceremony.

On certain South Sea islands, feeble male "senior citizens" were forced to inch their way to the tops of tall coconut palms. The trees were then shaken vigorously by the tribe's young bucks on the ground below. The old boys who managed to hang on were allowed to stay in this world a while longer.

In *Coming of Age*, Simone de Beauvoir tells an amusing story about the Greenland eskimos. When an old man's time had come, it seems, he was expected to paddle out to sea in his kayak. One day, a certain eskimo was too ill to paddle when his time came, and he asked his family to simply pitch him into the sea. They obliged. Then came an embarrassing hitch: The old man's parka filled with air, and he bobbed foolishly on the surface of the water. And so, writes Miss de Beauvoir, "a daughter who loved him much called out tenderly: 'Father, push your head under. The road will be shorter.'"

In the United States we have versions of the coconut palm shakeout and the long kayak voyage that are only slightly less subtle. Embedded deep in our culture is the belief that the old are worthless. Consequently, the man who is preoccupied with the stresses of midlife finds it less painful not to look ahead, let alone start making psychic provision. If he does look ahead, he sees the shadowy landscape beyond age sixty-five concealing a ghostly minefield: arteriosclerotic heart disease to the left, malignant neoplasms to the right, and you-name-it up ahead.

He has a nightmare vision: He's sitting blankly in front of a television set with other old crocks in the seedy common room of the Sunset Years Nursing Home—deserted, de-sexed, and demented.

Well, says Charlie, no thanks. "When my time comes, I hope it's early in the party."

Behavioral scientists tell me that Charlie's attitude is all but universal in this country. But they find his fear out of phase with the facts of aging.

I asked one of the nation's leading gerontologists about the American's terror of old age: Dr. James D. Birren, director of the Ethel Percy Andrus Gerontology Center at the University of Southern California.

"Now that we all know how to spell 'sex' backward, 'old age' and 'death' are just about the only taboos left in our society," replied Birren with a smile. "I think it's good that attitudes like your friend Charlie's are getting out into the open more and more. Perhaps now we can make some real progress."

Birren asserts that many of our fears of old age are rooted in ignorance. There is a great deal of mythical nonsense about old age abroad in this land of the young, he finds. We absorb it, and it strengthens our haphazard observations. Without trying to deny that the footing beyond the symbolic but essentially meaningless dividing line of sixty-five is chancy, Birren and the other gerontologists with whom I have talked say that it's both inaccurate and harmful to typecast the American over sixty-five as poverty-stricken, sexless, isolated, lonely, unhappy, crippled, and dotty. These stereotypes cause many people to keep their psychological distance from the elderly.

Dr. Thomas E. Anderson, chief of research in aging at the National Institute of Mental Health, says that much of the blame for this distorted picture can be traced to the gerontological profession itself. The distortions have come about because until recent years, research into the problems of aging has focused almost exclusively upon the poor, the ill, and the institutionalized.

"In our research, we've been too preoccupied with pathology and poverty; partly because these people are more readily available as subjects, partly because they are so visible, and partly because we all feel so guilty about them," says Anderson. Now that researchers have turned their attention to the aging process in individuals who are going about their everyday lives, a more hopeful picture of the twenty million Americans over sixty-five has begun to emerge. By the year 2000, half the U.S. population will be over fifty and one-third over sixty-five, according to some projections.

One National Institute of Mental Health study of old men, for example, shows them "as a whole to be vigorous, candid, interesting, and deeply involved in living. In marked contradiction to the usual stereotypes of 'rigidity' and 'second childhood' these individuals generally demonstrated mental flexibility and alertness. They continued to be constructive in their living; they were resourceful and optimistic."

Gerontologist Carl Eisdorfer has said, in this connection:

"We really don't understand the aged or the aging process, and so because there is a very high correlation between old age and illness, we have somehow got deluded into assuming it's all right for old people to be sick.

"But some of our recent work on blood pressure and intelligence has pretty well demonstrated that what a lot of people have accepted as a normal process of aging—the loss of intelligence between sixty-five and seventy-five—is actually related to hypertension; where it was controlled, we see no intellectual drop."[1]

Similarly, James Birren concludes from his research that "the average person need not expect a typical deterioration of mental functioning in his later years." If a man escapes severe illness, there's no reason why he won't click along on just about all his mental cylinders through his eighties.

Gerontologists Paul B. Baltes and K. Warner Schaie said recently in *Psychology Today* that after more than a decade of research, they're convinced that "general intellectual decline in old age is largely a myth. . . . Our findings challenge the stereotypical view, and promote a more optimistic one. We have discovered that the old man's boast, 'I'm just as good as I ever was,' may be true after all."[2]

Baltes and Schaie argue that during the 1930s, '40s, and '50s, intelligence testing was cross-sectional, and that this produced a false picture. Their research has been longitudinal. They explain:

> If we analyze the data cross-sectionally (comparing the different age groups at a given point in time) we see the conventional pattern of early, systematic decline. But when we look at the results longitudinally (comparing a given age group's performance in 1956 with its performance in 1963) we find a definite decline on only one of four measures, visuo-motor flexibility.
>
> There is no strong age-related change in cognitive flexibility. For the most important dimension, crystallized intelligence, and for visualization as well, we see a systematic *increase* in scores for the various age groups, right into old age. Even people over seventy improved from the first testing to the second.[3]

For some time now, there has been good news on yet another front. Research at Duke University and elsewhere reveals that healthy men and women enjoy love-making long into the twilight of their seventies and beyond. And they would doubtless be even more involved if it weren't for the lack of partners, opportunity— and fear of ridicule from the young.

Robert Butler's latest book, *Sex After Sixty*, should help bring this subject even further out of the closet.

The University of Chicago's Bernice Neugarten says research shows that most retired people are happy with their lot, and that most people over sixty-five think of themselves as healthy. A scant 4 percent of the nation's aged are confined in nursing homes, a bare 1 percent in mental hospitals.

Finally, Mrs. Neugarten maintains, it is simply not true that most American families isolate and neglect Grandma and Grandpa.

Probably more than men in any other field, professional athletes are subject to public, often callous, running commentary on their aging processes. A sports writer, for example, asked Johnny

Unitas toward the end of his career why he was having trouble with his knees. "They're old," snapped Unitas.

One afternoon, I left Nathan Shock's laboratory at Baltimore City Hospitals, and drove across town to Unitas's Golden Arm Restaurant to talk with him. Unitas was then in his late thirties, an old man by professional football standards, and what he had to say about compensation and adaptation goes to the heart of the aging process.

I asked him how he'd managed to stay on top of a game where physical strength and split-second timing were so critical. I knew that he had taken a pounding during his then sixteen or seventeen years with the Baltimore Colts: He had broken his arms, legs, collarbone, and back; sustained concussions, torn cartilages, and a punctured lung.

Unitas comes across as a very intelligent man, with the manner of a U.S. Marine colonel of infantry: brisk, to the point. (A rookie once said after his first game with Unitas: "It's like being in a huddle with God!")[4]

Unitas told me that he stayed in condition year round by playing paddle tennis, golf, and by jogging. He ate sensibly and drank sensibly. That was all there was to it, he said. He sounded like a Life Extension doctor prescribing a regimen for one of his middle-aged clients. As for what Unitas called his "quicknesses," he conceded that he could not throw the ball as "hard" as he once had, but that the ball reached his receivers just as fast because his long experience with reading defensive keys enabled him to release the ball sooner.

When men begin to slow down, they instinctively start playing a headier brand of handball, squash, tennis, and so forth. Sometimes the need to win diminishes in importance. They play the game for the exercise and sheer enjoyment.

A. L. Vischer, the eminently wise psychologist-philosopher, wrote that "the individual's powers of adaptation and compensation are quite as influential in matters of health as are involutive changes and functional disturbances."[5]

In a study of 300 biographies of outstanding individuals, psychiatrist Charlotte Buhler found that as a man's physical strength wanes in later life, his spiritual and intellectual life waxes.

Old age can prove to be a great adventure of the spirit, but it can be a torment of the soul if a man steadfastly refuses to think about it until it is upon him. For the name of the Aging Game, obviously, is "loss." And whether we win or lose depends upon how well we can handle loss when the time comes: loss of job and status at retirement; loss of mastery over events; loss of control over our children's destiny; loss of vitality—"the death of friends, or death of every brilliant eye that made a catch in the breath," as Yeats so beautifully expressed it.

Now we find out what we're made of.

 **"He's Not to
Be Allowed to Fall
into His Grave
Like an Old Dog"**

" 'Bᴙɪɴɢ me an apple and a pear!' "

"A hungry William Simon, millionaire-turned-money czar, shouts
a hasty lunch order to a harried secretary as he enters the private
conference room adjoining his office. Even though he skipped
lunch to save time, the Treasury Secretary is 15 minutes late for
his 2:30 ᴘ.ᴍ. appointment. In the conference room . . . five business executives wait. . . .

"The Cabinet officer takes his place at the head of the large
oval table. Silently, a young black man in waiter's uniform enters
the room bearing an apple and a pear on a gleaming china plate
from the Treasury Secretary's private dining room. He places the
fruit before the hungry official.

"As the businessmen begin explaining their complaints about
. . . tax regulation, Mr. Simon attacks his lunch. Chomp! The
crunching of the crisp apple punctuates the presentation by the
businessmen. Munch. Munch. Munch. The money czar devours
the pear, listening almost without comment. . . .

"After about 30 minutes, Mr. Simon signals the meeting is
over. . . .

"At this point, at 3:15 ᴘ.ᴍ. on Monday, June 24, the Treasury
chief is roughly half-way through a day that began with a 7:15 ᴀ.ᴍ.
interview on NBC's *Today* show and would end after 10 ᴘ.ᴍ.
over pizza in his office—a late working dinner attended by two
top aides. . . ."[1]

Thus began a recent "week in the life of" story in the *Wall*

Street Journal about that all-too-familiar figure on the Washington scene, the big businessman-turned-public servant; the "man in motion" who terrorizes secretaries—Simon has three—before breakfast, and obsequious underlings the rest of the day; a man who *gets things done.*

James P. Gannon, the writer of this chronicle, takes the reader through Simon's Monday-to-Friday week, hour by breathless hour. Indeed, Gannon spares us no details.

We're even informed that at 7:30 A.M. on Wednesday, Simon is in his bathroom and an aide is outside reading him a foreign intelligence report through the closed door, so that no time is wasted.

The story does not indicate when Simon, in the course of his fifteen-hour days, has a chance to think quietly. Obviously not in the bathroom. And there's little time for it on the weekend, apparently, for Gannon tells us that Saturday is devoted to backed-up paperwork and telephone calls, and that Simon is spending this particular Sunday entertaining Treasury employees on the presidential yacht *Sequoia.*

And what of Mrs. Simon? She is never mentioned in the story. And the little Simons?

It's difficult to pinpoint just when work became the *summum bonum* of American life, when we enshrined the go-getter, when we started equating social worth with the number of dollars a man had earned or inherited. That work has intrinsic value is a concept of relatively recent vintage. Even the Bible's authors described work as a curse, and our attitudes toward work carry penitential overtones to this day: "In the sweat of thy face shalt thou eat bread, till thou return unto the ground."

In his stimulating book *The Dynamics of Change*, Don Fabun speculates that "this idea may have had its first concrete expression in the sixth century when St. Benedict at his Monastery at Monte Cassino posted rules for the monks.

" 'Idleness is the enemy of the soul,' begins Rule XLVIII. 'And therefore, at fixed times, the brothers ought to be occupied in manual labor, and, again at fixed times, in sacred reading.'

"For the first time, not only work as such, but work for a stipulated time, became integral to Western thought. In later years we were to confuse the two, so that 'putting in time' became more important than the work. But what was new here at the beginning, with the monks of Monte Cassino, was that work was good for the soul. This was the myth that has become a monster in our times; it drives even the rich to maintain the illusion that they are working, and those who do not work into an incessant apologia for being alive."[2]

In his book *The American Idea of Success*, Richard Huber has traced the history of what has been variously called the Puritan Ethic, the Protestant Ethic, and the American Dream, a three-hundred-year-long attempt to resolve self-seeking and self-giving. Huber reminds us that Cotton Mather was the foremost spokesman for the Puritan Ethic during the late seventeenth and early eighteenth centuries. Quoting Proverbs, the fiery New England divine said:

" 'He becomes poor who dealeth with a slack hand, but the hand of the diligent maketh rich.' Such lessons are so frequent in the Book of God that I wonder how any man given up to slothfulness dare look into his Bible. Come, come, for shame, away to your business. . . ."[3]

Mather preached that a man should tithe a goodly share of his hard-earned income to church and charity. And he warned that laziness—and by implication, poverty—was sinful, but that material gain was even more sinful if not related to pious uses.

In today's world of the giant corporation and collective bureaucracy, the pure Protestant Ethic is an anachronism. Yet here and there it lives. It lives in the person of J. Willard Marriott, Jr., for example, chief executive officer of the worldwide Marriott Corporation—"Hot Shoppe" restaurants, airline food services, hotels, shipping lines—founded by his father.

Marriott is a non-smoking, non-drinking Mormon who gives between 10 and 20 percent of his annual income—his salary alone is $146,250—to the Church of Jesus Christ of Latter Day Saints, and devotes each Sunday exclusively to church business.

In a profile of Marriott, the *Washington Post's* Richard M. Cohen recently reported that religion, family, and work totally dominate the man's life.

" 'Social life?' he asked. 'I don't have a social life. Friendship is an investment and friendship takes a lot of time. My priorities are the church, the family, and business. After that, I have very little time left over.'

"The same holds true for many Marriott executives who, taking their cue from the boss, work six to seven days a week. If they have some free time, they can read the book Marriott gave them —*The Time Trap*. It tells them how to better use their time. . . .

"Marriott, forty-two, likes to call the double-time pace 'out-front hustle.' It's the effective corporate ethic. It so pervades the company that industry analysts and Marriott men themselves consider it as much a corporate asset as the items listed in the annual report. At the same time, though, some Marriott associates worry that Marriott men overdo it, that some decisions are made in a fog of fatigue. . . ."

At the company's headquarters in the Washington, D.C. suburbs, "Bill Marriott personally sets the pace. He's in by 7 o'clock in the morning and out around 7 or 8 o'clock at night."[4]

J. Willard Marriott would be at home with Benjamin Franklin as well as Cotton Mather, though Franklin leaned toward the secular side of the ethic with his admonition: "God helps those who help themselves." With sentiments such as these, says Richard Huber, Franklin "cut the cables holding the idea of success to its religious anchor and sent it drifting into a sea of pragmatism."[5] We've been bobbing about in this sea ever since.

How to pursue corporate profits and God simultaneously? We haven't resolved that one yet. Occasionally it surfaces in headlines such as the following in the *Wall Street Journal* in mid-February 1975: "Was Eli Black's Suicide Caused by the Tensions of Conflicting Worlds? United Brands Chief Tried to Combine His Business With Social Conscience." The *Journal's* Mary Bralove wrote:

"On a clear day, the view is breathtaking from United Brands Co.'s corporate office on the forty-fourth floor of mid-Manhattan's Pan Am Building. Majestically tall office buildings make a canyon of Park Avenue South, while their glass windows reflect the tiny blocks and the blurs of cars and pedestrians below.

"It was in an office overlooking this vista that Eli M. Black, chairman of United Brands, worked—as much as sixteen to eighteen hours a day. From this office, he had negotiated his $1.98 billion multinational corporation through a tight financial squeeze and steered it through a disaster-plagued 1974. On February 3, 1975, from every business point of view, the worst seemed behind Eli Black.

"At 8:20 that gray Monday morning, the fifty-three-year-old executive locked his office doors, smashed his attache case through his office window, and jumped to his death. He left no suicide note, no word to explain his inexplicable death.

"Eli Black's reach stretched him to an emotional breaking point. A rabbi by training, a businessman by inclination, he believed that he could straddle the two worlds successfully by combining business with a social conscience and sensitivity. In the end, the pressure from two worlds split him apart...."[6]

When the government investigated the circumstances surrounding Black's suicide, it discovered that his company had allegedly paid huge bribes to Central American and European government officials in connection with the company's trade in bananas. The press dubbed the scandal "Bananagate."

Though most Americans believe that this country discovered the success ethic, such is not the case. As early as the middle of the sixteenth century in England, precursors of Cotton Mather and Norman Vincent Peale were churning out "success" literature, Huber reminds us. The colonists brought the idea with them from the home country. We've taken it from there, and some believe we've taken it to extremes. Said a newspaper account of the killing a few years ago of Earl D. Rhode, a government official, by his wife Delores, who then committed suicide:

"According to friends and associates, the tragedy seemed to stem from the Washington phenomenon of an ambitious, outgoing man married to a shy, retiring wife who did not share his career drive.

"Neighbors said Mrs. Rhode had been unhappy over her husband's long hours of work.... A co-worker, saddened by the death, said he had known of Mrs. Rhode's dissatisfaction with her life and her husband's long hours and had advised him to 'spend more time at home,' adding 'He said it was no fun to go home.'"[7]

Rarely does the Rotarian or Lions Club speaker extol rugged individualism and the tough, self-made man, without mentioning the name of Horatio Alger, Jr. Alger (1832–1899) wrote scores of successful novels about plucky, lucky young boys who worked their way from rags to riches. His first big success came in 1868 with *Ragged Dick*, the tale of a bootblack who plunged into the waters of New York harbor from the deck of a ferryboat to rescue a drowning child, and was rewarded with a job by the child's rich father.

Only recently was it discovered, by Richard Huber, that Horatio Alger, Jr. was a homosexual. Huber learned Alger's secret when research for his book on the American success ethic led him to the Unitarian Church in Brewster, Massachusetts, where Alger had been a minister; thence to the century-old church records in the vault of a Cape Cod bank. There the former Princeton University historian found a report of a special parish investigating committee dated 1866 which stated that charges had been brought against Alger and that he had not denied them.

Alger's secret remained locked in the vault, however, and his books remained popular into the first decades of this century. The books did not make him rich, but they provided him a comfortable income and a unique place in the history of the work ethic. This symbol of the hairy-chested businessman, says Huber, was a sensitive, gentle, roly-poly little bachelor.

As early as the 1880s, the big corporation was transforming American life, and the Protestant Ethic was facing numbered days. By World War I, noted William H. Whyte, Jr., in *The Organization Man*, the ethic had suffered so many blows that it would never recover.

The publication in 1936 of Dale Carnegie's *How to Win Friends and Influence People* reflected the change that had been occurring in the work ethic for some time: Personality, and the ability to manipulate people, had superseded self-reliance, individuality, and other spartan virtues. To move up the ladder, one had to be a "team player" and submerge oneself in the greater corporate purpose—whatever that was.

A courageous individual can succeed against the group pressures of a big organization, but most genuine individualists must learn to adopt camouflage in order to survive. Says educator Eli Ginzberg:

"More frequently than not, an executive who gets along easily with others, who does not fight too hard for his position, who is willing to see the point of view of the other fellow, especially if the other fellow is his superior, gains a reputation of being constructive and cooperative. And that he is. But the question remains, what else is he?"[8]

The recession of the early 1970s wrought further changes in attitudes toward work. In the summer of 1975, a new production of *Death of a Salesman* opened in Manhattan, and some critics found Arthur Miller's drama even more relevant than in 1949 when the original production opened on Broadway.

For more than thirty years, Willy Loman, traveling shoe salesman, was "a man way out there in the blue, riding on a smile and a shoeshine," and he's in his early sixties when we meet him in the play. He's burned out, exhausted, on the brink of suicide. When he asks his unpleasant young boss for a quiet job in the home office, he's fired.

"I put thirty-four years into this firm, Howard, and now I can't pay my insurance," shouts Willy. "You can't eat the orange and throw the peel away—a man is not a piece of fruit."[9]

Willy's wife, Linda, voices Miller's message: "I don't say he's a great man. Willy Loman never made a lot of money. His name was never in the paper. He's not the finest character that ever lived. But he's a human being, and a terrible thing is happening to him. So attention must be paid. He's not to be allowed to fall into his grave like an old dog. Attention, attention must be finally paid to such a person."[10]

Critic Walter Goodman wrote recently: "Linda is trying to tell us simply that we are tolerating a society in which a great many must fail, but that failure does not make people any the less human. This play does not pick a quarrel with generally accepted notions of success—yet how can one raise questions about failure without at least implying questions about success? Willy had intimations of another life—working around the house, painting, looking at things. Weren't these healthy impulses quashed by a success-obsessed society? . . .

"The stooped figure of Willy Loman has entered our consciousness and is connected with our time. When things are going well for us, when jobs are plentiful and spirits are high, failure can be subsidized and shunted aside. But things are not going well; our vision of endless growth is clouded; many who played by the rules and thought they were secure are for the first time experiencing insecurity; salesmen are in trouble, and the country is not in a giving mood. Questions that have been submerged by years of prosperity are being asked again. Willy Loman is back with us, uttering his strange cry, 'The woods are burning.' Perhaps this time, more serious attention will be paid."[11]

12 *"Fifty-five —and Frightened"*

"IN OUR COMPANY, it's not who you know but what you've got on who you know that counts." Thus a midlevel executive for a major corporation reflects his distaste for a phenomenon that management experts say increased with the downturn in the economy: "office politics." Surveys and studies indicate that impatience with organizational politics is an important part of a larger dissatisfaction with life in the American corporation nowadays. This unhappiness flows from the factory floor to the executive offices.

A Research Institute of America study finds: "Today, when business can least afford a dissipation of effort, 'office politics' is on the rise within many companies. As a menace to individuals and organizations alike, it deserves more concentrated study than anyone has given it. The price of office politics is tremendous, both to management and the individual. That it has been encouraged by our present business structure of group management may be conceded. . . ."

Richard Huber believes the words "contacts" and "know who" have all but replaced "merit" and "know how" among those scrambling on the corporate ladder.

Life Extension Institute contends that the principal cause of tension among business executives is personality conflict associated with office politics and competition.

The trail led to Auren Uris, a top editor at the Research Institute of America in Manhattan, and author of a score of books on business management. Here's what Uris has to say:

"There is indeed a corporate tradition in which not the deserving but the faithful win the spoils. This is the seamy side of business, where justice doesn't always triumph, but power *always* does."

Dale Tarnowieski, who conducted a recent American Management Association survey entitled *The Changing Success Ethic*, says, "Frustration and dissidence in supervisory and middle management in particular are being traced more and more frequently to the effects of 'politics' at the policy-making level of the organization."

Among Tarnowieski's findings in a survey of nearly 3,000 U.S. businessmen—the largest survey in American Management's history—were these:

"Fifty-two percent of all respondents—including 58 percent of all middle managers, 69 percent of all supervisory-level managers, and 71 percent of all technical employees in managerial positions —believe that advancement and promotion . . . are most often based on 'a largely subjective and arbitrary decision on the part of corporate superiors in the position to decide who gets promoted and who doesn't.'

"Eighty-eight percent of all respondents say that 'a dynamic personality and the ability to sell yourself and your ideas is more of an attribute to the manager on the move today than is a reputation for honesty, or firm adherence to principles.'

"Eighty-two percent of all respondents believe that 'pleasing the boss' is the critical factor in determining 'promotability' in today's organizational environment."

On the broader question of life in the executive suite, only about half of those responding "believe that the organizations for which they currently work provide them, or are ever likely to provide them, adequate opportunities to realize their job- and career-related goals." And, says Tarnowieski, "An alarming 40 percent of all surveyed middle managers and 52 percent of the reporting supervisory managers say they find their work, at best, unsatisfying."

Psychoanalyst Franz Alexander has likened many of his patients —businessmen, engineers, bankers, and so forth—to men running in a marathon. Their faces are "distorted by strain," but their eyes are not focused upon the finish line; they're focused on each other, with a mixture of expression that includes hate.

Roger M. D'Aprix, a Xerox Corporation executive, says in his penetrating book, *Struggle for Identity: The Silent Revolution Against Corporate Conformity:*

"The idealized goal has always been made clear to the individual: He is supposed to scale his pyramid to the limits of his energy and talent. But in actuality, the game has never been that simple because, as with other human relationships, there are undefined boundaries and subtleties which the individual must discover for himself. Talent and performance are usually essential, but in themselves they are not always adequate. Sadly for those who throw themselves unreservedly into the race to the top and who measure their self-esteem only according to its outcome, the results can be devastating."[1]

D'Aprix and other students of organization man agree that office politics is a fact of life, and that it's sometimes more dangerous to stay totally aloof from the fray than it is to get into the front lines. "To ignore the existence of company politics, when others in an organization are dedicating much of their time to it, can be as impractical as assuming that the right-of-way is always an assurance of safety in traffic," says the Research Institute of America study, *Coping With Office Politics.*

Yet office politics is a subject all but ignored in the nation's great business schools. Alan N. Schoonmaker, a prominent executive counselor and faculty member at Carnegie-Mellon University in Pittsburgh, marvels that candidates for advanced degrees are taught "the principles of marketing, finance, corporate planning, communication, and supervision," while such a critical subject as organization politics is treated as though it didn't exist—though it exists, of course, within the faculty of the business schools themselves.

Most professors of management, says Schoonmaker in a recent issue of the publication *MBA,* "have assumed that the only way to succeed is to do one's job well, that virtue is always rewarded, and sin is always punished. But the most casual examination of organizations should convince you that job performance and career advancement are not perfectly correlated. Some men do advance on merit, but others do not. Some men do their jobs superbly but do not get ahead, while others contribute little but are highly rewarded."

Schoonmaker believes that company politics should be considered in its more general sense as "distribution of power." In this sense, then, "it becomes obvious that politics is unavoidable. Since power exists in every group or organization, politics must necesssarily exist in every firm. You can therefore get away from politics only by becoming a hermit. As long as you live and work in groups and in organizations, politics will influence your career —whether you like it or not."[2]

Auren Uris says there are two basic factors that give rise to such politics: genuine policy disagreements, and the career ambitions of higher executives.

"Let's say your company is producing chemical sprays that are destructive to the environment. One group within the company wants to modify production, or drop some of the lines, even if it costs the company money. The other group says: 'Well, the hell with it. We're in business to show a profit for ourselves, and for our stockholders. This ecology business is a lot of crap.' And so a power play begins within the company. People choose sides."

An individual might line up behind Executive A because he genuinely likes A's policy and thinks A will be the best man, says Uris. "Or it may be on a more acquisitive basis: 'He's the guy who can do the most for me.' Or, 'He always liked me, and he's the guy who, if appointed president, will see that I become a division manager or whatever, whereas Executive B doesn't like me and, if he gets in, I'm finished.' "

In this game, says Uris, one's *immediate* boss is critically important. You can agree with the course of action that he intends to take, and say, "I'm with you 100 percent on this, boss." Or you can disagree with him—"in which case you better damn well keep it a secret because you're susceptible to 'negative reward' as we Skinnerians say."

The man who chooses incorrectly often faces unpleasant consequences. He's forced out of the company, fired outright, or eased into a dead-end job.

"In *some* situations, the man who refuses to play politics gets a kind of respect from both sides," continues Uris. "It doesn't adversely affect his situation. He is the kind of man who knows his own ability and is confident of his worth to his company. He doesn't have to get himself involved in this political game to reinforce or secure his position. No matter who ends up on top in the power struggle, his situation remains secure because of what he has on the ball."

The neutralist, of course, should not expect plums from the eventual winner, Uris adds.

In uncertain times when companies set about pruning their staffs and ranks, politicking always increases markedly. "Not to be liked by a key man has immediate and very serious implications for a guy's future in the company, and his peace of mind," says Uris. "This is borne out by the fact that whenever there are recessions, it's the middle-managers who are always bounced out of an organization."

In recent years, a number of clever satirical books on office politics have been published, including Uris's own first sortie into humor, *How to Win Your Boss's Love, Approval—and Job*, written in collaboration with Jack Tarrant; *The Radovic Rule: How to Manage the Boss*, by Igor Radovic; and *Bravely, Bravely in Business: 32 Ground Rules for Personal Survival and Success in Your Job*, by Richard R. Connaroe. In early 1976, two such works were riding high on the best-seller lists: Robert J. Ringer's *Winning Through Intimidation*, and Michael Korda's *Power!*

While written in a humorous vein, the message of these books is serious: Before you can come to terms with corporate life, or life in any big organization such as the government, a university, armed service, or whatever, you must become a serious student of office politics.

"In every company there's an 'informal organization' on the upper levels with power centers that are often at variance with what the company organization chart suggests," says Uris. "Try to figure out what's going on inside this informal organization. Who are the big guns? Who are the little guns? Who's opposed to whom? Who's on top now? Who may be on top tomorrow?

"Consider your own personal interests. Do you want to get in the game or don't you? If so, where do you pack clout? Or is any move you make likely to result in doubtful gains?

"Remember that your immediate boss is the key to your own role. Obviously his situation has implications for what you can or can't do.

"Finally, take heart. Office politics are never forever. There's always change at the top—new turns in the wheel—developed by political activity."

Robert N. McMurry, who heads a Chicago-based firm of management psychologists, attributes office politics to the type of people who, he believes, are drawn to corporations—especially big corporations—to begin with. He tells me:

"People don't like to hear this sort of thing, but I'd say 75 percent of corporation employees, including a lot of presidents and vice-presidents, are very anxious, fearful people by nature, fundamentally insecure. Much of the internal conflict that takes place grows out of people's reactions to what they perceive as threats to their security.

"Many of the longest-service employees are the most frustrated, the most hostile. Many stay with one company not out of loyalty but because they lack the courage to quit and try something new. One of the biggest problems is the incapacity of many executives to tolerate strong subordinates. I can't tell you the number of companies I've seen composed of cringing wretches."

The blunt Mr. McMurry draws a depressing stereotype of a middle-range executive in today's corporation: "Fifty-five—and frightened":

"Let's say I've gotten where I am because of seniority. I've kept my nose clean. I haven't antagonized anybody. I'm 100 percent conformist. I've not thought any dangerous thoughts. Nor have I gone in for innovation—innovations have a way of going sour. So at age fifty-five, I'm vice-president in charge of something or other.

"I'm not really on top of my job anymore; things have accelerated so, the job is running me. About all I can hope for is that no one will discover how basically incompetent I am.

"I'm assigned an assistant. He's a real barn-burner. He immediately becomes a threat to me. Now, 90 percent of the jobs in industry are of such a nature that there's no objective measure of competence. My evaluation of my assistant is the only criterion that the men above me can go on. How do I cope with the threat?

"I can damn him with faint praise, see that he gets no promotions, and that he *does* get unpleasant assignments. I can make it obvious that he doesn't have a future. So he leaves. I am much happier with people who are not as good as me, who are docile, submissive, conformist."

Xerox's Roger D'Aprix takes a less gloomy—though no less realistic—view.

"The dilemma for the individual is this: How does he make his peace within an organization? I believe you can be your own man—and for the sake of your sanity you must.

"If my analysis is correct, then the individual is in a very tough psychological and philosophical bind in most companies. Specifically, he must answer the terribly difficult question of who he is and what he wants. And, further, he must relate that to a company abstraction difficult to define or understand. Then he must construct some sort of loyalty to people in power, people he rarely knows firsthand, people whose motives he can only guess at. And having done all this, he must be prepared to face an unrequited love affair because abstractions can't love back, and because people in power usually have other problems to deal with."[3]

All of this is amusingly described by Bob Slocum, the fictional hero of Joseph Heller's *Something Happened:*

> In the office in which I work there are five people of whom I am afraid. Each of these five people is afraid of four people (excluding overlaps), for a total of twenty, and each of these twenty people is afraid of six people, making a total of one hundred and twenty people who are feared by at least one person. Each of these one hundred and twenty people is afraid of the other one hundred and nineteen, and all of these one hundred and forty-five people are afraid of the twelve men at the top who helped found and build the company and now own and direct it.
>
> All these twelve men are elderly now and drained by time and success of energy and ambition. Many have spent their whole lives here. They seem friendly, slow, and content when I come upon them in the halls (they seem dead) and are always courteous and mute when they ride with others on the public elevators. They no longer work hard. They hold meetings, make promotions, and allow their names to be used on announcements that are prepared and issued by somebody else. Nobody is sure anymore who really runs the company (not even the people who are credited with running it) but the company does run. . . .[4]

Worker discontent nowadays goes deeper than annoyance with office politics and organizational red tape. Blue collar and white collar workers alike complain that most industrial plant and office labor is stupefyingly repetitive, boring, meaningless.

"Without work, all life goes rotten," said Albert Camus. "But when work is soulless, life stifles and dies."

There is strong evidence that work in industrial America has become soulless for the vast majority.

"The scars, psychic as well as physical, brought home to the supper table and the TV set, may have touched, malignantly, the soul of our society," says Studs Terkel in *Working.*[5]

Surveys by the score, government studies, and articles in the nation's newspapers and magazines substantiate Terkel's findings that Americans who really enjoy their work are in a small minority.

Psychologist Herbert M. Greenberg, head of a marketing and research firm in Princeton, New Jersey, has along with his associates interviewed 250,000 white and blue collar employees of 4,000 firms since the mid-1950s. Greenberg has found that four out of five workers were unhappy and frustrated.

A task force of the U.S. Secretary of Health, Education, and Welfare has concluded that "significant numbers of American workers are dissatisfied with the quality of their working lives. Dull, repetitive, seemingly meaningless tasks, offering little challenge or autonomy, are causing discontent among workers at all occupational levels."[6] The task force's candid report entitled *Work in America* pinpoints the principal reason for worker discontent.

Our economic, political, and cultural system has fostered the notion of independence and autonomy, a part of which is the belief that a hard-working person, even if he has little capital, can always make a go of it in business for himself. Or, to put it another way, if things get too bad in a dependent work situation, it has been felt that the individual could always strike out on his own.

This element of the American Dream is rapidly becoming myth, and disappearing with it is the possibility of realizing the character traits of independence and autonomy by going into business for oneself. The trend of the past 70 years or more, and particularly in recent years, has been a decrease in small independent enterprises and self-employment and an increase in the domination of large corporations and government in the workforce. In the middle of the 19th century, less than half of all employed people were wage and salary workers. By 1950 it was 80 percent, and by 1970, 90 percent. ... From 1960 to 1970, government workers increased from 12 percent of the civilian labor force to more than 15 percent....

As these data attest, the trend is toward large corporations and bureaucracies which typically organize work in such a way as to minimize the independence of the workers and maximize control and predictability for the organization. Characterologically, the hierarchical organization requires workers to follow orders, which calls for submissive traits, while the selection of managers calls for authoritarian and controlling traits. With the shift from manufacturing to services—employment has gone from about 50-50 in 1950 to 62-38 in favor of services in 1970—the tyranny of the machine is perhaps being replaced by the tyranny of bureaucracy.

Yet, the more democratic and self-affirmative an individual is, the less he will stand for boring, dehumanized, and authoritarian work. Under such conditions, the workers either protest or give in, at some cost to their psychological well-being. ...[7]

The assembly line has received the most attention. "You get kind of numb," said Dale Sirakis, describing his work at General Motors' trouble-plagued Chevrolet Vega plant in Lordstown, Ohio, a few years ago. Every forty seconds or so, all day long, Sirakis's sole duty was to snap a hook to the underside of another auto body, according to a *New York Times* story.

Niall Brennan says in his book *The Making of a Moron* that the unpleasantness of a job "depends solely on how many of the parts of man are used, and how well they are being used.... If only a part of a man is being used, the salvation of his sanity depends on what he himself does with the unwanted parts."

One day in a Ford Motor Co. assembly plant in Detroit, I saw how two workers had solved the problem of what to do with "the unwanted parts"—namely, their minds. They had placed a chess set on the floor beside the pit in which they were standing while working on the undersides of auto bodies moving down the line. Periodically, a seemingly disembodied hand would appear and move one of the chess pieces. A few auto bodies would go by, then the other man's hand would appear and he'd make his move.

White collar workers are no less disaffected. But they're rarely heard from unless—like the *Cleveland Plain Dealer's* Robert Manry—they do something that appears bizarre, or enter an exotic career totally unrelated to their previous Monday-to-Friday purgatory.

A recent *Harvard Business Review* survey found "burgeoning discontent" among the nation's 13 million clerical workers. The workers complained that they felt like robots working for faceless managements who were indifferent to them.

Other surveys and studies have reflected growing disenchantment among middle managers, including a disposition to unionize, especially in recent years when companies including Sears, Roebuck, Ford, Chrysler, General Electric, and Polaroid have been laying off these traditionally company-loyal individuals in record numbers.

The American Management Association's report on the changing success ethic emphasizes that if it "accomplishes no other purpose, it should serve to call further attention to the fact that a growing worker malaise in America has not merely spread to, but may even thrive in, the managerial suites of American business."

In the early 1970s, when Dale Sirakis and others in Lordstown were complaining to newsmen of the mind-numbing nature of their work on the Chevrolet Vega assembly line, the general manager of the Chevrolet division was John DeLorean, a motor industry Wunderkind, then in his mid-forties. Though DeLorean's world was light years removed from Sirakis's, he, too, complained that his work was mind-numbing when, in mid-1973, he resigned his $550,000-a-year corporate vice-presidency. Once he'd entered the hallowed fourteenth-floor executive suite, said DeLorean, he'd found that committee-think and bureaucracy had rendered the company costive.

"You were too harassed and oppressed by committee meetings and paperwork—you just had tons of it. You were cut off from the outside world. You saw only the men on the fourteenth floor. The corporate hierarchy was just reacting to some degree to the government and the public. It was like standing in a boiler room and tending a machine and you were just watching it instead of running it."[8]

The son of a Ford foundry worker in Detroit, DeLorean secured an engineering degree in 1948 and joined Chrysler, shifted to the smaller Packard company, then joined Pontiac and in 1965 at age forty he became the youngest general manager in GM's history. He earned a reputation as a designer of hot cars such as the Firebird; a stickler for quality who wasn't afraid to order a costly assembly line shutdown if he didn't get it; a great marketing man; a leader. He set sales records with Pontiac, then took over a fast-slipping Chevrolet division and turned it around.

GM made DeLorean a corporate vice-president in the fall of 1972 and many Detroit insiders saw him on a fast track to the presidency of the mammoth company. Within less than a year he had quit.

DeLorean has complained that the top GM executives lived as well or better than oriental potentates, that they moved around in chauffeured Cadillac Eldorados totally removed from the problems of the average automobile driver and the automotive tastes of the younger generations. He complained as well that the huge corporation was frighteningly slow of foot, and that despite his record of achievement, he could no longer get a hearing for his ideas. In vain, for example, did DeLorean and a few others argue years ago for the manufacture by GM of smaller cars in the face of rising gasoline prices and foreign car competition.

There's more to the story. DeLorean had been outraging GM executives and their wives for years with his refusal to conform. DeLorean, in fact, floor-boarded it through the midlife transition. Today, you might say, he's the answer to the "What kind of a man reads *Playboy?*" advertisement.

DeLorean dyed his graying hair jet black, let it grow long, and had it styled, complete with long sideburns. Though six-feet-four, he cut his weight from around 200 pounds to 170, started working out regularly with weights; pursued tennis, golf, and horsemanship; gunned a high-powered motorcycle around the countryside; divorced his wife of fourteen years and began going around with actresses such as Ursula Andress, and with sports and Hollywood figures. DeLorean was not playing the GM game. And when, in the spring of 1969, he married twenty-year-old Kelly Harmon, daughter of onetime Michigan football star Tom Harmon, he really put the cat among the pigeons.

"As his own life changed, DeLorean began questioning what

he calls the cloistered life at GM's upper levels," says writer Rush Loving, Jr. "As he saw it, the senior officers spent most of their days confined to meetings on the fourteenth floor of the corporation's headquarters in Detroit. Most executives worked ten-hour days, leaving for home around 7:00 P.M. lugging bulging briefcases. On Saturdays many reappeared in the office, this time in shirtsleeves, to put in a few more hours."⁹

DeLorean's marriage to Kelly Harmon coincided with his Chevrolet assignment, and he admits that he put his job first, working brutally long hours and traveling widely around the huge automobile division. Early in 1973, DeLorean divorced his young wife and a few months later married actress-model Cristina Ferrare, also in her early twenties. The men on the fourteenth floor may have decided that DeLorean's time for the long knives had come. The official company version is that DeLorean resigned, as he said he did, and that the company regretted his departure. DeLorean said he left GM because the automobile industry had lost its "masculinity." Obviously, DeLorean was determined not to lose his.

For a year after leaving GM, DeLorean headed the National Alliance of Businessmen in Washington, D.C., which helps members of minority groups find employment. Since then, he has formed the DeLorean Corporation in Bloomfield Hills, a marketing and consulting firm with clients such as W. R. Grace, Sears, Roebuck, and the French government. And he's still sending shockwaves through Detroit. The Soviet government has approached him to market its automobile in this country, a prospect which interests him.

More worrisome to his former colleagues are his plans to build a sports safety car which, he tells me, will enable drivers to survive accidents at closing speeds as high as 100 miles per hour, and have twice the fuel economy of a Chevrolet Corvette.

DeLorean says that Detroit is so "entrenched," it's easier to start a new company than to try anything revolutionary within the confines of an established one.

Early in 1976, he founded DeLorean Motor Co., and was busy trying to raise $70 million to get his dream car on the road in 1978.

"This is how I plan to spend the rest of my life," he said recently. "This is the reason I left GM."

DeLorean's midlife career change was cushioned by nearly $1 million in back-bonuses from General Motors. The average man, however, lives in a land where "Older person need not apply" advertisements have only recently been ruled illegal, but where age discrimination continues unabated, and remains socially if not legally sanctioned.

13 "... I Say, Let Them All Come Out of the Woodwork!"

ON JANUARY 2, 1975 President Gerald Ford sent a private letter of condolence to the widow of a Foreign Service officer. The man had committed suicide on April 12, 1971 after "a series of errors" in the Department of State's personnel and evaluation system had led to his firing for failing to earn promotion to the next grade within the time allotted. Accompanying the president's letter was a copy of a private law he had just signed: "An Act for the Relief of Charles William Thomas, deceased," promoting him posthumously as of April 23, 1967, and conferring upon his widow Cynthia, "The additional salary, annual leave, life insurance, and retirement benefits" she would have received had her husband died on active duty in the higher rank.

This is a truly remarkable letter—admission by the chief executive of the United States that his government had done grave injustice to one of its servants, and seeking to make amends. The Thomas case has been a *cause célèbre*, with far-reaching effects in government personnel policy. It has tremendous relevance as well for middle-aged men in private industry.

The State Department's most serious error involved the misfiling of a letter in 1966 from Ambassador Robert McClintock, inspector general of the Foreign Service of the United States, strongly recommending Charles Thomas's "immediate" promotion which he said was "long overdue" in light of the officer's outstanding record at posts in Africa, the Caribbean, and Mexico during the previous fifteen years. Thomas was serving as a political officer in Mexico City when McClintock wrote his letter, which found its way into the personnel jacket of another Charles W. Thomas, serving in Belgium, where it was not discovered until mid-1967. In the absence of the McClintock letter, Thomas was passed over for promotion at a highly critical turning point in his career, and in 1969, he was involuntarily retired for time in grade, having failed to gain promotion within the maximum eight-year period that had been arbitrarily put into effect in 1967. Even after the error was discovered, State refused to rectify it.

There was no grievance or appeals recourse for Thomas, the State Department being the only U.S. government agency without one at that time. His separation pay consisted of one year's salary: $17,000 before taxes. He was forty-seven, with a wife and two daughters to support, no outside income, and three years short of eligibility for a pension.

Until his death, he fought for reinstatement, meanwhile seeking permanent employment. Everywhere he applied, the answer was the same: He was "overqualified," the code word for too old. And, of course, he'd been let go by the foreign service.

On the day of Thomas's suicide, he had assets of $500 in the form of an old automobile, and he was $14,000 in debt. His death enabled his wife to collect a $325-a-month annuity.

Had Charles William Thomas been a mediocrity, his story would be tragic enough. But the evidence is overwhelming that he was an exceptionally fine foreign service officer. Yet except for his suicide, his was not an unusual experience for middle-aged men either in or out of government; it happens all the time. Few persons outside the Foreign Service of the United States would probably ever have heard of his case, had it not been for his widow's courageous battle to clear his name, and her continuing fight to change the system that has destroyed the careers of many fine men like her husband.

Thomas was born in Orange, Texas, on June 20, 1922, the son of working-class parents who died—his father of tuberculosis, his mother of cancer—when he was a little boy. He was raised by an older sister in Fort Wayne, Indiana, where he was president of his high school class and an honor graduate.

Thomas worked his way through Northwestern University on scholarship—busboy, onion-peeler in a Chinese restaurant, farm laborer, flower salesman—with a three-year interruption during World War II to serve as a U.S. Navy fighter pilot. In 1947 he was graduated with honors in economics. Two years later, he earned a law degree at Northwestern, again working his way through, again achieving honors. There followed a scholarship to the University of Paris where he took a doctorate in international law in 1951 before joining the foreign service.

Thomas's first post was as a consular, political, and public affairs officer in Monrovia, Liberia, from 1951 to 1953. There followed tours of duty in Accra, Gold Coast; Tangier, Morocco; Haiti; and Mexico City, with intermittent high-level assignments in Washington, D.C. and the United Nations. Thomas suffered his share of malaria and other tropical diseases; became fluent along the way in French and Spanish, and acquired a working knowledge of German, Italian, and Portuguese. He moved steadily up the career ladder, reaching "FSO 4" in 1961.

Once a year, fitness reports on each of the 3,000-odd foreign service officers are prepared by their supervisors, and their supervisors' supervisors. These reports are sent to the State Department personnel office, which makes its input before filtering them to seven-man selection boards. These panels have been likened by congressional critics to self-perpetuating boards of directors.

Based upon these reports from the field, the selection boards attempt to rate each man in relation to the others in his class. If a man is judged to be in the bottom 5 percent of his class he's subject to "selection out"—State's Orwellian term—if it happens twice. Depending upon the individual circumstances of the men being judged, departmental budgetary considerations, and ever-changing evaluation rules, the FSOs above the bottom 5 percent may be continued in grade for another year, promoted to the next class, or retired involuntarily.

The practice of rating individuals based upon pieces of paper sent in from scattered reaches of the globe is far from an exact science. Most fitness reports tend to be laudatory, for one thing. So selection board members try to read between the lines.

In private, foreign service officers say the system encourages round-the-clock politicking and a bland subservience on the part of men anxious for promotion, hence fearful of offending their superiors. Thomas stayed aloof from office politics, and this may have been his undoing. A few months after Thomas's death, Senator J. William Fulbright, then chairman of the Foreign Relations Committee, touched upon this side of Thomas's character in an angry exchange with William B. Macomber, then Under-Secretary of State for Administration. At that late date, Macomber, later ambassador to Turkey, was still defending State's treatment of Thomas.

Thomas, said Fulbright, "had a little imagination and was not perhaps as conformist as the Department required, and you don't like people like that.... He was a man of imagination and originality."

When Thomas left Mexico and his new post as an advisor to the U.S. Delegation to UNESCO, he had reason to feel confident about his future even though his time in grade was accumulating. His negotiation of some multi-million-dollar land claims had drawn the praise of Ambassador to Mexico Fulton Freeman, and had led to a job offer with the Mexico City branch of a big U.S. law firm at several times his government salary. Moreover, Ambassador McClintock had written a letter in his behalf that selection boards would have trouble ignoring.

But when Thomas reached the State Department in Washington, D.C. and checked out his file, his long, lonely entanglement in the toils of bureaucracy began. The McClintock letter recommending his immediate promotion was missing; hence the 1966 selection board, which had passed him over, had obviously not seen it. Worse still, he found in his file a negative fitness report, written in 1964, by a supervisor under whom he'd worked for a few months in Mexico City, one Joseph J. Montlorr.

Montlorr's report was only mildly critical of Thomas, saying that he was not ready for promotion because he lacked force of character and leadership qualities.

Thomas told his wife that he was stunned by Montlorr's report; that there had been no friction between them; that he had liked Montlorr and had thought the feelings had been reciprocated.

Every one of Thomas's supervisors, before and after Montlorr, had enthusiastically urged his promotion.

Now other events beyond Thomas's control were conspiring against him. The State Department's director of personnel at this time was Howard P. Mace, known behind his back as "The Executioner." Mace had reversed State's policy of thinning the ranks by selecting out the bottom-ranked men, and had placed the emphasis on involuntary retirement of men for time in grade.

Mace's rationale for this policy change are obscure. But to this end, Mace in 1967 reduced the length of time allowed to win promotion from Class 4 to Class 3 from ten years—which it had been when Thomas reached Class 4 in 1961—to eight years. This was followed up by a circular to the 1968 selection boards, instructing them to look hard and long before promoting anyone who had been in grade for a long time. A Senate Foreign Relations Committee report on the Thomas case later said: "This precept had the effect of removing Mr. Thomas and others in similar circumstances from serious consideration by the 1968 Selection Board. . . ."

In May 1968, Ambassador Freeman wrote a bristling, five-page, single-spaced letter to John M. Steeves, director general of the foreign service, reviewing the Thomas case and giving the back of his hand to Montlorr:

"The sketchy, perfunctory narrative statement prepared in December 1964 on the departure of the rating officer, Mr. Joseph J. Montlorr, containing the gratuitous (after only eight months in Mexico) remark that Mr. Thomas was not 'ready for promotion to Class 3 this year' was needlessly and unfairly prejudicial, and was directly contrary to my own judgment. . . ."

Selection boards meet in the fall of the year, and when the 1968 board fired Thomas, he was in Paris serving as chief spokesman for the U.S. government at the UNESCO General Conference, a position normally held by a higher ranking FSO. Even so, on January 7, 1969, Steeves wrote Thomas, making his separation official.

Thomas was stunned. He had loved the foreign service, said his wife, and to the last he never believed that he would be fired. But the foreign service is an abstraction, and as Roger D'Aprix, the Xerox executive, said in the context of the business world, "abstractions can't love back."

According to the unwritten rules of the game, Thomas's duty was now to slip quietly away. To protest was considered poor form. Like most middle-aged, middle-level executives and professional men, foreign service officers stood alone in Thomas's time. They had no union, no bargaining agent to represent them. Thomas tried to appeal his case—and got nowhere. In such situations, State Department officials are invariably polite, genteel, sympathetic, and understanding. They will "look into the matter." They will get back to you on it—but they never do.

Thomas, meanwhile, had been job hunting. He quickly discovered that Washington's many law firms were not in the market for generalists nearing fifty. So he took to defending indigents in the District of Columbia court system for $7.50 an hour—when he could get assignments. With characteristic thoroughness, he made studies of various industries; sent out 2,000 résumés and letters; subscribed to an executive search firm for $1,500; answered help wanted advertisements; worked through employment agencies; traveled around the country for interviews.

The self-respect that prevented Thomas from playing office politics prevented him from using friends and acquaintances in high places to help him find work. Nor did he let on to friends how desperate his economic plight was becoming with each passing day. Many diplomats have independent incomes; Thomas's friends assumed that he did, too.

"Isn't it about time to ask *somebody* for help?" Cynthia finally asked.

No, replied Thomas, his record should stand on its own two feet.

Humiliation was continuous, for a stigma attaches to forced retirement from the foreign service, and it followed him like a shadow on his job interviews. At one point, Thomas came close to securing a high-paying job with a major U.S. oil company which needed a man in Nigeria. He was asked to bring his wife to New York for what was to be the final interview. His interviewer asked a final question:

"Isn't fifty the magic age?"

Why, in other words, had he left the foreign service a few years short of qualifying for a pension?

Though creditors were dunning him, and the job situation was becoming ever more desperate, Thomas never let down the side, even with his wife. He and Cynthia even joked about hiring out as a live-in couple, then went ahead and placed an ad in the paper. She went so far as to prepare an elaborate dinner party for a wealthy, prospective employer as a trial run. But the Thomases decided they could not take the job; they knew too many people in Washington who might one day be guests of the would-be employer.

Thomas dropped no hint that he was contemplating suicide. On the day of his death, he discussed with Cynthia the possibility of opening his own law office in Washington. That morning, he'd been job-hunting on Capitol Hill. However, three more job rejections arrived in the mail on April 12, 1971, including one that said they'd hired "a younger man."

At about 3 P.M., Cynthia Thomas was writing letters in the living room of their rented house in Northwest Washington when her husband announced that he was going upstairs to rest. One hour later she heard an explosion. She ran upstairs and found her husband's body. Nearby lay a pistol that he had bought years before. Cynthia Thomas remembers that it still had the price tag on it.

Thomas's suicide had an impact on Washington. The White House called for an "immediate report." The Senate Foreign Relations Committee opened an investigation and summoned Howard Mace, William Macomber, and other personnel officials. A syndicated story by Clark Mollenhoff about Thomas's trials and eventual suicide made front pages in many parts of the United States and overseas. *The New York Times, Washington Post, Providence Journal,* and *Paris Herald-Tribune* carried stories. Letters now started arriving at State and Congress from men who'd known and admired Thomas, and from ordinary citizens. A number of foreign service officers and prominent citizens outside State formed the Charles W. Thomas Legal Defense Fund to aid men who wanted to fight their forced retirements or selections-outs, and to bring class action suits against the Department.

In the midst of all this, Macomber talked with Cynthia Thomas for two hours in his office. She told him she would never give up until her husband was promoted posthumously, the government admitted its injustice, and all foreign service officers were granted due process.

She says Macomber said he could do nothing about her late husband's status "because if I do, other FSOs will start coming out of the woodwork." And he said that he would have to defend "the system" before the Senate Foreign Relations Committee. Then he offered her a job in the State Department paying nearly as much as her husband had made.

Mrs. Thomas said she would accept the job on the condition that it did not compromise her campaign in behalf of her husband's name, and her cooperation in a congressional drive to reform State's personnel and promotion procedures. Macomber accepted her conditions.

The battle that Cynthia Thomas and her colleagues have carried on since April 1971 has relevance for middle-aged men and women everywhere who work, in fear, for big organizations. She's proven that it is possible to take on the system. Just as some middle-managers in the business world are coming to believe that they must organize for survival, just as age discrimination laws are beginning to embolden individuals to fight for their rights, so the Thomas case and its aftermath have encouraged many foreign service officers to stand up on their hind legs.

When Macomber went before the Foreign Relations Committee he defended the way Howard Mace and his other underlings had dealt with the Thomas case. The senators handled Macomber roughly. Into the record went the details of other cases as shocking in their way as Thomas's had been. Confidential memoranda between ambassadors in the field and personnel men in Washington were produced, indicating that the files of men considered troublemakers—those who were not "team players"—were manipulated to their disadvantage.

The upshot of the hearings was passage by the Senate of a bill, "To provide for a procedure to investigate and render decisions and recommendations with respect to grievances and appeals of employees of the Foreign Service. . . ."

With backing from the Thomas Fund, individual foreign service officers have taken their grievances to the courts and have won significant victories. In December 1973, U.S. District Judge Gerhard A. Gesell ruled that State's policy of firing people without due process was unconstitutional. He said that "full and fair hearing is all that is required."

Early in July 1975, State's personnel hierarchy suffered two body blows in succession. First, all seven public members of the Foreign Service grievance board quit when their recommendation that an official be reinstated was ignored by the highest levels of State. "The climate needed for good-faith resolution of grievances has been effectively destroyed," said board chairman William Simkin, former director of the Federal Mediation and Conciliation Service.

Second, the American Foreign Policy Association—traditionally an extension of State's "old boy" network—elected as its president John Hemenway, a former FSO who has devoted the last six years to attacking State's personnel system as corrupt. A Rhodes Scholar, and a specialist on Russian and German affairs, Hemenway had been involuntarily retired in 1969 because, his friends say, he spoke up when he disagreed with his superiors. Like Thomas, he fought for reinstatement, and he won the first grievance hearing ever granted an FSO. Though the grievance board came down on Hemenway's side, State still refused to take him back.

Since 1971, when it became the bargaining agent for FSOs, the Foreign Policy Association has been considered something of a company union. But even before Hemenway's election, it was showing signs of change. *The Foreign Service Journal,* which the association publishes, had run an editorial charging that "all kinds of political abuses and favoritism" were involved in promotions and assignments. In the State Department, the U.S. Information Agency, and the Agency for International Development, said the editorial, "who you know matters more than your qualifications for a particular job. . . ."

Cynthia Thomas is a petite, attractive woman whose eyes flash merrily when the tide of battle flows her way, as it has been doing of late. At such times she likes to recall Macomber's remark about FSOs coming "out of the woodwork" if he changed her late husband's status. She says:

"Well, everybody is coming out of the woodwork now; and they are coming out further; and I say, let them *all* come out of the woodwork! These are terrific statesmen, these men like Hemenway."

Early every morning, Cynthia Thomas drives to work at the Department of State in her battered old white Mustang after fixing breakfast for her children. Hers is a cheerful house, filled with paintings and furniture from around the world, unruly piles of books and magazines, a big English sheepdog named Abigail, a white cat. Mrs. Thomas is in the Foreign Service Reserve, Class 5, one grade below that of her husband at his death. With cost-of-living raises, she's making more than her husband ever did in his lifetime, and she finds this ironical.

It is certain that Congress will pass further legislation reforming the Foreign Service—a fitting memorial to Charles Thomas, says Cynthia. Meanwhile, she has President Ford's letter, and hereby hangs a final, ironic tale.

THE WHITE HOUSE

January 2, 1975

Dear Mrs. Thomas:

There are no words that can ease the burden you have carried over these years. The circumstances surrounding your husband's death are a source of deepest regret to the government he served so loyally, and well, and I only hope that the measures which came about as a result of this tragedy will prevent reoccurrences of this kind in the future. I also hope that the enclosed legislation will bring some comfort to you and your family.

Mrs. Ford joins me in sending you our warmest wishes and prayers at this holiday season and for the years ahead.

Sincerely,
Jerry Ford

Mrs. Charles William Thomas
5432 Wolf River Lane
Columbia, Maryland 21043

When it was announced in the White House press room that President Ford had signed the private bill clearing Thomas's name, and had sent, as well, a private letter of condolence to

Mrs. Thomas, a newsman phoned her at her State Department office. She closed the door and burst into tears.

As the days went by, however, she thought it strange that the presidential letter had not arrived at her Northwest Washington home. More days went by, and then it was delivered—not to her home but to her office. A quick glance at the bottom of the letter explained its two-week delay: 5432 Wolf River Lane, Columbia, Maryland was the address of the same Charles W. Thomas in whose personnel jacket Ambassador McClintock's letter recommending her husband's promotion had been misfiled in 1966— the very incident that set in motion the chain of events that led to his suicide.

14 "It Was a Blast, an Absolute Blast"

A DEEP-BLUE mountain lake in the Western wilderness. A small plane circles a craggy peak, dips, and crisps the reach of still water with its pontoons. The pilot cuts the engine, then rummages for a thermos of coffee, a sandwich, and a fishing rod. After his lunch break, he roars off into the sunny sky—a supremely happy man with a dream job.

The man is the chief pilot for a state aeronautics commission, which enables him to satisfy his twin passions: flying and hunting and fishing; passions that he'd had neither time nor money for as a desk-bound Army aviation colonel in the Pentagon. He found his new career even though he's in his late forties, and personnel men by the score had told him that his "service-acquired skills" were "not transferable" to civilian life.

He's one of more than 2,000 middle-aged men and women who've made their own successful career changes in the last fifteen-plus years after guidance from a highly unorthodox little career-counseling firm, Crystal Management Services, Inc. Located in the Washington, D.C. suburb of McLean, Virginia, the firm has begun to command national attention in the guidance field. It's run by John Crystal, a hearty individual in his fifties, a former Sears, Roebuck overseas executive and Army intelligence officer, who believes that personnel men should be skinned alive—preferably slowly.

"Anyone who looks for a job through the so-called personnel or placement 'system' ought to have his head examined," says

161

Crystal. "Personnel men were put on this earth primarily to screen you out on the basis of some detail in your résumé."

Personnel departments, for one thing, occupy the bottom of the pecking order in most companies. They're generally not even told about high-level openings; when and if they are told, they're rarely empowered to do the hiring. By the time a job is available, friends and relatives of people who work for the firm have the inside track.

So Crystal instructs his unemployed electrical engineers, restless government workers, soon-to-be-retired Navy men, and so on, to avoid all personnel and employment agency offices, executive search firms, help wanted advertisements, résumé writing, and most of the other standard operating procedures of the Great American Job Hunt; procedures that failed conscientious Charles Thomas despite the obvious transferability of his experience to other fields; procedures which fail the vast majority of men and women who follow them.

The placement apparatus fails the individual job-hunter because it is biased in favor of the employer with whom it has a continuing relationship. The employment agency or executive search firm will probably never see the job-hunter again.

The executive placement firm to which Charles Thomas paid more than $1,500 failed to get him a single interview. The firm did mail his résumé out in all directions, a demonstrably futile exercise. Some big corporations receive as many as 250,000 résumés a year.

Thomas's experience, furthermore, is the rule rather than the exception. The Federal Trade Commission has reported the success rate of private employment agencies is about 5 percent.

The placement runaround erodes a man's self-esteem—to say nothing of his finances—and often leads to serious marital problems as the unemployment period lengthens. Eventually, a man reaches the point where he'll accept any job, at any salary, anywhere ("Sure, my wife and I would *love* to move to Pittsburgh!"). He joins the ranks of the "underemployed," a word which probably describes most white collar workers in this country.

Crystal advises his clients to forget about the job hunt per se for the near term—his course includes 16 three-hour sessions spread over 21 weeks—and to concentrate upon what they want to accomplish with the balance of their lives. Toward this end, they spend the first three weeks writing a 25,000-word autobiography with the major emphasis on their working lives.

"This is the heart of the program; the hard part," says Crystal. "Finding a job is almost incidental."

The autobiography amounts to a focused, concentrated stocktaking. It's a method of talking to yourself on paper, helping you decide what you most enjoy; what you do best; what your real values are.

"We're really not in the 'job' business," says Crystal. "We're trying to help people lead 'whole' lives. We recognize that work as commonly defined is part of it, certainly. But that is not our major thrust.

"The trouble is that we're taught in school that it doesn't make any difference what we consider our values to be because we can't use that information anyway. The educational system beats it out of us, tells us we'll be lucky to get a job, any kind of a job. So we never try.

"My theory has always been that we can control our lives; not completely, not perfectly by any means; but more than most of us are doing. So our approach is based on (a) you can do it, and (b) in order to get started, you first have to figure out who you are. This has nothing to do with jobs; nothing at all—supposedly.

"So you define your values, and these will be lasting values. These are the things that really make you tick, that determine what kinds of environments—living environments and working environments—are congenial, and which kind are not. Now this may sound awfully metaphysical, but it isn't at all."

At the time Crystal's clients start to work on their autobiographies, they become unwitting disciples of Michel de Montaigne, who made himself the subject of intimate, objective, and prolonged study, trying to determine what life had taught him, as measured against the philosophy he'd acquired from books and professors, and the opinions of others.

"I presented myself to myself as theme and subject," he said. "It is a wild and monstrous plan."[1]

Montaigne was thirty-eight when he began the delightful, extended self-searching that has come down to us in his *Essays*.

"Each man is a very good education to himself, provided he

has the capacity to spy on himself from close up," he wrote. The trouble is, most men never develop this capacity, forever borrowing instead from the ideas of others.

"We seek other conditions because we do not understand the use of our own, and go outside ourselves because we do not know what it is like inside. Yet there is no use our mounting on stilts, for on stilts we must still walk on our own two legs. And on the loftiest throne in the world, we are still sitting on our own rump."[2]

Montaigne contended that each man is richer than he realizes. Crystal's clients reach the same conclusion. For though they're told to include their failures in the chronicle of their work lives, they are instructed to emphasize their accomplishments and enthusiams.

"Start thinking about the things you do well, the things you really like to do, even if they're sort of wild dreams," Crystal instructs them. "Start analyzing what you do in your spare time. Sometimes we do in our spare time what we really ought to be doing in our work. What about those community orchestras where you see a banker playing the violin and a department store clerk playing the French horn? Which is the real world? Which is the play world? Everybody thinks the real world is where we're employed. Which is the real world for the banker? The bank—or the orchestra?"

Because Crystal's method is a direct outgrowth of his unhappy experience with the employment system when he returned home to New York City after World War II, it's best described in this connection.

Before joining the army, he'd earned a bachelor of arts degree from Columbia University, with a major in economics. For five years he operated as a combat intelligence officer in Europe where he learned to speak French and German fluently, and to get along in several other languages.

In a general way, he knew what he wanted to do; he wanted to return to Europe in a well-paying job for a U.S. company; to do something "socially constructive" and enjoyable; something that would enable him to capitalize upon the information-gathering techniques he'd learned in military intelligence.

Naively, Crystal thought that the employment system would quickly match him up with a job. It didn't.

He filled out job application forms by the hundreds, wrote résumés, placed ads in newspapers, spent hours in the anterooms of personnel offices. Finally, he was offered a $65-a-week job as a researcher for a news magazine. He turned them down.

"I was a total flop as a job-hunter," he recalls. "But then I sat down and said to myself: 'Something's wrong here. I'm not that stupid; I just can't be. Maybe it isn't me; maybe it's the system.' And I made a key decision, which was not to do what everyone else does, and that is to become very defensive, and lose all my self-confidence, and just, you know, slip down, and down, and down, which is tragic. I said to hell with that. If I could get along behind the German lines, which I did, then I can sure as hell get along somehow in a system that is not actively out to get me. At worst it was neutral.

"The first requirement was intelligence with a capital 'I.' What is the employment system? How does it work? *Does* it work? If not, why not? And what can be done about it?

"I started out examining all the clichés we are brought up with: 'Obviously you get a job through the personnel department.' That is not true. 'You need a résumé.' Ask yourself why? A résumé is nothing but a glorified job application form—which throws you right back into the personnel department. And since the personnel department rarely if ever has the power to hire anyway, why put yourself in personnel channels? None of it makes any sense."

One day Crystal heard from one of his old army friends that Sears, Roebuck's president, General Robert E. Wood, was planning to internationalize the company's operations. By now Crystal knew enough to stay away from personnel. Instead, he cast about among his army friends and acquaintances for someone who knew Wood, a general in World War I. Crystal soon found a man who knew Wood well enough to pick up the phone and say:

"Bob, I've got a man here you ought to meet."

"Send him out," said Wood.

Crystal took the train from New York City to Sears's headquarters in Chicago. Within fifteen minutes after they'd started talking, Wood offered Crystal a job analyzing the market possibilities for Sears' products overseas.

"But General," said Crystal, "I must tell you that I don't know the first thing about retailing and marketing."

"Good, John," replied Wood. "You won't have to unlearn anything about retailing and marketing. You'll do it our way."

"Yes sir!" said Crystal with his big Irish grin.

On the spot, Wood made Crystal Sears's first manager for Europe, North Africa, and the Middle East at a high salary. Crystal says he thought he had died and gone to heaven.

"I had a home and an office in Frankfurt, an office in Bordeaux, and a villa on the beach outside town; and later on, an office and a villa in Beirut," Crystal recalls. "I deeply believed in Sears's Middle Western honesty, and in what I was doing. I was overseas nine years with the company, and it was a blast, an absolute blast."

Counting the war, Crystal had been abroad for fourteen years, and now he wanted to come home. About this time, General Wood retired, and Crystal and many of the other men who'd established Sears overseas left the company, too.

Crystal learned lifelong lessons from all this. For one thing, he'd found his *métier de rêve*, without reference to personnel offices, employment agencies, or any of the other traditional procedures. He realized that if he had submitted a résumé to Sears's personnel office, he'd probably never have set foot on General Wood's carpet. There'd have been nothing in his résumé, after all, about retailing and marketing experience. Instead, a résumé would have enabled personnel to label him: "Unemployed Army intelligence officer."

Furthermore, when Crystal talked with the Sears president, the general showed no interest in the young man's academic career at Columbia years before. For that matter, Wood was little interested in any of Crystal's background before his army experience.

Obviously, Wood knew what capabilities were required by Army combat intelligence, and how they were applicable to marketing research, especially in the hands of a man who knew the territory intimately and spoke the language.

It's safe to assume that Wood liked Crystal, and could tell that the young man's enthusiasm was genuine. ("You're a very per-suasive person when you talk about something you really love," says Crystal.) The two men also had something in common: both had served in the army during World Wars. But primarily, Wood was confident that Crystal could do the job, and that was really all he cared about.

There is an ancient proverb which goes: "Give me a fish, and I will eat for today; teach me to fish, and I will eat for the rest of my life." Based upon his experience with Sears, Crystal has dedicated his life since 1959 to helping frightened men and women in midlife learn to fish. He has been tremendously suc-cessful. A verifiable 85 percent of his graduates have found, on their own, jobs that they wanted, where they wanted them. More important, they've found themselves.

In *Where Do I Go From Here With My Life?*, which Crystal coauthored with the Rev. Richard N. Bolles as a teaching guide, he counsels job-hunters:

> Eliminating from your consciousness all the falsehoods taught to you throughout your life about how to get a job, is the beginning of wisdom. For the very practical purposes of your vocational sur-vival, you must understand that the so-called "employment system" does not exist. Finding a rational matching up with appropriate employment is solely up to you—aided by whatever persons *you* choose.
>
> You must determine exactly what it is you want to do. You must select precisely that organization which you find most attractive. You must identify the one official there who shares your major in-terest, and who does have the authority to create for you the position you wish. And then you must go about convincing him or her of the overwhelming logic of your thesis in order to get what you want. There is no other way.[3]

This takes time, patience, and hard work. There are no short-cuts. Experience has shown that finding a job at your highest skill level can take up to nine months or more, says Bolles, a Harvard-educated career deevlopment specialist based in San Francisco and author of *What Color Is My Parachute?*, a book which is also used in Crystal's course. Bolles is an Episcopal priest who be-

came interested in the employment system when he started helping former clergymen find work.

Crystal insists that the jobs are out there, and that unemployment statistics and Labor Department data on job availability
in various professions and businesses are meaningless to the individual and should be ignored.

For one thing, most jobs paying more than about $7,000 are
never advertised. As already noted, most personnel men are often
the last to hear about upper-level openings in their own firms.
Then there is that hidden job market in the minds of employers
who have problems that need solving, and who are prepared to
create jobs for people who can solve them.

"There are far more good jobs today—particularly for knowledge workers—than there ever have been before," insists Crystal,
echoing Peter Drucker, the management specialist, and other
experts.

Even if the scare statistics did have meaning, argues Crystal
with irrefutable logic, then it stands to reason that the men who
are going to get the jobs are the men best equipped for the job
hunt.

Crystal doesn't ask anyone to take his opinions on faith. "You
must think of yourselves as intelligence officers in an alien and
possibly hostile land," he tells his clients. "Don't believe me when
I tell you there is no such thing as job placement. Go out and
test it for yourself."

The clients come back from their field trips to employment and
personnel offices, with their aptitude tests and résumé writing,
convinced that he is right. "My God, why didn't someone tell me
this when I was still in high school. The whole thing's a fake!"

Lifework planning courses based upon Crystal's method are
now being taught in some Fairfax County, Virginia high schools,
and Georgetown University in Washington, D.C., has a noncredit
course.

The hard work in Crystal's course does not end with completion of the autobiography. At this point, Crystal and his small
staff help the client recognize and analyze his skills. No effort is
made to push an individual in any particular direction, but often

capabilities are pointed out to him that he hadn't realized he possessed.

Typical was a fortyish Catholic priest, who was leaving the church. He decided that he would like to get into financial management of a small university of some kind, but he feared he did not have the credentials. Yet analysis of the man's career revealed that he'd been almost continuously involved in "financial management" from the day he organized his first church bazaar, up to and including his recent completion of complicated dealings involving the sale of church property. Furthermore, his instinct about his new career choice had been a good one, for he'd demonstrated an obvious talent for money matters.

Buoyed by his newfound self-knowledge, the priest was able to market himself effectively, and come up with just the job that suited him: financial manager for a small university.

Crystal has seen so many men terrorized by arbitrary job specifications and credentials, that he gets exercised at the thought. "Credentialing is out. If he can do the job, he doesn't need a degree in it. If he can do the job, I don't care whether he once served in the Red Chinese Marines. I could care less. Why do we need all this idiocy?"

Crystal fondly recalls a former Navy jet-fighter pilot who was afraid of what he'd find "out there"; a man who had calmly flown into action from the heaving decks of aircraft carriers, yet had been made to feel by the system that he had little to offer private enterprise.

He revealed in his autobiography that he'd always volunteered for the post of maintenance officer at the various bases where he had served, and that he'd been commended for the high-level combat readiness of his squadrons' planes. Most fighter jocks are not interested in the assignment, which is analagous to managing a small factory, but this man loved the work.

Like so many of the military men passing through Crystal's course, the Navy man liked to go hunting in his off-hours, and he was an expert duck-hunter, with an appreciation of fine shotguns and other sporting firearms.

Finally, he wrote that of all the places he and his wife had lived during their Navy life, they liked Japan best of all, and often said they would like to return there to settle some day.

Today, the former Navy flier is happily managing an American-owned shotgun factory outside Tokyo, and winnowing Japan's flights of wild ducks on the weekends. . . .

One of the questions that Crystal clients are asked to answer is whether there is anything about the world around them they might like to change, or improve, in the years that are left to them. This line of thinking has led a number of men into worthwhile careers. A phased-out electrical engineer from Maryland decided that he would like to apply his experience to improvement of health care management, and that he would like to move to New Mexico. He was offered seven jobs before finally settling on one in Albuquerque that came closest to meeting all his requirements, psychic and financial.

A phased-out nuclear engineer from New York became attracted to the State of Virginia while taking Crystal's course, and decided he wanted to get involved in environmental protection in that state. He's now in the governor's office as a special assistant for environmental affairs.

These men all found their new lives the same way. Once they'd decided where they wanted to work and live, and had carefully assessed their personal strong points, they took field trips to scout the territory, talking with local people about the schools, the weather, recreational facilities, and opportunities in their chosen fields.

Like all good intelligence agents, they studied the terrain—in this case the employment terrain—long before they arrived, seeking out people who could refer them to the key men in the organizations that interested them. *Bob, I've got a man here you ought to meet.* They gathered information on the fields of their interest by writing to Chambers of Commerce, digging in their local libraries, writing or talking with the congressional delegations from the states involved. Then they surveyed the organizations that interested them, first taking the trouble to find out what problems the organizations might be having and trying to come up with solutions from their own experience.

They arranged for appointments with company heads or other

key men in the organizations, making it clear that they were surveying the field, not job hunting—which was true at that stage of the game.

Crystal calls these "low stress" interviews because they enable each man to size up the other without being forced to make employment decisions. Bolles has likened these "survey" or "proposal" interviews to cutting in on an attractive stranger at a dance. No commitment—just interest for now.

A retired foreign service officer, with experience as a commercial attaché in far-flung parts of the world, decided after his soul-searching that he'd like to go into banking in Washington, D.C. In his survey of the banking community, he came across one in particular that he believed could profit from establishing facilities for overseas transactions.

Through the friend of a friend, he arranged an interview with the bank's president, to whom he presented a carefully considered program for an overseas banking service.

The banker was interested. In fact, he said, he'd been thinking along these same lines for some time. There were more discussions. Finally, Crystal's client was hired to do the job that he had created for himself.

There was the Air Force officer, too, who rhapsodized in his autobiography about camping. For most of his career he had been in management, tied to a desk. Whenever he could spare the time, he went hiking and camping in the woods. He was forever buying new equipment from Orvis and L. L. Bean catalogues; trading it; experimenting with it.

"But nobody's going to pay me to do this," he wrote.

"Why not?" asked Crystal.

The Air Force man took it from there. First he made economic surveys of camping equipment companies in the Southwest, where he wanted to wind up his days. One of the companies asked him to establish a product development department to include field-testing of equipment. This, of course, requires him to do a lot of camping—on company time.

If Crystal's clients did not bring to their interviews a great deal of knowledge, experience, and genuine enthusiasm for the subject matter—and if they did not have a clear idea of where they were going—then it would be fair to say that the "survey" interview was contrived. And if such were the case, it would not work.

"One of the problems is that our people are forever being offered jobs before they've completed their surveys and found just exactly what they want," says Crystal. "I guess we're the only counseling outfit in America that has stood up and cheered when one of our clients turned down a $35,000 job. It wasn't just what he wanted."

Crystal's clients learn how to bargain. One former diplomat was offered a job as director of the foreign affairs council of a big Eastern city at a $19,000 salary. The offer came during luncheon with the directors of the council, and he politely rejected it. By midafternoon when he was about ready to take the plane back to Washington, the offer had been raised to $25,000, and he accepted.

A number of foreign service officers have passed through Crystal's course over the years, and they've increased in numbers since Charles Thomas's suicide. During the Foreign Relations Committee's hearings, it came out that the State Department's External Placement Division had done nothing to help Thomas find a new job beyond mailing his résumé to twenty-seven "carefully screened prospective employers," as William Macomber put it. Not a single job interview resulted.

As a result of the Thomas case, State for a long time did not dare to fire anyone, and the organization grew overloaded at the top with senior officials afraid to retire.

"Those men nearing retirement age, who needed to continue working, were terrified, and rightly so," says Crystal. "They had the example of Thomas's experience with the so-called 'job market.' Two thousand résumés! Here you have men who've spent their entire careers solving problems. Yet when it comes to applying their own analytical and planning and management experience to their own personal lives, they allow themselves to be told: 'You're a helpless victim of the system. Because you are a foreign service officer, you have gained nothing in the way of skills that are transferable.' The trouble is that most personnel people are so stupid they wouldn't know a 'skill' if they saw one.

"Let's take a man who has served as a commercial attaché in

Buenos Aires for a number of years. What has he been doing? He's been promoting American business in Argentina, and helping solve problems. Well, if he can promote American business and solve problems in Argentina, he can do the same thing in Wisconsin, or wherever."

In the wake of the Senate hearings on Charles Thomas's firing and suicide, the Department of State awarded Crystal Management a contract to put preretirement foreign service officers— those who wish to do so—through his course, with State paying part of the $1,000 fee for each man.

The problems faced by foreign service officers, Central Intelligence Agency men, servicemen, and other government workers, are little different from those faced by accountants, newspapermen, and whatnot. Crystal Management, for example, has also been under contract for a long time to the Institute of Electrical and Electronic Engineers, whose membership has been devastated by cutbacks in aerospace and defense contracts, and by the cynical hiring and firing practices of a segment of the volatile space-defense industry. It has become custom for many companies, for example, to hire an engineer and assign him to a highly specialized part of a project for its duration, which may be three or four years. The man works tremendously hard, under extreme pressure, only to be fired when the project ends. Then the company replaces him with an eager young engineer fresh from engineering school, and repeats the process.

Early one recent evening, a local minister telephoned Crystal and asked if he would talk with one of his parishioners, an aerospace engineer in his early forties, about whom he was concerned. The man arrived at Crystal's office in a highly emotional state. He said he'd worked for a number of years on a space program with a firm on Long Island, New York, and that the company's contract with the government was about to expire. Without warning, he received a telephone call at 4:45 P.M. on a Friday. His supervisor was on the line saying that he wouldn't be needed any longer, and that a security man was on his way to help him pack his personal files, and see that he didn't remove any classified documents.

The engineer went into a tailspin. For many months he searched in vain for a job. The strain on his marriage precipitated a divorce. He started drinking heavily. He'd finally found a job in Maryland that was far below his capabilities and previous salary level, whereupon the company went through a merger and the man feared that he might lose the job as a consequence. He'd told his pastor, and he told Crystal, that if he lost *this* job he was going to commit suicide.

Crystal sat up talking with the man until dawn. At last report, the engineer had not lost his job, and Crystal is convinced that the man is thinking more clearly now.

For many men such as this engineer, being laid off "is similar to a death sentence," says Crystal. "The person realizes that using conventional employment systems, he's never going to get back where he was. In our society, nothing is worse than failure. We can talk about venereal disease but not economic failure. The person out of a job has to understand that he has not failed, the system has."

Dr. Thomas Green of Syracuse University's Educational Policy Research Center, said in Congressional testimony sometime ago:

"Surely there is nothing more damaging to the human spirit than the knowledge—or belief—that one's capacities are unused, unwanted, or expended in something of no particular value. Who knows what human misery would be relieved and what human energies released if the possibility of multiple careers were the rule, and if there were, as a consequence, ready means of entry and exit to and from new avenues of work."[4]

15 *"Okay, You're Finished as of Right Now!"*

No ONE underestimates the risks, especially financial, of making a major midlife change. Even as John Crystal helps men pack their 'chutes, and cheers them on to make the leap, he does so with Christ's admonition to his disciples very much in mind: "Behold, I send you forth as sheep in the midst of wolves: be ye therefore wise as serpents and harmless as doves."

Our culture conspires against freedom to change direction in midpassage. Our immature and self-contradictory attitudes toward aging contribute to this, as does our private pension plan system that serves to lock some men in their jobs, lock others out with age limits on joining, and ultimately cheats the vast majority of pensioners of their retirement benefits.

We've managed to create a system which enables the powers that be to keep salaried men in psychological bondage once they've reached forty or thereabouts, to fire them easily for reasons other than cause, or to refuse to hire them. Similarly, many companies put age limits upon participation in training programs.

Dr. Harold Sheppard, one of the nation's top industrial sociologists, says, "A case can be made that our institutions do everything in their power to discourage and make it impossible to facilitate midlife change.

"A more charitable proposition would be that in our efforts to solve certain problems and to achieve other goals, we have developed solutions and mechanisms that—without malice or deliberate intent—function today as anachronistic obstacles to encouragement and facilitation of second careers. Typical examples are entrance requirements for training and education programs, provisions of pension plans, seniority rules, and early retirement.

"The trouble is, we have built up a system of investments in a job with a particular company, all those fringe benefits that go with the job, not the man.

"The original idea of the pension was to tie a guy to the company; the company might say it was to build up the guy's 'loyalty.' If it took him twenty years to earn vested rights to his pension, he couldn't leave for a better job after eighteen years, say, with two years to go, and start all over with no pension, and work twenty more years to build another pension with the other company.

"To the degree that a man is locked in, he is a less useful employee, and if you multiply that by the whole economy, we're all paying for it. The companies are not really winning by continuing these old practices; they wind up paying in other ways for not doing the right thing by people.

"I like to stress the argument that, the individual aside, we need mobility from the *economy's* point of view. The more rational utilization of manpower leads to greater productivity in the long run."

A middle-aged man, especially in these uncertain times, is caught between a rock and a very hard place. The leap to a new job, or new career, does entail risk. But it can prove even more dangerous to cling too long to an organization out of adherence to "company loyalty," or a misplaced confidence in its paternalism.

Industrial psychologist Harry Levinson of Harvard University notes that even in the best of times, there is a disposition on the part of corporations to downgrade employees as they get along in years, to clear the track for young people coming behind.

In the worst of times, such downgrading accelerates. By turning out an older man and replacing him with a younger one, the company saves money, not only on salary but also in pension and insurance payments. During the recession, supervisory and middle-management men have been fired in record numbers. Once out of work, they remain unemployed far longer than younger men. These victims will not soon forget how expendable they were, says a recent American Management Association study revealing both a growing sentiment on the part of middle-management men for unionization, and an intense "frustration and discontent" with life in the corporation:

> All around them, in the factory and now in many offices where clerical and some professional employees are represented by unions, they observe the relative security unionism provides to these employee groups. Too, top management seems relatively secure in the carpeted sanctuary that the authoritarian structure of much of the American business community provides for top executives. . . .
> Today's manager reports that his opportunities for direct participation in the decision-making process seem to be rapidly decreasing in the highly bureaucratic and authoritarian structure of the techno-corporation of the 1970s. Moreover, the sense of challenge and the feelings of personal reward and achievement seem to be diminishing, and for some, self-actualization seems entirely out of reach.[1]

Senator Charles H. Percy, Illinois Republican, speaking at a recent conference on second careers, said, "the American workplace has stubbornly remained the last redoubt of yesterday's values."

Betty Holroyd Roberts, as a doctoral candidate in gerontology at Brandeis University a few years ago, made a study of some 500 middle-aged individuals, mostly men, who dropped out of the system, much as many teen-agers did in the 1960s. They are loosely organized under the banner of an underground newspaper, *The Black Bart Brigade,* published from time to time in San Francisco. Black Bart was the alias of an obscure bandit of "good family" by the name of Charles E. Bolton, who operated in the old West. A onetime farmer, patent medicine salesman, and gold prospector, he turned to stagecoach robbery in late middle age after his disillusionment with legitimate work. He never harmed anyone, and liked to leave behind bits of doggerel such as this at the scene of his crimes:

> I've labored long and hard for bread,
> For honor and for riches.
> But on my toes too long you've tred—
> You fine-haired sons of bitches![2]

Bart was finally captured, imprisoned, and paroled into the obscurity whence he had come.

Mrs. Roberts concentrated her research upon thirty-seven white collar and professional people, nearly all men, between the ages of thirty and fifty-five, about half of whom had B.A. degrees or the equivalent, and half advanced degrees.

These individuals had been grossing annual incomes ranging from $8,000 to $40,000 when they dropped out of the rat race, and their incomes now range from $2,000 to $25,000, she reports. A number of her subjects increased their incomes after leaving their jobs. She tells of one professor who went from $10,000 to $25,000-plus by becoming an entertainer. Even so, he continues to lead a simple life in the country.

These former advertising men, bankers, engineers, and so forth, are working at part-time jobs such as ski instructors, waiters, farmers, consultants, and small businessmen, having greatly simplified their styles of living so that they can have more leisure, among other things.

The men left their careers for a variety of reasons, including boredom, lack of autonomy, a feeling that they were being exploited by the system.

Until recently, the subject of mid-career change has been largely an academic one, except for dropouts such as the Black Barts, the wealthy, and the would-be Gauguins.

"A few of us have been preaching the importance of helpful intervention for mid-career changers for the last twenty years, but John Crystal is one of the few people who has done anything practical about the problem," concedes Harold Sheppard who was for many years with the W. E. Upjohn Institute for Employment Research, in Washington, D.C.

Crystal notwithstanding, however, the mobility option will probably never become a reality for the average man until age discrimination has been made costly and publicly embarrassing to employers who practice it. This process has begun with the belated enforcement of the Age Discrimination in Employment Act of 1967 which had become by mid-1974 "an explosive issue," in the words of *Business Week*.

One reason it has taken so long for the issue to be joined in the courts is that Charlie has refused to think of himself as middle-aged. And he has not traditionally been the kind of person who joins picket lines or gets embroiled in court suits over his "rights." If he's fired, passed over for promotion, or turned down for a job, and knows or suspects it's because of his age alone, he takes his lumps in silence and in shame. He's been slow to grasp the cold reality that *he* is now a member of a minority—namely, the 37 million men and women in the work force aged forty through sixty-four, nearly half of whom are white collar workers. It's these middle-class, middle-aged white collar workers who've been hit hardest by age discrimination during the recession because they have not been organized, and have, until lately, been only half aware of what was happening to them.

Michael Batten, a former top official of the National Council on the Aging, Inc., a nonprofit organization in Washington, D.C., that concerns itself with such matters, likes to recall that Vicente Blasco-Ibanez, the author of *The Four Horsemen of the Apocalypse,* once observed that most individuals "regard aging as a sort of 'plague' or disease that occurs halfway around the world. We Americans who are encouraged to wash the gray out of our hair and gulp Geritol, tend to fall into that group. It should not be surprising, therefore, that the whole business of age and age discrimination ranks low in our catalogue of concerns. That is, until you or I run into the problem. Age discrimination in employment is no respecter of status or personal ability. It occurs in industry and government agencies and affects all occupations from executives to sweeps. This type of discrimination is pervasive in our society."

Thousands of age discrimination investigations carried out by the Department of Labor since the law took effect in mid-1968, reveal that age bias falls most heavily upon middle-aged males in middle management, followed by unskilled laborers. Employees with certain mechanical skills and union representation have been the least affected.

In May 1974, labor won its first headline-making settlement, one that involved middle-aged employees in all three of the above categories. Western Operations, Inc., a division of the giant Standard Oil Company of California, made news because of the

$2 million in lost pay and benefits it agreed to restore to 160 over-forty workers it had fired between December 1, 1970 and December 31, 1973. The company agreed, as well, to reinstate 120 of the 160 workers.

Standard Oil said the firings were simply part of an economy drive in which 1,600 jobs were eliminated, all but 500 through attrition. But after a two-year investigation, Labor Department "compliance officers," as they're called, concluded that age had been the sole factor in dismissal of the 160 men and women in question.

What made this case so interesting was that annual salaries of the workers fired ranged from $8,000 a year to $40,000, with individual penalty payments ranging from less than $10,000 to more than $50,000. As Michael Batten likes to emphasize, the $8,000-a-year blue collar worker and the $40,000-a-year executive in Western Operations undoubtedly had little in common before they were fired. "Rather quickly, they discovered some common ground. Both were in their fifties. Both realized they had job protection under the age discrimination law."

Labor Secretary Peter J. Brennan said of the case: "This agreement demonstrates clearly that age discrimination costs money. It deprives workers of income. It boosts our unemployment rate. And it swells the cost of unemployment compensation.

"Age discrimination is also expensive for employers. They are cheating themselves of some of the best talent in America. And they do so because of myths and prejudices that have no basis in fact."[3]

The California Standard case was the biggest settlement in the six-year history of the law up to that time. Earlier, Pan American World Airways paid $250,000 to twenty-nine former Miami employees.

In June 1974, one month after the California Standard payout, Labor went out for more bear, filing suit against the Baltimore and Ohio, and Chesapeake and Ohio railways in behalf of 300 present and former employees for $20 million—ten times the amount of the record California Standard settlement.

Labor's complaint against the "Chessie" system charges that since 1971, the railroads have willfully violated the law by "dis-

charging, refusing to hire, demoting, and/or otherwise discrim-
inating" against the employees because of their age. The complaint also alleges that the railroads' pension plan revision of
recent date calling for mandatory retirement at age sixty-two
violates the law which protects employees to age sixty-five.

Solicitor of Labor William Kilberg has stated that the Department seeks the rehiring of individuals who have been unfairly
fired; reinstatement of demoted employees to their original positions; payment of back wages plus interest; abolition of the mandatory retirement provision, "and other appropriate relief."

Throughout the remainder of 1974, 1975, and 1976, Labor's
enforcement increased in vigor, involving more and more of the
nation's biggest and best-known corporations. There was ample
evidence that elimination of age bias in employment would be a
long, hard, bitter struggle, like the civil rights movements involving race, religion, and sex, that began earlier, and from which
this movement sprang, almost as an afterthought of Congress.

Title VII of the Civil Rights Act of 1964 forbids employers,
employment agencies, and trade unions to practice discrimination
on grounds of race, color, religion, sex, or national origin. Age
discrimination, which affects individuals in each of these categories, was somehow overlooked during the early drafting of the
legislation. Though a few legislators, including Senator Jacob
Javits of New York, urged that age discrimination be included in
Title VII, Congress instead ordered the Department of Labor to
determine the extent of age bias in employment and report back
by mid-1965. Based upon Labor's report confirming what everyone already knew, Congress held hearings that led to the Age
Discrimination in Employment Act of 1967.

"In other words," exclaims Michael Batten, "age is the last, the
lowest, and the least of the equal employment civil rights, and
this lag is symbolic of the whole perception of aging in our
society."

Labor's report revealed that workers forty-five and older at
that time comprised nearly 30 percent of the nation's unemployed,
40 percent of the longterm unemployed, and were receiving three-
quarters of a billion dollars in unemployment insurance every
year. Labor estimated that at least one-fourth of all private job

openings were barred to men over forty-five, one-half to men over fifty-five, and nearly all jobs were closed to men over sixty-five. Senator Edward M. Kennedy observed at one point that since most presidents of the United States were age fifty or above at their inauguration, they'd be ineligible for most jobs in our system.

In the decade since that report, the situation of middle-aged workers has steadily worsened.

The Age Discrimination in Employment Act of 1967 generally follows the outline of the Civil Rights Act of 1964. The law's purpose is "to promote employment of older persons based on their ability rather than age; to prohibit arbitrary age discrimination in employment...." It empowers the Wage and Hour Division of the Department of Labor to carry out investigations, and to enforce its provisions by legal proceedings if voluntary compliance cannot be first obtained. Individuals may also bring suit, but must first notify the Labor Department and submit to a conciliation effort.

Effective May 1, 1974, the law's protection was extended to federal, state, and local government workers, with the U.S. Civil Service Commission given jurisdiction over federal workers, and Labor over state and local employees.

The law protects individuals forty to sixty-five years old from age discrimination by private employers of twenty or more persons, and public employers regardless of the number of employees; employment agencies serving such employers; and labor unions if they operate a hiring hall, procure workers for employers, or have twenty-five or more members in an industry affecting interstate commerce.

According to an official Labor Department summary, it is illegal under the law for an employer:

> ... to fail or refuse to hire, or to discharge, or otherwise discriminate against any individual as to compensation, terms, conditions, or privileges of employment, because of age;
> ... to limit, segregate, or classify his employees so as to deprive any individual of employment opportunities, or adversely affect his status as an employee, because of age;
> ... to reduce the wage rate of any employee in order to comply with the Act.

For an employment agency:

... to fail or refuse to refer for employment, or otherwise discriminate against, any individual because of age, or to classify or refer anyone for employment on the basis of age.

For a labor organization:

... to discriminate against anyone because of age by excluding or expelling any individual from membership, or by limiting, segregating, or classifying its membership on the basis of age, or by other means;
... to fail or refuse to refer anyone for employment so as to result in a deprivation or limitation of employment opportunities or otherwise adversely affect the individual's status as an employee because of age;
... to cause or attempt to cause an employer to discriminate against any individual because of age.

For employers, employment agencies, or labor organizations:

... to discriminate against a person for opposing a practice made unlawful by the Act, or for making a charge, assisting, or participating in any investigation, proceeding, or litigation under it;
... to use printed or published notices or advertisements indicating any preference, limitation, specification, or discrimination, based on age.

Exceptions:

The prohibitions against discrimination because of age do not apply:
... when age is a bona fide occupational qualification reasonably necessary to the normal operations of the particular business;
... when the differentiation is based on reasonable factors other than age;
... when the differentiation is caused by observing the terms of a bona fide seniority system or any bona fide employee benefit plan. This applies to new and existing employee benefit plans, and to the establishment and maintenance of such plans. However, no employee benefit plan shall excuse the failure to hire any individual;
... when the discharge or discipline of an individual is for good cause.[4]

The law appears to turn on the question of what is a "reasonable" *bona fide occupational qualification* ("BFOQ") for a job that entitles an employer to bar an older worker. An extreme example of a more than reasonable BFOQ would be an advertising firm that wanted to hire someone to model teen-age clothes. Obviously, the company has a right to restrict its hiring to teenagers; a middle-aged person could hardly claim age discrimination if turned down for the job.

On this point, the Labor Department states emphatically, however, that "an unmeasured but significant proportion of the age limitations presently in effect are arbitrary in the sense that they have been established without any determination of their actual relevance to job requirements; and are defended on grounds apparently different from their actual explanation." Carin Ann Clauss, the brilliant, driving associate solicitor who directs the Department's newly combative drive against age-bias, is a hard-liner on this critical point. "We take the position that there is really not a job in the country which, generally speaking, men and women between forty and sixty-five cannot perform," she emphasized during an interview in her office recently.

Consequently, Labor has been in court contesting the age-thirty-five hiring limit set by such companies as Greyhound, which nevertheless have sixty-year-old drivers in their employ, and, in Greyhound's case, exploit age and experience with a television advertisement of a gray-haired, fatherly driver leaning from his cab, saying, "Leave the driving to us." Labor is supporting a Massachusetts state policeman in a case that the U.S. Supreme Court—the members of which have lifetime tenure in their jobs—has agreed to hear, involving his rejection of mandatory retirement at age fifty. Labor has also joined a former test pilot of high-performance fighter planes in his case against McDonnell Douglas for grounding him at age fifty-two—after twenty-five years with the company—and then firing him for "insubordination."

For three or four years after passage of the law, however, Labor's enforcement was hesitant. Department attorneys knew what they were looking for, but not how or where to find it. Age discrimination proved highly elusive.

Miss Clauss points out that in race and sex discrimination cases, a government investigator can look around an organization and count the black people and women and decide whether to pursue the matter. Age discrimination is more difficult. There are usually quite a number of middle-aged and older workers in a company, but that doesn't mean there is no age discrimination.

Furthermore, public awareness of the law was almost nil. The drama that enveloped the struggle for racial equality was absent from the quiet drive that produced the age discrimination legislation. About the only thing that caught the attention of the newspapers during the hearings was the testimony of airline stewardesses from a handful of companies complaining of their mandatory retirement from flying at age thirty-two, an age bracket outside the scope of the legislation. The women's plight did serve to point up the absurdity of so many age limitations in employment. Remarking that pilots on the airlines are allowed to fly until age sixty, Congressmen issued a public statement which said in part:

"It seems anomalous to us that a stewardess who faithfully and efficiently performs her duties year after year through the age of 31 years and 11 months becomes, by the mysterious workings of company policy, too old or too feeble when she passes her thirty-second birthday. If the company policies of offering such girls 'other employment commensurate with their abilities' were to be taken literally, it is not impossible to imagine a situation in which a stewardess might be forced to leave her arduous duties in the galley at age thirty-two and retire gracefully to flying the plane for another twenty-eight years."

Labor attorneys also found they were battling a form of discrimination that was sometimes conscious, sometimes unconscious. Says my friend Michael Batten:

"When you ask an employer who his best worker is, he invariably says: 'Mr. Jones. He's been with me twenty years; hasn't missed a day. He's loyal, reliable, and he gives a day's work for a day's pay.'

"But when you ask him: 'How many Mr. Joneses have you hired lately?' he looks at you as though you were nuts. You're supposed to hire someone when he's young, and then he *becomes*

Mr. Jones, who is 'loyal,' 'reliable,' etcetera, etcetera. This is really unconscious discrimination.

"Then you have the other kind of employer who says, 'Look. It'll cost me money to hire a forty-five-year-old. I'll have to pick up a pension. I can't train him; it's harder for him to learn. I'll have to pay him a higher salary than a younger man, and he won't be with me as long.'

"Then he says: 'And anyway, why is this older guy unemployed? Did he get fired? Does he drink?' There are all kinds of images floating around in the mind of the prospective employer. And so the upshot of it is, in some cases, a very pronounced decision not to hire the worker over forty.

"Now the second major rubric is job retention. What happens to older people? Well, in the case of a reduction in force ('RIF'), who's the first to go? In some cases, it's the last hired, first hired, and these are usually young people. But most RIFs hit middle-aged people.

"The employer says, 'Look, Joe. Why don't you take early retirement? That alleviates my problems, and you'll get your benefits.' They call this 'reduction in force through attrition'—so-called 'attrition.'

"Sometimes there is even a little bit of a bribe put up front to get people out of the work force; they give them a money package. But oftentimes it's a reduced pension or annuity, and the older person is not so gently pushed out into 'voluntary retirement.' "

If Joe says that he doesn't want to be eased onto the scrap heap, he now gets to see the other side of his company's paternalism. The company can threaten to relocate him in Akron, give him a demeaning assignment, or cut his salary, which will in turn affect the size of his annuity. A favorite harassment tactic is to take a man's office away from him, especially if it has a window, and give him a less desirable space, without a window. McDonnell Douglas even took its test pilot's parking permit from him.

"So there's this age fifty-eight, fifty-seven, fifty-six, fifty-five early retirement trend," continues Batten, "and it leaves the older person out on the street really not able in many instances to live with today's inflation.

"Then there is this phony issue of 'skill obsolescence' that we saw so dramatically with the aerospace engineers, but it holds true in everything—the advertising business, the chemical business, whatever. Sure, skills become obsolete, but *people* don't. You simply have to make training or retraining available to them."

By early 1973, enforcement of the age discrimination legislation was gathering momentum, and at a symposium on the subject sponsored by the National Council on the Aging, a businessman named Frank P. Doyle mentioned an unmentionable cause of age discrimination in many corporations:

"It's amazing to discover the incidence of age discrimination in organizational life. It appears to be the only form of discrimination that has widespread social approval within the structure of corporate life. Racial and religious discrimination has never been touted as a good idea. But how many times have you known of a manager praised and promoted because he headed an organization filled with 'young tigers?'

" 'Old lions' just don't seem to boost managers up the corporate ladder.

"Such a philosophy appears to have become an underlying corporate value. I think that makes the age discrimination legislation different from any preceding legislation. Management, through annual reports, brags about reducing the average age of top management. Stock analysts will promote stock by praising a company's 'youthful management.' The action of managers reflects the values of their firms; their action is prompted by environmental pressures. Unless positive steps are taken to change values and control decisions, there will be case after case making us look bad as corporate leaders."[5]

The last part of Doyle's remarks has proven prophetic. Case after case *has* made the leadership of some of the biggest U.S. corporations look very bad indeed.

Doyle also observed that as yet there was no such thing as "middle-aged lib," that the middle-aged was a group that hadn't as yet defined and organized itself for political and economic action. "When that happens," he concluded, "I think it's going to be a lot more chilling than today."[6]

Already on the books at that time was one of the Labor Department's first victories in a case relating to age discrimination in hiring; a small one as far as the money settlement—$1,081.80 —but a big one as far as establishing precedent. The case involved Mrs. Betty Rose Hall, forty-seven, who was denied a job as teller by a Fort Lauderdale, Florida, savings and loan association, in the spring of 1969.

Airlines, of course, are not alone in putting attractive young women out front to deal with the public and glamorize the product, and such was the policy of First Federal Savings and Loan Association of Broward County at its main office in Fort Lauderdale, and branches elsewhere. First Federal had its share of over-age-forty employees in other parts of the organization—47 percent were in this age bracket, in fact—but it nevertheless systematically excluded older persons from the category of teller, hiring, with rare exceptions, teen-age girls and young women up to the age of twenty-five.

Mrs. Hall was unaware of the organization's illegal policy when she applied for the position of teller on April 25, 1969, a $75-a-week job for which she was well qualified, having worked as a cashier on and off for nearly a decade in supermarkets, school cafeterias, and whatnot. Besides, it was a no-experience-necessary position.

Mrs. Hall was on the plump side—five feet five and something over 145 pounds—when she was interviewed by First Federal's personnel man, Joseph Bunsfield, who told her that she might find the teller's job too tiring as it required standing all day. She left, and later mailed in an application. Unbeknownst to her, Bunsfield scrawled the words "too old for teller" across the bottom of his interview notes, and promptly forgot her.

In the court case, Bunsfield claimed that Mrs. Hall's age had not been a factor, that he had meant to write "too heavy," when he'd written "too old." Labor's investigation of First Federal's employment records, however, revealed that in another instance, the observant Mr. Bunsfield had written "heavy girl, may make teller" on his interview notes of a twenty-five-year-old woman the same height as Mrs. Hall—and nearly twenty pounds heavier.

Labor also discovered that between June 12, 1968, the effective date of the Act, and July 14, 1969, First Federal had hired thirty-five tellers or teller-trainees, all of whom were under forty, and all but three of whom were in their teens and early twenties. Moreover, the savings and loan had filed a standing order with an employment agency for teller candidates, stipulating that they be between the ages of twenty-one and twenty-four.

The court ruled that Mrs. Hall had been rejected for the job because of her age. She was awarded $1,081.80 representing $75 a week in lost pay between April 25, 1969 and August 27, 1969, when she went to work for the circulation department of a local newspaper.

One of the Labor Department's first big wins involving age bias in firing was the Pan American World Airways case alluded to earlier, a case that illustrates the vulnerability of non-unionized white collar workers in their middle years.

During 1970, Pan Am went through a big shakeout. Older, unionized workers were protected by their seniority. Older, non-unionized middle-management men, engineers, and other professionals, found themselves under the ax. At Miami International Airport, Pan Am fired twenty-nine individuals in the latter category, all aged fifty-nine or older, claiming that their skills were obsolescent, technology had passed them by, and younger, more competent employees were taking over their jobs.

Labor Department investigators checked through the performance ratings of the former employees and found them higher than those of their younger replacements. Refusing to admit that it was guilty of age discrimination, Pan Am nevertheless settled out of court, agreeing to pay $250,000 in damages.

"Another significant aspect of the Pan Am settlement was that these people were protected by Pan Am's extension of their insurance benefits," said Labor's Carin Clauss early in 1973. "Also, their pensions will be recomputed, meaning contributions will be made into the pensions, and when these individuals reach mandatory retirement at sixty-five under the plan, they will receive pension benefits as much as $500 a year better than if they had taken early retirement at the time they were laid off.

"In other words, these employees were treated as if they had not been fired. In computing their pensions, the years of service will extend up to their retirement age, as if they had never been let off, and their salaries will continue for compensation purposes."[7]

A volatile and continuing issue under the age bias law concerns the legality or lack thereof of maximum age limits imposed by employers upon applicants for certain jobs. Of equal interest is the question of age limits that employers set upon the performance of particular tasks.

In February 1973, Labor won a hard-fought district court case enjoining Greyhound Lines, Inc., from refusing to consider applications for the position of bus driver from men over age thirty-five. In April of the following year, an appellate judge reversed the decision of the lower court, and in January 1975, the U.S. Supreme Court refused to review the case. The issue may eventually reach the high court, however, because a similar case brought by the government against part of the Trailways interstate bus system is still wending its way through the courts.

Greyhound first established the age-thirty-five hiring cutoff for its drivers in 1928, and until the age-bias law went into effect forty years later, the company maintained maximum hiring age limitations for *every* category of worker: age forty-five for mechanics, and age forty for all other positions. After June 1968, the company abolished all the hiring limitations except that affecting bus drivers.

Greyhound's defense of the age-thirty-five cutoff was that degenerative changes in the human body around that time begin to impair a man's ability to drive safely.

A Labor witness argued that chronological age was not a reliable index of a person's physical or psychological condition, and could not be a basis for determining the ability of a man to drive. The government's medical witnesses said that an applicant should be judged as an individual on the basis of his functional age, his ability to do the job. This theme runs through case after case.

Labor's attorneys were also quick to draw attention to Greyhound's greying drivers, many of whom are in their fifties and sixties, and the company's "leave the driving to us" advertisements that portray its drivers as fatherly, mature men. How could Greyhound have it both ways?

Greyhound's attorneys replied that the seniority system enabled its older drivers to compensate for physical decrements by choosing the easier, scheduled runs. New employees, regardless of past experience, were assigned so-called "extra board" runs. These are unscheduled trips, charters, extra-sections of scheduled runs, dead-heads, and so forth. Greyhound maintained that these irregular trips were more grueling than the scheduled ones, and that an older man was not flexible or strong enough to adapt. To corroborate this claim, the company trotted out a number of veteran drivers. The government countered with its own driver-witnesses who pooh-poohed the company position.

Greyhound had to concede that the age-thirty-five cutoff was not based upon "surveys, inquiries, research studies, statistical studies, or any other study to our knowledge." Greyhound said it was based upon "good basic common sense."[8]

The U.S. district court judge ruled against Greyhound, saying:

"I believe strongly that functional capacity and not chronological age ought to be the most important factor as to whether or not an individual can do a job safely. This determination must be made repeatedly throughout the employee's employment experience. The human variances involved are myriad; there is no way to generalize as to the physical capability and physiological makeup of an individual. Nor is there a way to project how an individual will be affected by the aging process...."[9]

Government attorneys were shaken when a three-judge appeals court overthrew this decision, saying that Greyhound's age cutoff was a "reasonable" safety precaution.

So as it now stands, a thirty-six-year-old man with ten years' experience as a Trailways bus driver, or driver of oil trucks, or munitions trucks, or trucks loaded with onions, cannot even apply for a job at Greyhound, no matter how perfect his record behind the wheel. And because this is industry-wide with a few exceptions (though most companies draw the cutoff line at forty rather than thirty-five), the Greyhound driver who has passed through the shadow line pretty much has to stick with Greyhound if he wants to keep driving a bus. Never mind that he hates his supervisor, wants a change, thinks he's being underpaid, or senses an opportunity to advance himself elsewhere. Union seniority protects him, but seniority, in combination with the age-thirty-five or age-forty cutoff, forges his chains.

Almost certain to reach the appellate stage, and possibly the U.S. Supreme Court, is the case that Phillip W. Houghton, former chief production test pilot for McDonnell Douglas Corporation, has been pressing against his onetime employer. The case could set an important legal precedent concerning an employer's right to reassign an individual because of age in a way that adversely affects his status and pay as an employee. And like the Greyhound and Trailways cases, the litigation tests the legality of establishing age cutoffs for jobs involving considerations of safety.

Houghton was fifty-two when, on December 31, 1971, McDonnell Douglas removed him from flight status over his objections, thus effecting a one-third reduction in his annual salary. On December 12, 1972, McDonnell fired him. Houghton had been with the company for twenty-five years, twenty-one of them spent test-flying a number of the world's highest performance jet fighter planes, most notably McDonnell's famous F-4 Phantom in its various configurations, and earlier, the F-101 Voodoo.

Regardless of the suit's outcome, the case has already provided one of those rare glimpses inside a big, authoritarian corporation. In the Houghton affair, McDonnell has unwittingly provided business schools with a classic, textbook example of how not to treat a valuable, long-time employee. Houghton was an especially proud and courageous man whose day-to-day duties for more than two decades—3,700 test flights, 4,200 test flight hours—involved risking his life as a matter of course.

Houghton's background is similar to that of the astronauts, many of whom are his friends. He was graduated with honors in aeronautical engineering from the University of Minnesota, then flew combat missions in fighter planes with the U.S. Army Air Force in the Pacific Theater during World War II. After leaving the service, he joined McDonnell as an assistant aerodynamicist—there being no test flying jobs open at the time—and flew on his off-hours with the Missouri Air National Guard. After four years, he won a place on McDonnell's test flight staff.

In 1956, McDonnell was experiencing problems with the engine and hydraulic systems of the F-101 Voodoo which the U.S. Air Force had ordered in great quantity. Because of Houghton's extensive experience with the twin-engined jet, he was promoted to chief production test pilot, and rewarded with his own office.

"It was an office adjacent to the chief pilot's office, similar in size and location, with a large window overlooking the remainder of the pilots' office," he testified recently. "There was a picture window running clear across the wall of the airport side overlooking the flight ramp and the airport."[10]

During the 1960s, Houghton worked with the F-4 Phantom in its numerous versions, a twin-engined, twice-the-speed-of-sound machine that many authorities considered the best multipurpose fighter plane in the world. Houghton was the company's acknowledged expert on the F-4, and on production test flying in general.

Early in the 1970s, McDonnell was readying its new F-15 Eagle—an air-to-air fighter capable of flying more than twice the speed of sound—for the U.S. Air Force. At the same time, says Houghton, the company was going through one of its periodic budget squeezes. Houghton says he was a victim of the squeeze.

Faced with twice-yearly physical examinations conducted by the company as a requirement of the military services and the Federal Aviation Administration, Houghton led a highly disciplined life, religiously adhering to a strenuous exercise schedule. In 1971, as usual, he had no problem passing his physicals. One outside physician found him physiologically more than ten years younger than his chronological age, which inspired Labor Department attorneys to dub Houghton "Super Phil."

Then one day in July 1971, Houghton was summoned to the office of his supervisor, Joseph Dobronski, director of flight operations, who told him without ceremony that his flying days were over. Dobronski explained that he had been "getting pressure" from G. C. Covington, vice-president, engineering, to trim the fifteen-man test flight staff to twelve, said Houghton in his testimony.[11] Because of their age, Houghton and two other pilots had been selected for the cut. Houghton says that he politely registered a negative reaction to being grounded, and departed. One of the other two pilots eventually accepted a desk job at McDonnell, and one left the company.

Dobronski said nothing at this first meeting about another job for Houghton within the company. Apparently no one had given it any thought at this point. Nor did Dobronski express any dissatisfaction with Houghton's flying or administrative work.

One month later, early in August 1971, Dobronski called Houghton to another meeting, this time including W. S. Ross and Joseph Shields, vice-presidents of McDonnell Aircraft Company, the McDonnell Douglas division for which Houghton worked.

Ross did the talking at this session, says Houghton. "He informed me that he had bad news and that my flying was to be terminated by the end of that month. He told me a decision had been made that at my age I should stop flying... and that I should find another position within the company...."[12]

Someone had forgotten to tell George Graff, president of McDonnell Aircraft, about the Houghton matter, however. When Graff did hear about it, he called Houghton in and said he thought the decision to ground him had been "hasty," that he was rescinding the directive.

Some time went by, and then Ross summoned Houghton again. The vice-president said that Graff's decision to rescind notwithstanding, "Mr. Covington was not finished with his efforts in cutting the flight staff, and that he thought I should continue looking for another job."

In September, Houghton's big office was taken from him, and he was assigned to a tiny office. The handwriting was now easily legible on Houghton's now windowless office wall.

In early December 1971, Ross told Houghton that he'd be grounded as of the end of the month, and that this time, the decision had the concurrence of president George Graff. Ross said the company was offering Houghton two job possibilities, one in flight safety, the other in flight simulation. In these jobs, he'd no longer receive flight pay, which accounted for more than one-third his salary. Houghton looked into the jobs and tells me he found them demeaning. He worked at various chores in flight operations while the situation festered.

In March, Houghton told Ross that in removing him from flight status, the company had violated the Age Discrimination in Employment Act of 1967. And on June 26, 1972, Houghton filed with the Secretary of Labor a "Motion of Intention to Sue" as required by the law. The Labor Department undertook informal conciliation with McDonnell Douglas, but it came to naught, and on September 12, 1972, notified Houghton to that effect.

The ax fell on December 12, 1972, when, in a discussion with Joseph Shields, Houghton said he firmly believed that McDonnell had violated the age bias act.

"Okay, you're finished as of right now!" exclaimed Shields, according to Houghton's testimony. "Clear out immediately."[13]

Early in January 1973, Houghton filed suit against McDonnell, alleging that the company had transferred him to a lower-paying job and had thereafter discharged him because of age. The Labor Department joined him as a co-plaintiff, alleging that the aircraft company had violated the age-bias act "by limiting, segregating, or classifying" Houghton because of his age in a way that adversely affected his status as an employee.

McDonnell Douglas maintained that age had been only one factor in Houghton's dismissal, charging that his administrative work left something to be desired, and that he had failed to "remain current" in jet flight technology; in other words, his skills were obsolete.

During the opening phase of the case early in 1975, company attorney Veryl Riddle said, "plaintiff was not removed from flight status solely because of age, but age was a factor considered, and in any event, under the circumstances, age is a bona fide occupational qualification of flight status, and that is the position of McDonnell Douglas in this case."[14]

Riddle then cross-examined Houghton and this exchange resulted:

Q. . . . Well, you have experienced body changes, physical changes, have you not, in the last several years?

A. No, I don't think of any. I'm not real sure what types of changes you're referring to.

Q. Well, let me talk about, for example, I notice that you have a number of wrinkles on your forehead.

A. Uh-huh.

Q. You didn't always have them, did you?

A. I had some wrinkles there from the time I can recollect, and from the pictures that the family album had showing me from fifteen years old, I had most of these wrinkles you see across there now. . . .

Q. Has your hair coloring changed as the years go by?

A. It has changed somewhat.

Q. Are you dying it these days?

A. I use a darkening agent on it, yes, sir.

Q. And without the darkening agent, what color is your hair?

A. I would say it would be about fifty percent gray, fifty percent dark brown.

Q. Do you put the darkening agent on there to maintain the appearance of youth?

A. I put it on there to bring my appearance more into line with what I feel is my physiological condition, plus I think it improves my appearance. . . .[15]

Not long after this, the case was recessed to mid-July 1975, only to be postponed for another month because a key witness for Houghton was detained—he was orbiting the Earth as one of the three U.S. astronauts who linked up in space with two Russian cosmonauts in the Apollo-Soyuz Test Project. At fifty-one, Donald K. Slayton, Houghton's witness, was the oldest man ever to fly in space. (For that matter, the other two American astronauts on the mission, Thomas Stafford and Vance Brand, were forty-five and forty-four respectively.) Thirteen years before, as one of the original Project Mercury astronauts, Slayton was scheduled to fly the second U.S. manned orbital flight when doctors discovered an abnormal heart rhythm, and dropped him from flight status.

Slayton had never lost his determination to fly in space. He remained with the space administration as astronaut training officer. Like Alan Shepard before his moon flight, Slayton fought against disability and the aging process. In 1972, Slayton's heart condition returned to normal and he was cleared to fly.

"To some people, life begins at forty," said Slayton before the Apollo-Soyuz flight. "To me, it's more like fifty, but I guess I'd rather be a fifty-year-old rookie than a fifty-year-old has-been." He said that he would like to continue flying in space in the years ahead, and when asked whether his age might not be a handicap, he replied with an edge to his voice. "I've never figured that age was any criterion for anything. If I pass the physical, I fly."[16]

As chance would have it, neither Slayton nor Alan Shepard, another Houghton witness, was able to testify. After the U.S.-Russian flight, Slayton underwent an operation for a benign tumor on his lung, then had to leave on a world tour. Shepard couldn't make it for other reasons. Had they shown up, they'd have given a boost to the drive against age discrimination, for Houghton's case would then have been front-page news across the nation.

Even so, a handful of the most prominent men in aerospace medicine and aerospace safety did appear at the August 1975 hearings in Houghton's behalf, including Dr. Charles A. Barry, former director of the National Aeronautics and Space Administration's astronaut medical program. They said that Houghton was mentally and physically fit to resume test flying, and that chronological age should not be the criterion for determining such fitness; men age at different rates; it should be an individual matter.

A medical witness for McDonnell said that in his opinion, men of forty and forty-five should not be test-flying high performance airplanes. John Schluetter, Houghton's private attorney, noted that nearly all of McDonnell's twelve remaining test pilots were over forty, several were over forty-five, and that if the company were to take its own witness's advice, it would have to recruit a new flight test staff.

In his suit, Houghton seeks reinstatement to flight status at McDonnell, back pay, and court costs, which have been extremely high, even with Labor sharing the burden. If he wins, he would accept a pension in lieu of reinstatement.

 **16** *"An Institution Built Upon Human Disappointment"*

THE PROBLEMS of age discrimination, compulsory retirement, and pensions are intertwined. If they can be solved, middle-aged man will one day walk with a lighter more confident tread.

"Many middle-aged begin to see that they have been living under a dangerous illusion that their Social Security, private pension, savings, and investments will provide them a decent, secure old age," says Robert Butler. "Neither existent government programs nor personal providence guarantee this. Even if one were able to put together enough resources to provide for retirement income equal to actual earnings in one's middle, prime years, it could mean a massive step down in living standards twenty to thirty years later at age sixty-eight or eighty, according to current inflation projections. Thus the middle-aged feel pressure not only by the need to care for their older and younger family members, but also to accumulate funds for their own needs in old age."[1]

Few domestic problems are more charged with emotion, complexity, and confusion than the private—as opposed to governmental—pension plan system. It is this system that Senator Javits has called "an institution built upon human disappointment." It had combined assets of more than $150 billion in the summer of 1974 when the pension reform act was passed, and covered between 23,000,000 and 35,000,000 employees (pension authorities disagree over the total). These assets are expected to reach $225 billion by 1980, and cover 42 million employees.

Even though these tremendous sums are tax deductible, they had gone virtually unregulated until passage of the Employment

Retirement Income Security Act of 1974. By the most conservative estimate, anywhere from one-third to one-half of the men and women enrolled in these plans prior to 1974 found their pensions a mirage.

Merton C. Bernstein, a professor at Washington University School of Law in St. Louis, and perhaps the nation's leading pension authority, has likened pension-plan enrollees to men betting on a 10-to-1 shot at the race track:

> If every year a company gave an employee the funds representing his retirement savings for the year on the condition that he go to a race track and bet on a horse with 10-to-1 or longer odds, we would be shocked. If the Federal Government gave such a scheme a tax subsidy, we would be aghast. Yet that is essentially what our . . . private pension system does with workers, aided and abetted by . . . a subsidy from the U.S. Treasury.
>
> Employees under private pension plans forego part of their wages every week, every month, every year, so that they may be devoted to employee retirement, although the odds are that the great majority of them will not realize benefits under such plans. . . . The hazards employees bet against are that their company, division, department, or job, will not disappear, that they will not find it advantageous to shift from a declining company or industry to an expanding one; or that injury, ill health, or obsolescent skill will not force them out of their pension-covered employment.
>
> The way the plans are now designed—with heavy emphasis upon long, uninterrupted service with one company, or a group of companies—achieving a decent pension means staying with the same company throughout a work career of thirty or forty years. Any less means a less adequate pension, or none. But the realities of the world of work make it utterly unlikely that most employees can run this maze successfully, and no one can foretell which routes will turn out to be blind alleys.[2]

Before 1974, most plans required ten, fifteen, or twenty years of unbroken service—and achievement of a specified age, usually forty, forty-five, or fifty—before a pension plan member became "vested"; that is, before he earned irrevocable rights to full or partial pension benefits upon retirement, even if he left the employer before retirement age. As we've seen—and statistical studies confirm—most men and women can't meet these criteria in these days and times. Then, when a person leaves a pension-covered position, especially if he's forty or older, his chances of finding pension coverage in his next job are remote. And in his new job, of course, he's among the first to go if the company's fortunes nose dive. A vicious circle.

"Pension plans are an intricate and reasonably boring topic, at least until the day when, to our surprise, we turn sixty-five, and when, to our even greater surprise, we find that the promised pension isn't waiting for us," says David Hapgood in his delightfully irreverent book *The Screwing of the Average Man*. He continues:

> The pension disappeared somewhere along the years, and it's too late now to go back. . . .
> Pensions have blossomed into a major industry that supplies great benefits to employers and banks, some pickings to a few unions, and a living to the parasitic pension administration industry that has attached itself like a $4-billion leech to the nation's . . . pension funds. To the employer, the primary value of the pension fund is that it offers him an opportunity to con his employees out of wage increases in return for a promise he need not keep. The employer says: If you will give up all or part of a wage increase, I'll put some money aside in a fund, and I'll pay you a pension, in addition to your Social Security, when you retire. The employer gets the hard cash and the employees get the promise that will be broken; all of them give up the raise, but only a very few will ever collect the pension. . . .[3]

In 1875 the American Express Company founded the first formal private pension fund in this country, the railroads having developed some informal retirement benefits earlier. The movement grew slowly, and at first companies made it clear that these funds were voluntary rewards for long and faithful service— rather like the monies that the grateful Roman state bestowed upon its victorious generals to ease their declining years.

Unions long remained wary of pension plans, seeing them as paternalistic management efforts to woo workers' loyalty from the unions which eventually created their own pension funds with contributions from the members. In 1927, however, the American

Federation of Labor changed its policy and began to bargain for employer-supported pension plans. The Depression, and the establishment of Social Security in 1935, gave impetus to the movement. Even so, the great surge of private pension plan growth didn't get under way until World War II brought labor shortages, high personal and corporate taxes, and restrictions upon wages and prices. Companies hit upon pension plans as a means of luring workers into their fold—and holding them there. Since that time, workers have come to look upon pensions as their right, a form of deferred wages.

In 1947 the late John L. Lewis, leader of the United Mine Workers, won the right of the union to a say in the management of an employer-financed pension and welfare plan, establishing yet another precedent. Ironically, the drive for pension reform in the 1960s and early 1970s was inspired in part by alleged irregularities in management of the mine workers' pension fund by Lewis's successors.

The way in which some unions and employers—in league with some banks and insurance companies—have abused the private pension plan system in recent decades is a national disgrace, and one that went largely unpublicized until the early 1970s. During the years of debate and hearings culminating in passage of the 1974 pension law, individual and collective horror stories found their way into the newspapers, along with the results of statistical studies that thoroughly substantiated the seriousness of the problem.

In 1971 the Senate Labor and Welfare Committee completed a study of 1,500 representative pension plans from the estimated 34,000 then in existence. These 1,500 plans had 6,900,000 participants during the years 1950 to 1969. During these nineteen years, 5,200,000 workers left the plans and only 3 percent of them ever received any retirement benefits; only 1 percent achieved vested rights.

The Senate committee discovered that 92 percent of participants in plans with fifteen-year vesting provisions left before achieving pension eligibility; 73 percent of those in plans with ten-year vesting also left empty-handed.

Thousands of pension-plan victims wrote to Senator Javits, to

Senator Harrison Williams, New Jersey Democrat, Javits's co-sponsor of the pension bill, and other congressmen concerned with the recent legislation. I plucked two letters at random—one from a blue collar worker, one from a white collar worker—and checked them out.

A man wrote from a city in California, saying that he'd soon be retiring after more than forty years' work and would receive no pension. He outlined his employment record as follows:

> Twenty-five years and two months' employment with a steel company in the Midwest, working up slowly and painfully from the ranks of common laborer to the position of metallurgist. On leaving the company, my monthly salary was $575. There was no pension plan for salaried workers, but an employee-paid annuity fund had been set up during the last ten or twelve years of that time. Total accruement was $3,100.
>
> Two years and two months in an aerospace firm in the State of Washington. This company had a ten-year minimum plan. Employee was not eligible because he would reach the age of sixty-five in less than ten years.
>
> Employed since October 1969 by another California aerospace firm. Again not eligible for a pension plan. . . .

Just as many victims are loyal, one-company employees.

A man from a town in New York worked up from office boy to a supervisory position at a gas company in Manhattan during nearly twenty-four years of continuous "not sick a day" service. Yet he was denied a pension when he left the company because he had not reached the minimum qualifying age of forty-five; he was only forty.

The man says he resigned for compelling personal reasons when the company closed its Manhattan headquarters in 1970, and ordered him to relocate in Ohio.

The company confirmed that the man's record had been "excellent" but said that nothing could be done about his pension.

The purpose of the Employee Retirement Income Security Act of 1974 is to regulate the multibillion-dollar pension industry so that such injustices become the rare exception. It's doubtful that the law will accomplish this objective. Worse still, says pension expert Bernstein, the law presents the illusion of reform and hence will delay a new effort at real reform probably for a decade.

While the law requires that the employer provide his workers with a description of his pension plan "written so as to be understandable by the average plan participant," the 208-page pension law that Congress has composed is all but unreadable. Joseph P. Leary, executive director of the Association of Private Pension and Welfare Plans, Inc., who serves as a nonpartisan observer, says he doubts that half a dozen Congressmen really understand what's in the new law. For that matter, Leary says, even the legions of pension experts who've monitored the bill's progress for years, can't understand great chunks of the fine print.

Merton Bernstein wrote, in a stinging critique of the legislation for the *Cleveland Plain Dealer:* "The new law is fantastically complicated. It should be called the 'Full Employment Act for Actuaries and Lawyers'—who will be its chief beneficiaries. A more protective law could have been simpler and more straightforward. As a result, the non-benefit costs of plans will go up, thereby discouraging new plans, especially for small companies. They and their employees need a national, simple, low-cost plan which could be operated by private enterprise."[4]

Consumer advocate Ralph Nader has charged that union, management, and the pension fund management industry including banks and insurance companies, formed an unholy alliance to denature the pension bill.

"We all know that there is a lot of corruption, conflict of interest, and mis-management in pension funds, so that the Teamsters fund doesn't want any more sunlight on it than the corporate pension fund," said Nader. "The result was that labor and industry closed ranks on the issue, formed a juggernaut, and wore down meaningful legislation."[5]

The importance of the private pension plan system to a man in or approaching midlife is clear. Yet with the exception of Bernstein, Nader, and a few others, the middle-aged, middle-management man was not represented among the special interest groups such as the American Bankers Association and AFL-CIO—both of which were enthusiastic about the bill as it finally emerged—that lobbied so long and so hard on Capitol Hill. As Nader and Kate Blackwell say in their book *You and Your Pension,* "Up to now, pension legislation has been formulated in the virtual absence of constituent pressure—that is, pressure from employees who hope to benefit from the system. Without their involvement, legislative reforms will continue to do too little."[6]

Michael Batten and a number of other men knowledgeable about the politics of aging, believe that creation of an advocacy group for middle-aged men would speed up the drive for pension reform, the movement against age discrimination, and the like. For the near term, at least, such a possibility appears remote. In any event, it behooves everyone to educate himself about the new pension law, the better to understand the changes that will be coming in his company's pension plan.

To begin with, the Employee Retirement Income Security Act of 1974 does not require a business or union to establish a pension plan where one does not exist; the law concerns existing and future pension plans.

The law requires that all employees who are at least twenty-five years of age, and have worked for a company for one year, must be made eligible for the pension plan. If a man joins a company before age twenty-five, he must be granted up to three years' credit toward eventual vesting rights once he's reached age twenty-five. On the other end, the act permits a company to exclude a man from its pension plan if he's within five years of the stipulated retirement age under the plan. (The Age Discrimination in Employment Act does not force a company to take an older man into its pension plan, but it forbids a company from using its pension plan as an excuse for not hiring him at all.)

The pension law offers employers three alternative vesting formulas to choose from. *National Journal Reports,* an authoritative, objective weekly that covers such major legislation, has summarized the vesting formulas and other principal parts of the law as follows:

> ... at least 25 percent vesting at the end of five years of service, gradually increasing over the next 10 years until the employee becomes fully vested at the end of 15 years with the company;
> ... full vesting at the completion of 10 years of service with no interim vesting;
> ... at least 50 percent vesting when an employee's age and years

of service total 45, increasing 10 percent for each of the next five years. However, an employee with 10 years of service must be 50 percent vested even if his age and years of service do not total 45.

Funding:

... the bill would require employers to fund each year's current service costs and amortize any unfunded liability (vested and non-vested). Single employer plans would have 30 years to amortize their unfunded accrued liabilities, while multi-employer plans would have 40 years. Funding requirements could be waived, however, if an employer demonstrates a substantial "business hardship."

Termination insurance:

... the conference report generally followed the Senate version ... in creating an insurance program to pay pension claims if the sponsoring company goes bankrupt or runs short of funds, although both Senate and House bills set up a Pension Benefit Guaranty Corporation in the Labor Department to administer the program. The corporation would be directed by the Secretaries of Labor, Commerce and Treasury. . . .

Fiduciary responsibility:

... the bill would tighten existing law regarding fiduciary responsibility to prevent the misuse of pension funds. No more than 10 percent of a fund could be invested in an employer's securities. . . .

Reporting and disclosure:

... (requires) plan sponsors to supply enrolling participants with a summary of provisions and benefits to be updated at least every 10 years. If there is material modification in the plan, however, a new summary would have to be distributed within 210 days after the end of the plan year in which the change is made.

... companies would also be required to give an employee a statement of his vested rights and, effective in 1976, a summary of his pension benefits when he leaves his job.

Administration:

... the Labor and Treasury departments are given joint authority in such a way that it is hoped there will be no overlapping jurisdiction. Generally, Labor will be concerned with individual rights, while Treasury will be handling overall pension problems.

Retirement accounts:

... conferees accepted the Senate version on establishment of individual retirement accounts for employees not covered by pension plans. An individual would be allowed to set aside 15 percent of his annual income or $1,500, whichever is less, in a retirement account. The contributions would be tax deductible when made, and would be taxed only when withdrawn, at which time the individual presumably would be in a lower tax bracket.

Portability:

... the bill provides that an employee leaving a job could transfer his vested pension benefits to an individual retirement account within 60 days. If his next employer agreed, he then could transfer the funds in the account to the employer's pension fund.

Self-employed:

... (the bill) would raise the amount that self-employed persons could deduct from taxable income for retirement plans. The amount would be 15 percent of annual earnings, or $7,500, whichever is lower. At present, self-employed individuals can deduct only 10 percent, or $2,500 a year.[7]

After President Ford signed the bill into law on September 2, 1974, saying that it would do more for the workers "than almost anything in the history of the country," Bernstein wrote his critique for the *Cleveland Plain Dealer*, concluding that in many respects, the law was a step backward.

From the employee's point of view, early vesting and "portability"—a system whereby a person takes his pension credits with him from job to job—are the ideal. Bernstein says the 1974 law does not represent a significant step toward this goal, and it's hard to argue with his arithmetic or his analysis.

"The new law does not have any portability worthy of the name," wrote Bernstein. "It *permits* the transfer of the value of vested benefits to the next employer's plan, if both the old and new employer agree to do so. And the law instructs the Secretary of Labor to work on technical services to stimulate such transfers. But the former employer has no financial incentive to agree to such a transfer, and the employee has no leverage to compel him to do so...."

Concerning the three vesting formulas, Bernstein noted that the employer will obviously choose the one that's least costly. He dismissed out of hand the first formula—full vesting after ten years—because of the statistical data showing that most individuals leave such plans without a dime. Then he wrote:

A second formula requires 25 percent vesting for employees separated after five years of service—growing by five percent for each additional year of credited service to 50 percent after 10 years, then by 10 percent increments yearly to 100 percent vesting after 15 years of service. As most employees separate with fewer than 10 years service, the utility of the formula must be assessed at the lower end of the scale.

According to a Bureau of National Affairs survey published in the fall of 1973, a typical blue collar plan pays a benefit of $5 a month per year of service. So a 20-year retiree would get a benefit of $100 a month—modest but not insignificant. Under the 5-year-25 percent formula, an employee separated from such a plan after five years service would get a monthly benefit of $6.25 (25 percent of five years multiplied by $5) or a yearly benefit of $75. A benefit for a $10,000-a-year white collar worker would be $150 a year—a paltry income replacement, to put it politely.

With this formula working perfectly (which it wouldn't) an employee with eight such experiences in a 40-year work life would obtain a monthly benefit of $50—the equivalent of a full-time benefit for 10 years service despite 40 years of pension credits! In practice, the average employee will get less because he doesn't have to be taken into a plan after age sixty. . . .

But, if the first two formulas are poor, the third is disastrous. Under it, an employee whose age and service total forty-five must be vested with 50 percent of the normal benefit (provided he-she has at least five years service) and after 10 years service 50 percent must vest in any event. For a young group of employees that formula provides less protection than the 5–25 percent formula. Pension experts pleaded for a vesting formula that completely omitted any age element so as to avoid adverse impact upon older employees and, even more, applicants for employment. . . . This formula is subject to terrible abuse; it provides a direct incentive to employers to make employment arrangements that discourage the employment and continued employment of older people. . . .[8]

In this fashion, Bernstein plods methodically through the small print. He notes that the legislation provides no real protection against layoffs and firings aimed at defeating pension expectations:

Instead, it declares it illegal to fire an employee "for the purpose of" interfering with attainment of rights under the act or the plan—apparently requiring the employee to prove such intent—a nearly impossible thing, as any labor lawyer can attest. And enforcement depends upon private lawsuit, an expensive, time-consuming effort . . .

The law should ban firings and layoffs that lack just cause, as most collective agreements do. But the nonunionized work force (the overwhelming majority of employees are not unionized) lack effective protection against discharges whose real but unprovable purpose is to defeat vesting. Executive and managerial employees are the most vulnerable because they have the biggest, most expensive potential pensions but no union protection.[9]

The law, furthermore, does nothing to discourage the coziness between employers and trustees of the pension plans.

Bernstein says that a proper pension reform would:

> ... Enact more protective vesting standards that improved automatically—moving by stages to 100 percent vesting after one year of service. ...
> ... Provide a national, single, inexpensive plan requiring no lawyer, actuarial and consultant fees to obtain standard coverage and no administrative expenses to employers beyond sending contributions. ...
> ... Create a national pension clearing house to collect and invest vested benefits. ...
> ... Ban any party-in-interest from serving as a plan trustee; ban any financial dealings between parties-in-interest and trustees.
> ... Establish neutral administration of the law.
> ... Amend the National Labor Relations Act to empower retirees and their survivors to choose bargaining representatives and require employers to bargain with those representatives over post-retirement adjustments. ...[10]

Observing that the Treasury loses more than $4 billion in tax collections annually because of the private pension system, Bernstein concludes that if the private system can't do the job of supplying supplemental benefits to workers, and survivor benefits to their spouses, then the tax subsidy should be withdrawn, and these monies used to enhance Social Security.

Eli Ginzberg, a Columbia University economics professor and one of the nation's foremost authorities on manpower matters, has been preaching pension portability for years.

"It is a scandalous matter that we have not moved on this front up to this date," said Ginzberg. "A person can be employed for

19 years, lose the job, and thereby lose 19 years worth of bene-fits. We have some good qualities left in American society, but we really handle some things with unbelievable ineptness, inade-quacy, and indecency. . . . This is one of those areas that is simply outrageous. . . . Pension portability should have a much higher priority."[11]

Ginzberg is among the 350,000 academics in the United States who are enrolled in a private portable pension plan with 2,500 colleges, universities, and research institutions as its members. Inaugurated in 1918, the plan evolved from a pension fund for teachers originally supported by philanthropist Andrew Carnegie.

When a man such as Ginzberg is first hired by a university, he signs contracts with the Teachers Insurance and Annuity Associa-tion, which provides him a fixed annuity at retirement; and the College Retirement Equities Fund, a variable annuity institution founded in 1952 in an attempt—successful for a time—to keep pensions abreast of inflation.

Each new employer in the system contributes to the two con-tracts as does the man, and when he retires, his benefits reflect the years he worked at each institution. And even if he leaves academia temporarily, or permanently, a mechanism is provided whereby he can continue to contribute to his pension fund.

Dr. William C. Greenough, chairman of the Teachers Insur-ance and Annuity Association in Manhattan, says that his fully funded retirement system with immediate vesting and portability, has functioned smoothly for nonprofit educational institutions for fifty years. He sees no reason why the same kind of system couldn't work for men and women in private industry and other lines of work.

17
"The Leisure Problem Is Fundamental"

ALDOUS HUXLEY wrote in his foreword to *The Complete Etchings of Goya:*

> ... the longer he lived, the more frightful did the world seem—the more frightful, that is to say, in the eyes of his rational self; for his animal high spirits went on bubbling up irrepressibly, whenever his body was free from pain or sickness, to the very end ...
>
> Realistically, or in fantastic allegories, with a technical mastery that only increased as he grew older, Goya recorded it all. Not only the agonies endured by his people at the hands of the invaders, but also the follies and crimes committed by these same people in their dealings with one another. . . .
>
> As a very young man, he paints like the feeble eclectics who were his masters. The first signs of power and freshness and originality appear in the cartoons for the tapestries of which the earliest were executed when he was thirty. As a portraitist, however, he achieves nothing of outstanding interest until he is almost forty. But by that time, he really knows what he's after, and during the second forty years of his life he moves steadily forward towards the consummate technical achievements, in oils, of the *Pinturas Disparates.* Goya's is a stylistic growth away from restraint and into freedom, away from timidity and into expressive boldness.[1]

Throughout Robert Butler's career as a psychiatrist, he's studied the phenomenon of creativity in middle-aged and older men, and has been struck by how few manage to lead "open, evolving, and changing lives"; how few, like Goya for dramatic example, grow from "timidity into expressive boldness" with the passage of years.

Butler and other thinkers have long been convinced that social

210

and economic factors in advanced industrial societies such as ours conspire to dampen the creative spark with which each of us is born. Just as the ocean ebbs and flows, man experiences surges of creativity and effectiveness, followed by fallow periods when he needs regeneration. Our society rarely provides this opportunity. Work-obsessed Americans, he argues, must rediscover the meaning of leisure if they're to restore their creativity.

Butler believes that we must have a complete reordering of the life cycle to place work back in proper perspective. He calls for a "reshuffling" of our present stultifying lock-step of a twenty-year block of education, followed by a forty-year block of work, followed by a period of retirement and leisure. The trouble with this cycle is that it works in the long run against the individual's growth.

In the first place, the adolescent often as not hasn't the maturity to get what he should out of higher education. He hasn't had a chance to work, to live, to do much dreaming.

At the other end of the cycle, most men after forty years of solid work in the corporate vineyard—with no chance to really relax and enjoy themselves—are generally incapable of making creative use of their leisure. En route to retirement, many of them even suffer "vacation neuroses," returning early from the beach, the mountain, the lake, or wherever, because they are unhappy and restless when not working.

As for the man in midlife—struggling under the heaviest responsibilities and expenses—he'd often like to change his career, or just have a respite from the continuous pressure, observes Butler. But how many men have the money to take a year off? Even if they do have money, they don't dare leave their jobs that long for fear they'll find a younger man sitting at their desk when they return. Besides, most Americans look askance at men who want to change careers in their forties; such men tend to be looked upon as losers.

In former, less frenetic times, it was in the natural course of events for a man to start slowing down in middle age. Not today; now he dyes those gray hairs and, if anything, steps up the pace, for he feels as though he's being "tailgated," to use Butler's term, by younger men.

Butler believes we must start thinking of education, work, and leisure as running "concurrently and continuously" *throughout* our lives.

"Existing financial supports—private and public funds for education, unemployment insurance, in-service training funds, Social Security, pensions, etcetera—would have to be reallocated, of course, to support such a basic reshuffling of life-cycle activities. Youth would then feel free to work or loaf as well as attend college. The thirty-five-year-old would be encouraged to take time off to study, change directions, or relax. The seventy-year-old, in part because he would have had these constantly refreshing experiences throughout life, would be as prepared for work and study as he would be for a true enjoyment of leisure."[2]

Butler suggests that the federal government, as the nation's largest employer—there are three million individuals in federal civil service—could serve as the laboratory for such an experiment, allowing workers to accumulate greater amounts of annual leave, encouraging them to use this leave for travel, study, leisure.

"We must attack the whole complex of laws, customs, union and management rules that discourage adolescent work and encourage compulsory retirement. We must reappraise all of the supposed social 'advances'—such as job tenure, career ladders, and seniority rights—that tend to lock people into 40 years of work, and devise new ways of stimulating men to use more of those years for learning and leisure."[3]

For many years, Butler has been an activist in causes of the aging, testifying before Congress and so forth. His *Why Survive? Being Old in America* won the Pulitzer Prize in 1976. In his capacity as director of the National Institute on Aging he will be in a stronger position to work for change and reform.

Butler's commonsensical utopia will come in the fullness of time. Age discrimination in employment will collapse under the pressure of litigation, inevitably forcing a healthy change in our basic attitudes toward aging. Portable pensions will come, too, despite the powerful special interests arrayed against the concept. Mandatory retirement at age sixty-five will go by the boards, having long been an anachronism.

The significance of age sixty-five became implanted in our

psyches in 1882 when Germany's Prince Otto von Bismarck based Europe's first comprehensive social security system upon it. Man's life expectancy at birth in those days, however, was half what it is today. In 1935 this country anchored its social security system on age-sixty-five retirement, further entrenching it in our consciousness.

A number of congressmen wanted to erase sixty-five as the upper limit of the protected group in the age discrimination in employment legislation, but yielded to the lobbying of unionists and others, and postponed the decision by ordering the departments of Labor and Health, Education, and Welfare to make a longterm study of the question.

Constituent pressure for abolition of age-sixty-five retirement was strong, however. And Senator Javits said in mid-1975 before the American Bar Association that "mandatory retirement at age sixty-five can no longer be regarded as a sacred cow and, accordingly, we should begin to grapple with all that implies in terms of pension design, and the manpower situation."

There are other scattered signs that the American's rigid work-life cycle is beginning to loosen up. Many universities now allow —nay, encourage—deferred admissions, and leaves of absence. In one recent year, 125 Yale University students were on leaves.

Too, higher education has belatedly come to realize that Thoreau was right a long time ago when he said:

"It's time that we had uncommon schools, that we did not leave off our education when we begin to be men and women. It is time that our villages were universities, and their elder inhabitants the fellows of universities with leisure—if they are indeed so well off—to pursue liberal studies the rest of their lives."[4]

Notre Dame University's Center for Continuing Learning recently published a study calling for the United States to become "a learning society" in which formal education "would be spread throughout one's lifetime. This reflects a recognition that people learn more readily when they see a clear need to do so, and also that some learning is more appropriate to one age than to another. It makes little difference where or how the learning takes place, whether it occurs in the classroom or on a job, at age twenty, fifty, or seventy, as long as it does take place, and under circumstances appropriate to the learner. . . ."[5]

The study points out that millions of adult Americans are involved in continuing education, but that it's a haphazard business. The authors criticize universities, politely, for not asserting leadership of the movement, and for failing to adapt their institutions to the needs of individuals:

> The increasing involvement of adults in furthering their learning is an encouraging sign. Unfortunately, the traditional educational system does not readily accommodate them. Peter Drucker refers to an imminent conflict between extended schooling—conventional education for 18-to-22-year-olds—and continuing education. "If educators give any thought to the question, they assume that we should have both ever-extended schooling and continuing education. But the two are actually in opposition. Extended schooling assumes that we will cram more and more into the preparation for life and work. Continuing education assumes that school will be integrated with life.
>
> "Extended schooling still assumes that one can only learn before one becomes an adult. . . . Above all, extended schooling believes that the longer we keep the young away from work and life, the more they will have learned. Continuing education assumes, on the contrary, that the more experience in life and work people have, the more eager they will be to learn and the more capable they will be of learning. . . ."[6]

The authors of the study are all prominent university presidents: Theodore M. Hesburgh of Notre Dame; Paul A. Miller of Rochester Institute of Technology; and Clifton R. Wharton, Jr. of Michigan State University.

In a parody of the types of courses offered in adult education classes, comedian Woody Allen once listed a make-believe catalogue:

"Yeats & Hygiene, a Comparative Study: The poetry of William Butler Yeats is analyzed against a background of proper dental care."[7]

Despite the hit-or-miss nature of so much adult education, there have of late been a number of imaginative programs for the middle aged. In the mid-1960s, while at Columbia University's School of General Studies, Dr. Alan Entine directed a highly successful program whereby eighty-five men and women—with the aid of a $100,000 grant from the Ford Foundation—attended Columbia for a year of study. Most of the participants earned masters degrees in new fields that they subsequently entered with help from the university. Since then, Entine has been working to adapt the curriculum of the State University of New York to the growing numbers of middle-aged men and women who have enrolled.

Yet another encouraging straw in the wind is the fact that hundreds of corporations today sponsor tuition-aid plans and graduate study fellowships for employees—though it should not be inferred that this stems from an upwelling of humanism on the part of management. J. Robert O'Meara, an executive of The Conference Board, a business research organization in New York City, says that the information explosion combined with the need for corporations to stay competitive, spawned the support of education. Before the recession deepened, these programs were on the rise. O'Meara made a survey of fellowship plans of sixty companies which in one recent year spent $6,000,000 to support 1,182 fellowships of wide variety, many of them in engineering and science. The dean of one engineering school told O'Meara: "A graduating engineer today faces the prospect that half of his professional knowledge will be obsolete in ten years, and half of what he will need to know ten years from now hasn't been discovered yet." O'Meara says that a handful of companies in his survey are considering establishing formal sabbatical programs similar to those enjoyed by university professors. But rare is the company that will grant a man a sabbatical for regenerative purposes alone, as Butler recommends.

"No sir," said a former top personnel man for American Telephone & Telegraph Company in Manhattan awhile back. "That would be escapism."

"You mean a sixty-two-year-old who wants to spend a year studying ballet?" said a General Electric executive. "Forget it."

Washington, D.C. psychologist Michael Maccoby, who has been making a study of businessmen—"I must be the first person who ever gave Rorschach tests to corporation leaders"—says: "There *are* guys in business with vision and a certain amount of humanism who are secretly in favor of the kind of sabbatical you and Dr. Butler are talking about. But they feel that they have to justify company fellowship programs in terms of money; otherwise people would think they were crazy."

Of course many corporation heads look upon an employee who wants to take a year off as disloyal. They also fear that he will learn to love his freedom and fail to return.

Then there is at least one type of man who wouldn't consider taking a fellowship or sabbatical even if it were offered to him, says Maccoby: He's the high-level engineer or general manager in a big company, whom he likens to a fiercely competitive quarterback in professional football.

"Sure, they know they're going to burn out, but they want to get it while they can. They are highly motivated and stimulated by their work. They don't want to return to their company after a year and find someone else sitting at their desk. They look upon the sort of guy who takes a year off as a loser."

Not so, says a man who at age forty, won the Howard S. Cullman Fellowship of the Port of New York Authority a few years ago. He used his fellowship to spend a year traveling through seventeen West African countries exploring U.S.-West African trade possibilities—and returned home to a promotion.

The Port Authority does not limit its educational sponsorship to white collar personnel. A retired Manhattan policeman joined the Authority, for example, took an engineering degree on the side at the agency's expense, and now holds a key engineering position. The Authority also allows employees to change jobs within the organization.

IBM rewards a handful of its top technical people every year with fellowships that free them for five years, to pursue company-related subjects that interest them.

O'Meara has come across *one* employer who does give time off without strings attached. He's the president of a small Manhattan textile firm who stipulates that his top executives take every seventh week off—in addition to their annual vacations—to do whatever they like. As a result, the executives return to their

work refreshed and alive with new ideas. A wise man, and perhaps another harbinger . . .

In the 1960s, writer Don Fabun saw this coming. "When and
where will we begin to chip away at the antiquated work ethic
and come up with new systems and institutions in which leisure,
not work, is the desirable and socially acceptable goal of man?
One scans the horizon of two decades ahead and sees the almost
inevitable collision of two great forces—exploding population and
exploding technology—and one of the results of that collision
will almost certainly be a society in which some other ethic than
the sanctity of work will have to be found."[8]

Amitai Etzioni, the prominent Columbia University sociologist
and writer, finds evidence fast accumulating today that Americans are losing interest in working and consuming hard. Psychiatrist Alexander Reid Martin goes even further, saying that
we're moving far more rapidly from a "work" to a "leisure" society
for which we are ill prepared. In any event, there has been a
Eureka-like realization on Good Old Charlie's part that the
harder he works, and the more he produces, and the more he
consumes, the less time he seems to have for enjoyment.

Why, he asks himself, can't he ever seem to relax any more
without a martini or two—or three?

Why does he bring work home with him every night, then
allow it to taunt him silently from his unopened briefcase?

Why does he feel compelled to go into the office on Saturday
mornings?

And why does he feel depressed and restless on Sundays and
holidays?

Charlie is tyrannized by a time machine. The more money he
earns, the more so-called "leisure-time" goods, and time-saving
gizmos that he and his wife acquire, the less leisure he has.

Charlie had a sailboat, but he soon found it time-consuming
and costly to maintain. He rarely found the energy to drive fifty
miles through freeway traffic to the bay, drag the boat into the
water, then tack through another traffic jam before finding clear
sailing. Finally, he sold the craft.

Same thing with golf. For a while he'd enjoyed his Saturday
afternoon foursome. But this left his wife with all the chores.

Their daughter had to be driven to her ballet lessons; their son to the orthodontist. There was all manner of work to be done around the house and yard.

The company made extra demands on his time, too. Business luncheons. Business dinners. Out-of-town trips. In addition, it was made clear to him that a man in his position should get out in the community and *contribute*—good "PR." So each January, Charlie's grinning countenance appeared in the local newspaper heading up a new charity drive.

Charlie did know what leisure was. It was something he never had. Leisure was doing something for its own sake, not for a secondary motive. Leisure meant doing what he, Charlie, wanted to do; not what his company, his wife, his children, his conscience, his ambition or whatnot, wanted him to do.

As a child, Charlie used to lie on the backyard swing in the summer and wonder at the shooting stars and the heat lightning playing on the distant, silent mountains. He could lose himself in a good book or in his stamp collection for hours on end. He'd had, as Rafael Sabatini put it in one of his swashbuckling tales, "the gift of laughter and the sense that the world was mad."

No longer. Charlie had lost something terribly valuable along life's way.

The rediscovery of leisure is the most important thing Charlie has to do. For as Julian Huxley has said:

"The leisure problem is fundamental. Having to decide what we shall do with our leisure is inevitably forcing us to reexamine the purpose of human existence and to ask what fulfillment really means. . . . This involves a comprehensive survey of human possibilities and methods of realizing them; it also implies a survey of the obstacles to their realization."[9]

Like the word "love," the word "leisure" is subject to individual interpretation and can't be measured. But free time can be measured, and its loss can be explained in economic terms. In his entertaining book, *The Harried Leisure Class*, Swedish economist Staffan B. Linder emphasizes that economic growth and higher standards of living mean less free time. It's as simple as that, says Linder, and even many economists tend to forget that consumption and maintenance of goods and services gobble up time:

"We had always expected one of the beneficial results of economic affluence to be a tranquil and harmonious manner of life, a life in Arcadia. What has happened is the exact opposite. The pace is quickening and our lives in fact are becoming more hectic.

"It used to be assumed that, as the general welfare increased, people would become successively less interested in further rises in income. And yet in practice, a still higher economic growth rate has become the overriding goal of economic policy in the rich countries, and the goal also of our private efforts and attitudes."[10]

Linder turns a skeptical eye on the "culture boom." He considers it largely myth. Many books are sold, he argues, but there is no proof that they are read.

"We have long expressed the hope that the elimination of material cares would clear the way for a broad cultural advancement. In practice, not even those endowed with the necessary intellectual and emotional capacity have shown any propensity for immersing themselves in the cultivation of their minds and spirit. The tendency is rather the reverse...."[11]

There is a way out, says Linder, but it presupposes that people desire "to spend their time in a way that does not involve consumption centered upon goods. If the entire economic process were something subsidiary, something that it might be possible to disengage from material activities, then it would be conceivable to achieve our economic targets rapidly in order to devote ourselves thereafter to matters outside economic analysis.

"We would then have achieved complete satisfaction of our material wants. We would find ourselves in an intermediate position with fewer goods, but as many as we needed; and plenty of time out with sufficient economic resources to devote it to noneconomic matters."[12]

In this way, we would be following Aristotle's prescription:

> Nature requires that we should be able, not only to work well, but to use leisure well. Leisure is the first principle of all action, and so leisure is better than work and is its end. As play, and with it rest, are for the sake of work, so work, in turn, is for the sake of leisure.

However, Linder fears that the opposite trend—toward ever higher production—will continue. In the past, when given the choice of taking their productivity increases in the form of money or free time, most Americans have opted for money.

Mrs. Janice Hedges, a Bureau of Labor Statistics economist, tells me that U.S. workers gained a mere fifty extra free time hours during the 1960s, mostly in the form of more frequent holidays and longer vacations. These fifty hours represent only 8 percent of the free time that would have accrued had the fruits of increased productivity been taken in shorter hours instead of raises.

Can Americans expect more free time in the future? The prospect is that they'll probably continue gaining it at the same rate as they did in the 1950s and 1960s, some economists speculate. Between 1950 and 1970, productivity increased about 3 percent annually. If productivity continues at this pace, then Americans could have a twenty-nine-hour work week in 1980—if they elect to take all of this productivity in the form of free time, which, history has shown, they won't.

Productivity fell off in the early 1970s because of the recession —which brought in its train unwanted free time in the form of unemployment—but productivity rose in mid- to late-1975. While Bureau of Labor Statistics officials shy away from productivity projections, one top official said he believes the 1970–1980 decade will show an average productivity increase comparable to that of the two previous decades.

Since the early 1960s, senior employees at U.S. Steel have been entitled to three months off, with pay, once every five years, and like the executives of the New York textile firm mentioned earlier, they're not required to devote this time to company matters. The blue collar workers must take most of the sabbatical, but office workers have the option of staying on the job at premium pay. Lending support to Linder's contention that Americans will take dollars over leisure every time, more than 80 percent of the white collar workers choose to stay on the job at extra pay.

Dr. Peter A. Martin, a Detroit psychiatrist who has long studied the use and misuse of leisure, believes that many Americans take second jobs, or turn down opportunities for vacations and time off, simply because they don't know what to do with themselves. Still others fear being left alone with their subconscious. In his view, too, much if not most of the charity and community work carried on by executives is a form of moonlighting.

"In these big auto companies, they don't know what the word 'leisure' means," says Martin. "The executives work sixty hours a week, then are forced by their companies to take community and charity jobs in their free time. They do good work, but it's not leisure; it's not completely a free choice."

American Telephone & Telegraph Company is another organization that requires its executives to get visibility, for public relations purposes, in community charity activities. But the practice is widespread, and includes small firms as well.

A body of intriguing literature on the subject of leisure has grown up in recent years. The foibles of Americans-on-the-run have been getting a thorough going over. Critic Walter Kerr, for example, laments the American's attempt to "use" time by cramming it with activity.

"We have had Music to Read By, Music to Sleep By, Music to Make Love By, and as one humorist has had it, Music to Listen to Music By," says Kerr in his book *The Decline of Pleasure*. "What is interesting about these titles is that they so candidly describe the position of the popular arts in our time. They admit at the outset that no one is expected to sit down, for heaven's sake, and attend to the music. It is understood that, while the music is playing, everyone in earshot is going to be busy doing something else."[13]

Poet Kenneth Fearing has described the lives of many of us, notes Kerr:

> You have forgotten the monthly conference. Your four o'clock appointment waits in the ante-room. The uptown bureau is on the wire again.
> Most of your correspondence is still unanswered, these bills have not been paid, and one of your trusted agents has suddenly resigned.
> It is an unlikely plot, a scheme, a conspiracy you helped to begin but do not, any longer, control at all . . .

When they dig you up, in a thousand years, they will find you in
   just this pose,
One hand upon the buzzer, the other reaching for the phone, eyes
   fixed upon the calendar, feet firmly on the office rug.

"Only the feet on the rug are firm, and someone is pulling at
the rug," continues Kerr. "Any man on his way to the office in the
morning is a man wondering what is going to go wrong today.
Any man on his way home in the evening is a man wondering
what has gone wrong today....

"He has, from the time he married, been working for stability
there. He has done everything humanly possible to insure it: he
has gathered his family under a roof (the roof needs repair, taxes
are up again, the cat was killed), he has clothed, fed, and helped
educate his children.... He has established a small human community that is constantly threatened with dissolution—by death,
by temperament, by termites. The foundations seem to have
cracked anew each time he sets foot in the door...."[14]

Kerr goes on and on in this vein, and the bells continue to ring.
How to keep the keel even, the decks dry? he asks.

Poet Michel Quoist puts it this way:

> Good-by, Sir, excuse me, I haven't time.
> I'll come back, I can't wait, I haven't time.
> I must end this letter—I haven't time....[15]

Economist Linder has a hunch that love-making is suffering in
the society we've created. ("I haven't time."):

> To court and love someone in a satisfactory manner is a game
> with many and time-consuming phases.... Affairs, which by their
> very nature occupy a great deal of time, become less attractive; the
> time spent on each occasion of love-making is being reduced....
> The mistress, as an institution, is disappearing. Who has time these
> days for intimate lunches in conversation with an attractive woman?
> The French institution of the *cinq-à-sept*—two hours for which love-
> seeking husbands do not always feel bound to account—is reported
> to be disappearing in the increased hustle of life even in France....[16]

Heraclitus, the sixth-century Greek philosopher, said man must "listen to the essence of things." This was easier for man, of course, when he lived on the land and responded to the seasons. He experienced time as a cyclic, plentiful commodity. When he moved to the towns and cities to engage in commerce, he began to experience time as linear, rather than cyclic, and in short, rather than abundant supply. By the fifteenth century, public clocks in Italian cities were striking every hour. Thus, centuries before Ben Franklin, man was looking upon time as money.

"One of the most important cultural consequences of man's changing attitude to time in the late Middle Ages and High Renaissance, was its effect on the visual arts, causing painting *a secco*, to replace *a fresco*, or true fresco," says Britisher G. J. Whitrow in his little volume *The Nature of Time:*

> For the very long apprenticeship that pupils had to serve before they became proficient in fresco painting could not be maintained when social changes and pressures stimulated the desire for speed.
>
> Whereas, formerly, an artisan could linger over the execution of his work, a painter who had risen in the social scale, and had thereby acquired a new prestige, had to work fast in order to handle all the commissions he received. Even Michelangelo's example was in vain. Originally, it had been planned that the *Last Judgment* in the Sistine Chapel should be painted *a secco*, in oil, but Michelangelo objected that oil painting is only "fit for women and slovenly people" and so he carried out the work *a fresco*. But this proved to be against the current of the age, and the glorious art of the true fresco died out, its practice being incompatible with the new social attitude to time.[17]

We have the Puritans to thank for the notion that we must, like Longfellow's blacksmith, *earn* our "night's repose," and feel guilty when we haven't.

Then came industrialism. "At first, that merely meant that if one worked in a factory, one had to adjust oneself to the rate of the machine," says economics writer William V. Shannon in a fiery essay entitled *The Death of Time:*

> Gradually, however, the ever-accelerating inhuman pace of technology has invaded every domain of life. The values of the factory

—efficiency, speed, total use of available resources—have become the values of the home and of leisure. It is as if the time-and-motion studies of the efficiency expert took up their inexorable watch in each man's soul.

The consequences are now all around us. It is illegal to drive slowly on an expressway; the law commands a minimal speed. Railroads and ocean liners decline, while the jet plane races overhead. . . .

Resenting death, we murdered time. Now, time vanquished, we lie exhausted alongside our victim. Almost too late, we see that what we have slain is not time but our sense of ourselves as humans. Left alone with our machines, we know not how to wait, to prepare, to discipline, and deny ourselves.

Therefore, we know not the rejoicing which comes when we have reaped and consummated and brought to fulfillment, all in good time. . . .[18]

It's not surprising that the American today has trouble recapturing his innate capacity for leisure—or even really understanding what the term means. Yet his salvation depends upon it, especially as he grows older. Compulsive work can lead to self-alienation and sterility. Leisure, on the other hand, fosters creativity, self-respect, and such happiness as man is capable of, when it is kept in balance with work. Most exceptionally creative individuals sense this. Said Albert Einstein:

"I believe, indeed, that over-emphasis on the purely intellectual attitude, often directly and solely on the practical or factual in our education, has led directly to the impairment of ethical values. I am not thinking so much of the dangers with which technical progress has directly confronted mankind, as of the stifling of mutual consideration by a 'matter-of-fact' habit of thought which has come to lie like a killing frost upon human relations. People in all practical walks of life should keep in mind that deep in their hearts they also need pure enjoyment of impractical pleasures to live a balanced life."[19]

What, then, is leisure? A number of distinguished thinkers have written on the subject in recent decades, most notably Dr. Josef Pieper, a German theologian, in *Leisure the Basis of Culture:*

Leisure, it must be clearly understood, is a mental and spiritual attitude—it is not simply the result of external factors, it is not the inevitable result of spare time, a holiday, a weekend, or a vacation.

It is, in the first place, an attitude of mind, a condition of the soul, and as such utterly contrary to the ideal of "worker". . . .

Compared with the exclusive ideal of work as activity, leisure implies, in the first place, an attitude of non-activity, of inward calm, of silence; it means not being "busy," but letting things happen.

Leisure is a form of silence, of that silence which is the prerequisite of the apprehension of reality: only the silent hear, and those who do not remain silent do not hear. . . .

Leisure is not the attitude of those who actively intervene, but of those who are open to everything; not of those who grab, and grab hold, but of those who leave the reins loose and who are free and easy themselves. . . .

. . . When we really let our minds rest contemplatively on a rose in bud, on a child at play, on a divine mystery, we are rested and quickened as though by a dreamless sleep. Or as the Book of Job says, "God giveth songs in the night." Moreover, it has always been a pious belief that God sends his good gifts and his blessings in sleep. And in the same way his great imperishable intuitions visit a man in his moments of leisure. . . .[20]

In this country, Alexander Reid Martin has spent nearly three decades decrying the loss of leisure and the consequences thereof to our society. Until recently, Martin's voice has been a lonely one.

In 1948, Martin formed the American Psychiatric Association's first committee on leisure, and headed it for many years. After several name changes, it became the Committee on Leisure Time and Its Uses. For a long time, the psychiatrist tells me, many of his colleagues thought the committee's function was to organize recreation for the association's annual meetings.

Martin's strong feelings about leisure stem from treating, on his Manhattan couch, many of the casualties of our leisure-less society. Martin talks with passion on the subject. "We are only just beginning to appreciate the great strangling of the human spirit that has resulted from our total immersion in the world of work," he says.

In his writings, Martin likes to point up the parallel between therapeutic insight, and everyday creative insight in the arts, sciences, and other fields, a process that follows a rhythmic pattern.

First, notes Martin, there is "a phase of conscious work and struggle lasting for days, months, or years; this is followed by a leisure phase variously described as a relaxation of conscious effort, an abandonment of logical work and reason, a period of 'leaving it alone'... of intimate involvement with the real self, of allowing natural biological rhythms to assert themselves, of getting in touch with the darker reaches of ourselves, and 'letting the spiritual, unbidden and unconscious, rise up through the common.'

"Suddenly, after a variable time, *but only during this leisure phase,* there occurs the inductive leap, the creative flash, the imperishable intuition, the new synthesis. Following this comes a period of conscious effort to improve and refine what emerged during the creative flash.

"Psychologists have named these phases 1) preparation; 2) incubation; 3) illumination; and 4) verification. Phases 1 and 4 are expressions of our inner capacity for work; 2 and 3 are expressions of our inner capacity for leisure. In the creative cycle work and leisure complement each other. Creative growth depends upon the maintenance of this cycle. It is not achieved through leisure alone, but is impossible without it....

"In work there is a focusing, a contraction of faculties, and acuteness of consciousness. During the true leisure phase there is an unfocusing, a relaxation of faculties, a greater diffusion of consciousness. Using the analogy of the action of the human heart, conscious work, effort, and exertion represent the systolic phase, and leisure the diastolic phase of the creative process...."[21]

Whenever we have even a minor decision to make, or problem to solve, we pay obeisance to our subconscious when we decide "to sleep on it." At other times, revelations come unbidden.

The late Arnold Toynbee was keenly attuned to the rhythms of his creative cycle, and likened the subconscious "to a child, a savage, and even a brute beast, which is at the same time also wiser, more honest, and less prone to error than the conscious self.... The subconscious, not the intellect, is the organ through which man lives his spiritual life; is the fount of poetry, music, and the visual arts...."[22]

Toynbee was able to recall in later years the moment when the inspiration came to him for *A Study of History,* his unique interpretation of the rise and fall of twenty-six civilizations since the dawn of man: it was on September 17, 1921, while he was riding the Orient Express westward from Istanbul. As the train sped through the Thracian countryside, Toynbee fell to musing about the region's tumultuous history.

"That evening," Toynbee remembered, "I was standing in the window, overwhelmed by the beauty of the Bela Polanka Gorge in the light of the full moon, as our train bore down upon Nish. If I had been cross-examined on my activities during that day, I should have sworn that my attention had been wholly absorbed by the entrancing scenes that were passing continually before my outward eye. Yet before I went to sleep that night, I found that I had put down on half a sheet of notepaper, a list of topics which, in its contents and their order, was substantially identified with the plan of the book as it now stands."[23]

Writer Alden Whitman noted at the time of Toynbee's death, in the fall of 1975, that the plan for the work germinated for six years before the historian expanded his notes into a detailed outline and started writing. Forty years later, Toynbee completed his monumental, 3,500,000-word history of mankind. . . .[24]

In the United States, especially, the "strangling of the human spirit" that Martin speaks of often starts early—in our schools and colleges. Determined to reverse the tide, and restore play and leisure to their rightful places in the scheme of things, a thirty-year-old doctor of philosophy at Emporia State College in Kansas by the name of Bill Harper has mounted a one-man crusade that has begun to attract national attention. The principal medium for his ideas is the monthly *Play Factory Advocate;* his principal weaponry, humor and common sense. A recent issue contained this quiz which he says is a takeoff of an alcoholism pamphlet:

> Answer the following questions HONESTLY, and finally discover the truth about yourself—whether you are a worker: 1) Do you lose time from drinking due to working? 2) Is working making your home life unhappy? 3) Is working affecting your reputation? 4) Do you often "sneak" your work in so that others will not know how much you work? 5) Do you want to work right after (or instead of) having sex? 6) Have you lost interest in everything other than

work? 7) Do you avoid activities which might interfere with your work? 8) Do you prefer moonlighting to moonshine?

If you have answered YES to any one of these questions, there is warning that you may be a worker. If you have answered YES to any two of these questions, there is good probability you are a worker. If you have answered YES to any three, you are definitely a worker. If you were too busy working to even answer the questions, you are quite pathetically beyond any help whatsoever.[25]

"Play is voluntary, spontaneous, light, and one of the traditional sources of pure pleasure for humans," says Harper. "Real play is an in-itself, not an in-order-to activity; an end, not a means. In play a human recognizes and celebrates his humanity, recognizes and celebrates the humanity of others. Play is expansive. Lack of play turns a person inward, makes it more difficult to experience and perceive the reality of the world."[26]

The minute a person plays for a secondary purpose—reward, social status, publicity, therapy, or whatever—he is no longer playing, says Harper, echoing psychiatrist Martin.

Harper saw his first clear chance to put his theories into action in 1973 when he was asked to take over direction of Emporia College's intramural cultural and athletic program. It was no small assignment, as Emporia has 6,500 students. The young philosophy instructor—a University of Southern California graduate —stirred things up when he published the first edition of the *Advocate*, in which he announced that he was abolishing the intramural program. As it turned out, he was simply giving the program a new name, "The Play Factory," and making it much more informal and much more fun. Harper was convinced that competitive sport, even of the intramural variety, with its system of reward and punishment, serves to kill the spirit of play. So he abolished all trophies, removed most eligibility requirements, loosened up the rules—and even had the boundary lines removed from baseball diamonds, touch football fields, and so forth. He considers arbitrary white lines inhibiting. The groundskeepers thought he'd gone crackers.

For all his foolishness, Harper is on sound philosophical ground. The late Shakespearean scholar Harold C. Goddard saw leisure as the central message of *The Tempest*. He believed that Shakespeare

> must have come to realize what creative minds in the end are almost bound to see: that the arts are to man only what toys are to children, a means for the rehearsal of life. And so, paradoxically, the object of art is to get rid of the arts. When they mature, the art of life will be substituted for them—as children outgrow their toys.
>
> > Merrily, merrily shall I live now
> > Under the blossom that hangs on the bow
>
> Perhaps Shakespeare had himself in mind when he wrote those lines of Ariel's. I picture him retired to Stratford lying under a plum tree in May. . . .[27]

Shakespeare valued three things in life above all else, said Goddard: liberty, love—and wonder.

And so, not surprisingly, Bill Harper's program at Emporia has been a wondrous success. But with the downturn in the economy, the tide that he's trying to breast is mounting daily. In the fall of 1975, a survey reported that college students were abandoning the humanities in droves for "job-related" courses such as business administration, economics, and accounting. Caught in the economic squeeze along with their students, some universities have let the Hun within the gates: They've opened their classrooms to courses in how to manage a Holiday Inn.

"What do I expect out of engineering and accounting?" asked a junior at the University of Texas. "A good job and lots of money."[28]

Wonder, said Socrates, is the beginning of philosophy; and a capacity for philosophy is one of leisure's most valuable by-products for the man in his forties. For without a philosophy to measure his present actions and past experience against, a man's life comes through to him as a succession of often meaningless, disconnected events. Chaos. This can prove devastating when as an old man he undertakes—as every old man does—a continuing "life review," as psychiatrists refer to late-life stocktaking. W. Somerset Maugham once said that what made old age a trial was not one's physical and mental deterioration but the heavy burden of his memories.

In the course of my own erratic journey through the forties, I've talked with any number of men who've developed philosophies appropriate to the afternoon of their lives. Without exception, their stories have been interesting, invariably dramatic. Montaigne—whom every man pushing forty should read for enjoyment and stimulation—was correct, as usual, when he said, "You can tie up all moral philosophy with a common and private life just as with a life of richer stuff."²⁹ And there should be solace for all of us in his conclusion, reached after nearly two decades of stocktaking in the tower of his chateau not far from Bordeaux, that if we manage to live "appropriately," we accomplish a great deal, a very great deal; and that, "All other things, ruling, hoarding, building, are only little appendages and props at most."³⁰

Of all the men I've talked with about their midlife stocktaking, three strike me as particularly interesting: an artist who found an idyllic life on an island in the New England sun; a self-made multimillionaire who first listened to "the essence of things" during a vacation beside Lake Michigan; and a Trappist monk who went to a mountain to seek a vision, only to find, at first, a loneliness approaching terror in its intensity. Leisure was the key to their eventual successful passage through the most critical years of their middle life.

Looking back now after years of studying the midlife male— all the interviews, all the reading, and my own observations and personal experience—it is difficult to escape the conclusion that with leisure his possibilities are infinite.

"Be still and know that I am God," says the forty-fifth Psalm.

In his translation from the German, Josef Pieper makes this read:

"Have leisure and know that I am God."

18 "... He Just Looked So Great Going Up to the Blue Sky...."

AL HARTIG lives in a flower-bordered house on Nantucket Island off the Massachusetts coast where he makes possibly the most beautiful, imaginative, and aerodynamically stable kites in the United States, perhaps the world. Since he quit his job in a Bronx, New York, ceramics factory in mid-1967, he has designed, tested, and assembled—with his wife Betty at the sewing machine and handling the finances—more than 35,000 kites: tailless triangular or delta-wing kites; kites shaped like bats, like eagles, like pterodactyls.... He has shipped them to mail-order customers as distant as Singapore and as remote as the Trucial States; to wholesalers and to retail outlets in Manhattan and San Francisco. Each kite bears his patent number and trademark: "The Nantucket Kiteman 'N Lady."

Robert Ingraham, head of the American Kitefliers' Association, has said of Hartig's *Valkyrie* model, "For sheer simplicity and superb flying ability, we've never seen the equal of this kite." Ingraham is the last word on such things, but Hartig was thrilled even more by an accolade of a radically different sort in the fall of 1968. He'd just designed his *National American Eagle* model and was test-flying it near his Nantucket home when a speck appeared in the sky high above the lifelike creation at the end of his line.

The speck grew into a bird, and into a larger and larger bird, as it circled downward toward the kite. And then Hartig couldn't believe his eyes: a rare, magnificent male golden eagle was circling within a few feet of his kite. After a few seconds, the eagle circled upward again and resumed his flight path.

On another occasion, Hartig was reeling in one of his damaged eagle kites and as it flip-flopped earthward, an Audubon member came running, fearful—before he caught sight of the string— that a real eagle was in distress. And a number of eagle kite owners have told Hartig that hunters have riddled their kites with shotgun fire before they could retrieve them from the sky. His bat-shaped kite has caused consternation, too. One of Hartig's customers wrote from a little village in Spain saying that the local *caribinieri* had asked him not to fly his bat kite in the evening any more: its hovering and fluttering in the twilight had frightened many of the superstitious peasants.

Since Hartig's arrival on Nantucket, he's nearly overtaken the sperm whale as the island's symbol. One of the first things that passengers see from the mainland steamer when it enters Nantucket harbor is one of Hartig's weathered kites bobbing in the sky high above his little clapboard shack on Old South Wharf where he sells his wares.

The kiteman is tall, dark, and lanky, in his mid-fifties, with a moustache and heavy, horn-rimmed eyeglasses. He generally wears a black Derby hat with bright red band, and an old rumpled shirt with its tail outside his pants. He has an easy, off-hand manner with children who come to his shop. After establishing rapport, he tries to determine whether the child has ever built a kite of his own. If the child hasn't, which is usually the case, Hartig tries to talk him into doing so.

If the child insists upon buying a kite, fine. But if the child comes back to buy another kite the next summer and still hasn't made one of his own, Hartig will take down an old two-stick, brown-paper kite from the wall of the shack, give him a lesson in kite construction, and send him away empty-handed.

"Every kid should know the joy of flying a kite he has made with his own two hands," says Hartig, who made his first kite when he was eight years old, with tissue paper wrappings from oranges, bamboo teeth from his father's rake, and paste made from water and flour.

The kite that changed Hartig's life now hangs in a place of

honor in Hartig's basement music room. It's a sun-bleached red, delta-shaped kite with Iron Crosses on the panels. He calls it "The Red Baron," and he speaks of "the Baron" as though it were a person. The Baron was the result of a creative flash in the summer of 1963.

For a number of years, Hartig had given up kite-flying to concentrate upon model clipper ships which he sailed on Conservatory Pond in Manhattan's Central Park on weekends. But when the pond dried up temporarily during the summer of 1963, Hartig returned to kites. When the Hartigs went on vacation in August at Lake Florence in New York's Catskill Mountains, Al took along a red plastic kite that he'd bought.

"We got up to Lake Florence on a Saturday, and I don't think my suitcases were even unpacked," recalls Hartig. "I took the kite right out and tried it and within the first half hour, the first damages began to show. I tried to fix them with Band-aids but it didn't work. But for some reason, I didn't throw the damaged kite away as I normally would have. I rolled it up in the bedroom closet in our cottage.

"And the next day, Sunday, I took a half-hour nap after lunch, and when I woke up, the first thing I saw out of the corner of my eye was the plastic kite. And being a model-builder—I'd been building models since I was a kid—I said to myself, I wonder if rather than making it out of paper or something, I can make it out of fabric, and make it a little bigger?

"So the next day when we went into town to buy groceries and all that, I bought a couple of yards of red cotton fabric and four birch dowels at a hardware store. And I made the Baron. I finished him in about an hour and a half. That day at noon—I know I hadn't eaten yet—I said to Betty: 'I'm going to try him out.' And I took him up on a hill.

"What an exhilarating moment! The wind wasn't strong, and he just looked so great going up to the blue sky, and he flew so effortlessly. Normally, you run with kites. Here I made a motion to run but within three or four seconds, I realized I didn't have to run. He was just doing his thing; he was going up! It was just great!

"Betty had come up about twenty minutes earlier. I know I was in a great mood; it was just fantastic. As I brought the kite in—as he got about ten, about eight feet above the ground where the wind wasn't as strong—he suddenly started to glide, which was great for the moment; and then he came right over Betty and I put one finger out to turn him, and then he just floated gently to the ground.

"I went back to the cottage, talking about making more kites. But one thing bothered me, which was that it had glided; because when it glided, I no longer had control. And because of my being a model-builder, I said: 'I can put a hunk of lead on the center strut in the back and make it tail-heavy.' But then, just on intuition, because the cloth on the front end was a little loose, I thought: 'Maybe there's too little drag at the apex, and if I shorten the wing struts and increase the drag area, maybe that'll be just enough.' So I took two inches off each end. And then I hand-launched it in the cottage and it stalled. There it was. That's the only big change the Baron ever went through."

The Red Baron became something of a sensation at the resort, and Hartig spent his time loaning it to other vacationers. When he returned to New York City and flew it in Central Park, he was besieged by kitophiles who wanted to buy it. At Betty's insistence, Al patented elements of the Baron's design and, using it as a prototype, made other delta-wing kites and began to sell them. One day in Central Park the late Surendra Bahadur, owner of a shop called Go Fly a Kite, asked Hartig to supply his shop with kites on a regular basis, which Hartig has done ever since.

By the mid-1960s, the Hartigs had grown desperate to escape New York City. Every morning, year in and year out, Betty had gone to an office job, and Al had made his way from his apartment house on a depressing street in the East Nineties, to his job designing tiles in Harris G. Strong's ceramics factory on another depressing street in the Bronx. During the winter months he'd leave before sunup and return after sundown. Hartig loves to paint in oils, and there never seemed to be enough light or enough time for it except on Saturdays and Sundays.

Nearly ten years earlier, when Hartig was in his mid-thirties, he says he began to realize that he was "not immortal," and he began to wonder what his life was adding up to.

" 'Jeez,' I said to Betty one day, 'the idea of dying in New York City is so frightening.' I got very depressed, and she got me this book by Albert Einstein, *The World As I See It,* and it just made so much sense to me." Hartig's favorite passage:

> To begin with, I believe with Schopenhauer that one of the strongest motives that lead men to art and science is escape from everyday life with its painful crudity and hopeless dreariness, from the fetters of one's ever-shifting desires. A finely tempered nature longs to escape from personal life into the world of objective perception and thought; this desire may be compared with the townsman's irresistible longing to escape from his noisy, cramped surroundings into the silence of high mountains, where the eye ranges freely through the still, pure air and fondly traces out the restful contours apparently built for eternity. With this negative motive goes a personal one. Man tries to make for himself, in the fashion that suits him best, a simplified and intelligible picture of the world; he then tries to some extent to substitute this cosmos of his for the world of experience and thus to overcome it. This is what the painter, the poet, the speculative philosopher, and the natural scientist do, each in his own fashion. He makes this cosmos and its construction, the pivot of his emotional life, in order to find in this way the peace and security which he cannot find in the narrow whirlpool of personal experience.[1]

In the world as Hartig now began to see it, the beauty of art was life's one constant. But while Einstein gave Hartig the beginnings of a new philosophy, the book made Hartig even more anxious to flee the city.

His chance came a few years later. One of the men in Hartig's factory returned from a trip to Nantucket. He said the island, with its broad, wild beaches and glorious moors was beautiful.

"Al, *that's* the place for you."

Moreover, he gave Hartig the name of a New York man he'd met on the island who owned a shop in Nantucket town and was looking for someone to provide him with ship models to sell there. Hartig got in touch and was soon turning out models of *Pequod,* the Nantucket whaler in Herman Melville's *Moby Dick.* Later, the man asked him to make kites as well. And in the early spring of 1967, he asked Hartig if he'd like to move to Nantucket and work for him full time.

"I'm packed!" exclaimed Hartig.

"No, no. Take your wife up there and see if you two like it."

For the Hartigs it was love at first sight. "It was like a movie set," he recalls. The stubby old lighthouse at Brant Point. The gull-screaming waterfront with its thickets of sailboat masts. The gray clapboard fishermen's shacks. The cobblestoned streets. The queenly houses built by the Macys, Starbucks, and other nineteenth-century whaling lords.

Hartig gave notice to the ceramics factory and moved to Nantucket in June. No sooner had he arrived than the rains came. All summer long it rained, cutting down drastically on the number of "day trippers" from Woods Hole on the mainland, the kind of people who buy models of the *Pequod*. There were other problems with the shop. And some eight months later, it went out of business. The Hartigs were stranded on a fifteen-mile-long island in the Atlantic Ocean, thirty-five miles from land, with a total of $500 to their names.

"Let's chance it and stay on Nantucket," said Betty.

The Hartigs did hold one ace: a big back order from the Go Fly a Kite shop in New York City. But they had to buy back from the defunct Nantucket shop kite-making materials valued at $750. This left them, on paper, minus $250—and winter was coming on.

The Nantucket shop agreed to accept a $200 down payment for the materials, leaving the Hartigs with $300. With this, Al bought a $44 round-trip airline ticket to New York City and flew down to buy $200 worth of cotton broadcloth. While in town, he went out to the ceramics factory to see his friends and his former boss, Harris Strong, the owner. Strong asked Hartig what he thought he'd need to get started in the kite business properly. Hartig said he'd need $500 to $1,000, and was about to leave when Strong told him to wait a moment. Strong went to his desk and wrote out a check for $1,000. He was in no hurry, he said, to be repaid.

The Hartigs' kite business took off like the Red Baron on its inaugural flight. In recent years, Hartig has turned down several six-figure offers to put his kite operation into mass production. As he sees it, kites are the medium that allows him to lead the kind of life he loves. He doesn't want to spoil that. His is a life of leisure in a pure sense. He has time for his oil painting, his sculpting, model-building, chess, and classical music ("I'm into Sibelius now, but I don't know for how long"). And, of course, kite-flying.

"Flying a kite is silent poetry," says Hartig. "Each kite has its own way of flying, its own personality; it's almost as though it had a separate life out there at the end of that string. There's an essential honesty. . . ."

Especially during the summer season, the Hartigs work long, hard hours. A perfectionist, Hartig designs and assembles the kites, hand-sanding the struts, inserting brass eyelets. He throws away about a third of the struts he buys because they are not strong enough or willowy enough. Betty and a number of helpers cut and sew the sturdy cotton-and-polyester material from which the kites are now made. As a result of scrupulous workmanship, the kites are practically indestructible.

But while the Hartigs work hard, they don't work compulsively.

"At first, I had real trouble adjusting to Nantucket," says Hartig. "Something was strange, and I couldn't figure out what it was for a long time. And then one day, I realized: It's the sun! On Nantucket, I was seeing the sun all day long. What a difference that makes. And so if it's a particularly nice day, Betty'll come in around 11:30 and say: 'I'm going to make some sandwiches; let's go down to the beach.' And so where normally, in New York, you'd have a half-hour for lunch, here we might find ourselves taking two and a half hours."

Hartig's commuting days are far behind him. During the tourist season, he tries to put in a few hours every morning in his shack on Old South Wharf, but it's just a few miles from his mid-island home. His workshop is a few steps from his second-floor bedroom, with windows opening to the Atlantic breezes.

From a workshop window he points to a blue pond on his sandy 2¼-acre property where he tests his ship models before racing them against those of his neighbors at a bigger pond down island. He says that his 11-inch ketch *Whisper* has never been defeated, either on Central Park's Conservatory Pond, or on Nantucket.

"I had a great childhood, a fantastic childhood," says Hartig, though he was raised during the Depression, and his family had little money. He remembers his father, a onetime merchant seaman, as "an immense symbol of authority"; his mother as a kindly soul who fed him and tucked him into bed at night.

"But the main thing about my parents was that they left me alone. Between the ages of about seven and fourteen, I was never home. My imagination was allowed to run wild."

Al and his parents lived in Clifton, New Jersey, a town anchored on the west bank of the Passaic River, about twelve miles from the New York City line. In those days, the town had a population of about 20,000 and was surrounded by farming country. With his gang, Hartig roamed over some twenty-five square miles. They rigged rowboats with makeshift sails and shoved off to explore "islands" in the Passaic River; crawled through caves in nearby hills; and fought with slingshots for weapons and garbage-pail tops for shields. "There was a big garbage dump covered with dirt, and this became our desert where we played 'Foreign Legion.'"

In the early 1940s, Hartig went off as an Army enlisted man to a real war in New Guinea, returning to take courses under the G.I. Bill at the Art Students League in Manhattan. Then came the job at the ceramics factory, and in 1952, marriage. Through it all, life's realities have not deadened his childlike sense of wonder.

One day Al took me to his music room to view the Baron. Wonderful sounds of battle were booming from his stereo system. It was Eric Wolfgang Corngold's background music to Errol Flynn's swashbuckler, *The Sea Hawk.*

We had sprawled out on easy chairs to listen, and Hartig said: "Can you imagine giving a kid a name like *Eric Wolfgang Corngold?*"

I couldn't. But as I observed this delightful individual, it wasn't at all difficult to imagine him, forty years ago or more, charging over that dirt-covered New Jersey garbage dump brandishing a wooden sword.

Hartig has recently been hard at work on a secret kite design. "Every kid over about eight is going to want one," he said mysteriously. I asked him about the design and he dodged the question. He said that there were research and development problems yet to be solved. I pressed him.

Finally, he said, he would give me a hint. I knew that one of his friends on the island was writer Peter Benchley, who had a home on the north bluffs.

"Let's just say that when I get it finished, I'm going to give the first one to Peter," said Hartig with a big grin.

 **"When They Get There, They Find There's No There, There. . . ."**

SUCCESS American style has never meant simply *being* rich or famous. Success has meant "*attaining* riches, or *achieving* fame," says historian Richard Huber. "You had to know where a man began in order to judge how far he'd come."[1]

If you applied this criterion to investment banker William Henry Donaldson in September 1973, you had to conclude that he was a success American style. At forty-two, he was the founder, chairman, and chief executive officer of Donaldson, Lufkin & Jenrette, Inc., with total assets of more than $312 million, a firm that he'd started less than fifteen years earlier with an initial investment of $100,000, most of it borrowed from contemporaries. He had come through the "go-go" years of the 1960s on Wall Street with his reputation for personal integrity and intelligence intact, along with his considerable fortune.

Nor was Bill Donaldson, as they say, "narrow gauge." At forty-two, he was a trustee of the Yale Corporation; a director of the New York Stock Exchange; a member of the Ford Foundation's executive committee; a member of the Council on Foreign Relations; a trustee of the Bowery Savings Bank, Wesleyan University, and the German Marshall Fund; a director of the Hudson Institute, the Museum of Modern Art, the Robert Joffrey ballet. . . .

For some time, he'd been a familiar backstage figure in New York Republican politics, carrying out special assignments for Governor Nelson Rockefeller and future governor Hugh Carey. Donaldson's name had been floated as a mayoral prospect. "You know, Bill who?" he says with a grin. The boomlet was serious, however, but little came of it because he didn't feel that he could leave his firm at the time to devote himself to politicking. If there was such a thing as an Eastern Establishment or "Power elite," in other words, Donaldson's credentials were in order.

There had been a storybook quality to Donaldson's life to date. Like Monroe Stahr, the Hollywood producer in F. Scott Fitzgerald's *The Last Tycoon,* his successes came early, and he retained much of his youthful idealism. And like Stahr, Donaldson was an individualist, one whose career had an aura of glamour.

Monroe Stahr was the last of the princes of a "lavish, romantic past" in Hollywood that Fitzgerald believed would probably never return. The same can be said, without unduly straining the analogy, of the Wall Street that Donaldson and his partners had taken by storm while still in their late twenties and early thirties. When the 1960s decade had run its course in the catastrophic stock market plunge of 1969–70, the glory days of the New York Stock Exchange were clearly over.

There was something of Tom Sawyer and Frank Merriwell about Donaldson's childhood and adolescence. In his hometown of Buffalo, New York, he'd founded a make-believe company with one hundred or so children as employees—he called it, rather grandly, "United Enterprises"—and cornered the lawn-mowing, house-painting, and car-washing business in his neighborhood.

Eames Donaldson, Bill's father, who died in 1960, had suffered business reverses during the Depression and while the family was not poor by any means, its circumstances were modest. From the beginning, Bill was a scholarship student, a well rounded individual who was popular with both sexes in his own age group, and especially popular with older people, a quality that he still manifests.

"Bill somehow represented what every father wants his son to become," says a former associate at DLJ.[2]

Donaldson won the headmaster's award at Nichols, a private day school in Buffalo, and a scholarship to Yale University where his father had graduated. He won his freshman numerals in hockey, and soon became a big man on campus: business manager of the *Yale Daily News;* a member of the Torch Honor and

St. Elmo Societies; Skull and Bones. . . . Upon graduation in 1953, he served for two years as a first lieutenant in the U.S. Marine Corps in Korea and Japan.

Among Donaldson's friends at Harvard Graduate School of Business Administration were his future partners, Dan W. Lufkin, a Yale classmate, and Richard H. Jenrette, a graduate of the University of North Carolina. Lufkin was outgoing, a charmer. Jenrette was a quiet, solid South Carolinian, an organizer.

After receiving their MBAs in 1958, the trio served brief apprenticeships in separate Wall Street firms before forming Donaldson, Lufkin & Jenrette in 1959. DLJ's timing was right, its success almost immediate.

The young fire-eaters would lose their virginity in the 1962 stock market break, correctly predict the ensuing bull market, and foresee the 1969–1970 crash and make provision.

For twenty years and more after the 1929 crash, Wall Street had not been high on the list of career choices of hard-charging young men. The aging bulls and bears who were occupying the Street as the 1960s dawned had grown weary and soft as ripe pears. The three young men from Cambridge were like Goths feasting their eyes upon ancient Rome.

Their arrival coincided with the rise of the big institutional investors which were to transform the character of the market— the mutual funds, foundations, pension trusts, insurance companies, and the like. The young men saw that the old-line brokerage houses were growing ever fatter on commissions from buying and selling huge blocks of stock for the institutions. And they saw something else: the investment research and advice that the brokerage firms were providing the institutions in return for windfall profits was often slapdash at best.

"Wall Street was trying to serve the growing institutional market with mere reporting—plus a handshake and the old school tie," recalls Donaldson. "We felt that the institutions themselves were becoming more professional, more competitive. . . . We felt that they needed, and would buy, a new kind of analysis, more like that offered by a management consultant. . . .

"We tried to talk to competitors, suppliers, customers—interview a whole range of people, not simply content ourselves with asking the financial vice-president of a company what his earnings were going to be the next quarter. We tried to apply business analysis to Wall Street."[3]

The three partners put in man-killing hours. They went into manufacturing plants and talked with the men at the lathes as well as the men in the front offices; they listened as carefully to the casual, insightful remark of a crane driver as they did to the formal statement of a company officer. DLJ's research proved first rate, and more and more institutional investors started giving them their brokerage business.

DLJ was behind the acquisition of the giant United Fruit Company by AMK, a meat-packing firm headed by the ill-fated Eli Black. Chris Welles, in *The Last Days of the Club*, describes what happened.

> The idea that AMK and United Fruit would make a good marriage did not originate with Eli Black, but with Donaldson, Lufkin & Jenrette, the ambitious Wall Street investment house. DLJ, along with several other Street firms, had been a big booster of United Fruit stock since 1967. Though the Boston-based management team led by John M. Fox, former president of Minute Maid Corporation, had taken over in 1965 and had begun what was widely felt to be a substantial revitalization. DLJ . . . had distributed several glowing reports on United Fruit's progress and had put several major institutional clients into the stock. Though Fruit had zoomed from 17 to 62 in anticipation of improved management, by the middle of 1968 it had become clear that the revitalizers were not much better than their languid predecessors. The stock began to slide back down.
>
> The new managers were not the only ones embarrassed by this development. The stock had been pushed by the analysts at DLJ, who now began to receive calls from anxious clients. . . .[4]

Donaldson tells me he met repeatedly with Fox, who kept assuring him that all was well. With the stock vulnerable, it would have been hurt even more if DLJ suddenly advised its clients to sell, Donaldson recalls.

Continues Welles:

> Not very many of them would be able to unload their positions at anything close to the prevailing market price. Those who suffered losses would no doubt be angry.
>
> A more advantageous strategy, Donaldson decided, would be to

promote a take-over. A take-over, the firm knew, would almost automatically boost United Fruit stock—most acquiring firms typically pay a 10 to 50 percent premium for the acquired concern's stock—thereby giving its customers a chance to get out at a very attractive price. The customers would make profits and reward DLJ for its cleverness. Donaldson approached Eli Black with the idea. Black was attracted, for United Fruit was the sort of quiescently affluent concern that conglomerates dearly love. . . .[5]

The successful maneuver began in the Fall of 1968 with DLJ's investors selling only a portion of their stock in United Fruit, and was completed in early 1969. About this time stock averages started their slide-plunge-slide that continued into the mid-1970s. Alas, as Welles observes, AMK—renamed United Brands—went downhill under Black's management, the company losing $60 million in 1974.

As noted earlier, the hard-driving, overworked Black plunged to his death from the forty-fourth floor of his Manhattan office building in early 1975.

Long before DLJ's United Fruit caper, Donaldson had begun to sense that the footing on Wall Street was becoming treacherous. They were calling this the "go-go" market, so named for the quick in-and-out block trading by certain "high-performance" mutual funds, and for the small investors who stood around in the back of brokerage offices shouting "go, go, go!" when the symbols of the glamour issues blipped across the tape. These were the days of the conglomerateurs, of the sure-fire electronics stocks, of the back-office paperwork breakdown, and the new-issues craze.

With a handful of others, Donaldson spoke out publicly, to no avail. So he took steps to shore up his own company's capital base for the heavy weather he knew was coming. One of the first things he did was to announce that DLJ was going to go public, the first brokerage house to do so. This move shocked the New York Stock Exchange old guard, but other, more serious shocks were on the way.

"The whole time that we were building DLJ, I was somewhat of a self-flagellant," says Donaldson, looking back now. "I was always working on the problem side of things, and so maybe I didn't get as much pleasure as I should have out of our quote success unquote. I was always preparing for the next battle, and I think that's why I saw problems coming to Wall Street years before it all hit the fan; earlier than a lot of other people, and that's what induced us to go public, and lay in our capital base, and do a lot of other things that would allow us to survive and redirect our efforts into businesses with a promising future."

By the time everything had made its way through the fan in 1970, about one hundred brokerage houses had either merged or sunk beneath the waves. Millions of investors large and small had lost billions of dollars. The party was over. And the rules of the game were changing; the New York Stock Exchange was losing ground to other exchanges, and to computerization.

Lufkin was the first to leave DLJ. In 1971, he was named Connecticut's Commissioner for Environmental Protection. (He would return to DLJ three years later.) Jenrette considered a career in historic preservation, but never did succeed in making the break, and stayed with the firm. For some time, Donaldson had been leaning toward politics or government service when, one morning in September 1973, his secretary exclaimed:

"Mr. Donaldson, somebody's on the phone and he says he's Henry Kissinger. And you know—I think it is!"

And it was. The soft German accent, the measured tones that Donaldson had heard on the evening news hundreds of times was coming through the earpiece. Could he come to Washington for a chat?

Donaldson was taken aback. He had never met Kissinger. And he had not been maneuvering for a job in Washington. On the contrary, when the Nixon Administration had come to power the year before, he'd resisted a few offers. With Lufkin gone, he was deeply embroiled in DLJ; and besides, he had had an uneasy feeling about some of the Nixon principals who had talked with him.

In Donaldson's mind, a caution light blinked on. The Watergate scandal was well under way at this time. There was little stardust to be harvested by going down to Washington.

Kissinger made a direct, simply stated appeal. The nation, he said, was in a period of political and economic turmoil. . . . There would be foreign policy repercussions not easy to foresee.... President Nixon had appointed Kissinger Secretary of State, making him an offer he couldn't refuse. He, Kissinger, was making Bill Donaldson an offer he hoped Donaldson couldn't refuse; namely, he wanted someone, an outsider, an independent person, to help him run the Department of State and foreign policy; someone like "Cy" Vance who'd played such a role for "Bob" McNamara in Defense awhile back.... The business of a title could be worked out; it would be a job that would provide "flexibility," and leave him relatively free for "special assignments"; i.e., trouble-shooting. Well?

Another caution light blinked. When Kissinger spoke of a "partner," he obviously meant *junior* partner. Donaldson hadn't been born yesterday. He knew that there was no room in Henry's psyche for an equal partner, and he couldn't have expected such an arrangement anyway.

"Even so, it was heady to feel that the most popular man in the world had singled me out to help him," says Donaldson. "He could have had anybody, but he had picked *me*."

Bill Donaldson was being asked to help run the world. Even so, instinct held him back. He talked with Kissinger a number of times over a three-week period. Donaldson was well aware of Kissinger's reputation as a taskmaster. He even twitted Kissinger about this, making the point that he'd always been an entrepreneur and that while he knew he could work for someone else, he also knew that he could never become a yes man.

The last thing in the world that he wanted, replied Kissinger, was a yes man. That was the whole point.

Donaldson was still agonizing about his decision when the Arab-Israeli Yom Kippur War broke out on October 6, 1973. Kissinger invited Donaldson to come down to Washington and sit in with him during the crisis. Donaldson says he felt like a young man being rushed for a fraternity—and right in the middle of a war. Six days later, Kissinger called Donaldson at his Manhattan office and asked for a final yes or no. Donaldson said yes. Kissinger thereupon announced Donaldson's appointment as one of his three Undersecretaries of State, effective December 1.

As it turned out, Donaldson would not have a breaking-in period.

"He sees himself on a railroad station platform," said writer John S. DeMott in a perceptive article in *Institutional Investor's* May 1974 issue. "A train representing the government of the United States is approaching. It doesn't slow down a whit for Donaldson, let alone stop. He must board it on the move—a lurching experience indeed. 'This job,' he says, 'is like riding that train out of the station at 100 miles per hour from a standing start.' "[6]

Donaldson moved his wife Evan, his six-year-old daughter Kimberly, and his four-year-old son Matthew, into a big, high-ceilinged house in the fashionable Kalorama section of Northwest Washington, D.C., but he saw very little of them. DeMott's article in *Institutional Investor* described his work schedule:

> Donaldson's days begin at 7 A.M. and grind on until 8 or 9 o'clock at night, frequently later. There is first the 15-minute drive to the State Department. . . . Then there is the stack of overnight cables on his desk to be attended to. Then there is the "seventh floor principals" meeting, a daily feature of Donaldson's routine, at which high State officials brief each other, are briefed by other officials, sometimes Kissinger himself. And then, as Donaldson says, there is a drumfire of varied events for the rest of the day. . . .
>
> But overshadowing any prearranged schedule, of course, is the Catch-22 of Henry Kissinger. He telephones at 8 P.M. and wants a report by 8 A.M. the next day. He gives a speech in London (it went through 28 drafts) calling for a conference of energy-consuming nations and tells Donaldson to orchestrate it; the session, which normally would have required a year to arrange, was held in Washington . . . only weeks after Donaldson was given the assignment. . . .[7]

The article hinted that the relations between Kissinger and Donaldson were becoming strained.

Indeed, things had not been going well. And one morning in May 1974—less than six months after starting work at State—Donaldson quit. That very morning, a messenger flipped the May issue of *Institutional Investor* into Donaldson's office. DeMott's extensive article began on page 65. Its title: "Is Bill Donaldson in Washington to Stay?"

Donaldson and Kissinger are the only ones who really know what happened to cool the warm promise of their working relationship, and neither has said. The *Voortrekkers* who settled South Africa had a saying that Jan Smuts liked to apply to his political critics: "The dogs may bark, but the caravan moves on." Donaldson decided, wisely, that nothing would be gained by criticizing Kissinger. Besides, Kissinger's caravan was moving too fast. So Donaldson bit his lip and remained silent. It was the first time in his life that he had not finished something he had begun, and finished it in style. And for the first time, he'd lost face.

"I left Kissinger for all the right reasons, and I feel better about my personal integrity for having done so," says Donaldson today. "But the net bottom line of that is that I became, in some peoples' minds, another typical businessman who couldn't hack it in government. I'm sensitive to that."

Donaldson did have basic disagreements with Kissinger, and when he did, he spoke up. Kissinger, apparently, took offense. Some say that there was miscalculation on both sides, Kissinger failing to sense the steel fiber that lay beneath Donaldson's youthful, Ivy League mien; Donaldson not prepared for the tempo of in-fighting, intrigue, and bureaucratic chaos that pervades the seventh floor of the Department of State.

Donaldson's false start was to prove a blessing in many ways. For nearly fifteen years he'd been working fifteen-, sixteen-, seventeen-hour days much of the time without a real vacation. He'd never had time to ask, "to what end?"

After leaving State, Donaldson made what he considers one of the most important decisions of his life. He decided to do nothing; to walk away from it all; to forget, for the moment, about what his next step would be. With Evan and the children, he headed for Lake Michigan in July 1974.

All July, he sailed, played tennis, read quantities of books, and had fun with his children. When the month was over, he hadn't had enough. Evan rented the family a cottage on Cape Cod for August.

September found Donaldson back in Washington, his stock-taking well under way, and some important decisions already made. For one thing, he was not going to return to DLJ and Wall Street....

One brisk morning late in the month, we sipped hot coffee and talked in the cheerful porch of his Kalorama house while sun-shine streamed through the windows. He was not what my mind's eye had pictured. The former Wall Street tycoon and Under-secretary of State was wearing Topsiders with the marks of sum-mer upon them; a T-shirt, sweater, and weathered slacks. "Boyish" isn't exactly the word, but it won't go away.

Donaldson proved to be an open, easy conversationalist, with a lively curiosity about Dan Levinson's theories as I outlined them, and Robert Butler's writings, and about what I'd learned from talking with other men in their forties. Nor did he appear reluctant to talk about his own inner world.

"In the broadest philosophical sense, after a summer of reju-venation, I've convinced myself that I'm not burned out; that I'm not tired of the world. I'm not ready to retire somewhere. Quite the contrary. I've convinced myself that I'm at the prime of my life at forty-three. At forty-three, I'm experienced, but not tired. I'm young, I think, in terms of my rapport with the younger generation."

He was obviously aware that he had fared very well indeed in life's battles to date, and that while the State Department thing had proven frustrating, it had not disillusioned him. He obviously wanted to put something back in the pot by spending the rest of his life in public service of some kind.

Donaldson said that at the risk of sounding "Boy Scoutish," he was convinced that each generation had its particular challenge— World War II, Korea, Vietnam. . . . He felt that the nation's eco-nomic system was in trouble, and that this was probably going to prove to be his generation's challenge.

"I would like to have a role. I'm just not sure where to find the leverage."

We talked about how difficult it was for the average man in midlife to change careers, and of Fitzgerald's oft-quoted line that appears in the back-notes of his unfinished novel, *The Last Ty-*

coon: "There are no second acts in American lives."[8] And I asked Donaldson what it was like to have reached the mountaintop so early.

Donaldson smiled. "Someone has said of men who get to the top: 'When they get there, they find there's no *there*, there.' In a way, I have the advantage of having gone through a lot of things that other guys take a lifetime to do. I've gotten there— you know, 'there' in quotes—and I've had the fun of that, and also the disillusion of that. So I think this is a great opportunity. I'd hate to have the feelings of a job undone and so forth that I have right now, when I'm sixty-one, sixty-two, sixty-five. That would be really frustrating. Really, I'm being given another chance."

Bill Donaldson moved back to New York City and I lost track of him for about a year while I waited for the other shoe to drop. I knew that he'd been busy. After Hugh Carey's election as New York Governor in November 1974, Donaldson had directed his transitional government team. He was also advising the governor of Puerto Rico on fiscal matters. And for a long time, he moved into Vice-President Nelson Rockefeller's Foxhall Road home in Washington to work on President Ford's $100 billion Energy Independence Authority legislation. But these were all temporary things.

Then on October 1, 1975, the *New York Times* carried a front page story concerning Yale University's establishment of a Graduate School of Organization and Management to train leaders for both business and government service. Bill Donaldson was to be its first dean, as well as Professor of Public and Private Management.

"The dilemmas that our country faces on the eve of its 200th Anniversary, underscore the need for a major new initiative in leadership training," said Donaldson's formal statement issued at Yale. "Public attitudes are at a new low in terms of respect for and confidence in private and public business and government leadership. . . . It is not that we as a nation suddenly lack leaders, but rather that the explosive and accelerating pace of change has led people to question our traditional attitudes, and has placed a greater burden on the store of knowledge and practice in the field of administration and management.

"The lines between the public and private sector are being rapidly blurred. Young men and women, reflecting the pace and mood of the times, increasingly seek the variety and satisfaction of multiple careers, including private and government posts.

"In the private sector, business managers spend an increasing percentage of their time attempting to cope with the expanding role of government. At the same time, public officials and managers—federal, state, and local—find that the size, scope, and complexity of their operations require increasing reliance on private sector management techniques.

"In the twilight zone between the public and private sectors, managers of 'independent institutions'—hospitals, symphony orchestras, charitable foundations, and universities, struggle with organizations that must respond to a striving for artistic merit or social utility, while surviving in a world of more mundane profit and loss. . . ."

Bill Donaldson had, as they say on Wall Street, found his "leverage."

20 *"... There Is a Depth to the Human Heart...."*

FIFTY MILES west of Washington, D.C., the main highway leading to Winchester, Virginia, crosses the Blue Ridge Mountains and sweeps down over the Shenandoah River. At the far end of the bridge, the unmarked gravel road that leads to the Trappist abbey doubles back beside the span to the sun-sparkled river. The road follows the stream northward for about a mile beneath an archway of trees, then meanders through rich bottomland and patches of quiet woods. On the crest of a sudden rise, an easily missed sign marks the entrance to Holy Cross Monastery, out of sight across ascending fields where beef cattle graze. Moments later, the white cross on the monastery chapel jumps into sharp relief against the blue October sky. Originally known as "Deep Spring," the antebellum farm house that serves as the abbey stands on a hill commanding a glorious view of the mountains— a deep shade of blue today, even in the near distance—and of the valley, with its open, rolling fox-hunting country off to the southwest beyond the nearby town of Berryville.

It's late morning and the sun is shining brightly, puffy white clouds drifting here and there across the sky. There's not a sign of life. I shut off the Volvo's engine and wait, enjoying the moment. These fields, I knew, had not always been so peaceful. Where solitary monks now stroll and meditate, Confederates and Yankees fought a fierce engagement in the summer of 1864. Dozens of bullets bearing the teeth marks of wounded men have been turned up by the monks along with other relics of the battle.

The door of the abbey opens, and Father Matthew Killian's beaming face appears. Though he's in his early fifties, Father Matt, as he likes to be called, could easily pass for the early thirties; his responsive, youthful manner softening the austerity of his white habit and close-cropped hair. He's a tall, fit man—six feet or more—and it's not difficult to imagine him in his earlier role as a flying officer during the second World War.

The Cistercians of the Strict Observance, or Trappists, are a practical as well as contemplative lot, known for their skilled use of the land and, among other things, their breadmaking. Father Matt has been at work since 3:30 A.M. in the bakery down the hill behind the abbey. At noon, a truck will leave laden with still-warm loaves of "Monastery Bread" bound for Washington Safeway stores. Then Killian will be free until Vespers to pray, rest, study, and roam the fields—he's an inveterate jogger—and counsels visitors in the Pentecostal movement, his passionate concern. At 8 P.M., it's lights out in his spare, dormitory cubicle.

"May the outward and the inward man be at one," was Socrates' prayer. Father Matt is "at one." He came to terms with life, however, only after a dramatic crisis of the spirit in his late thirties. On an Indian Summer day in 1965, Father Matt made his "special bet," leaving the monastery to live as a hermit in the Vosges Mountains of eastern France. He was a few months short of his fortieth birthday. Nearly three years would pass before he returned to Holy Cross.

Killian was raised on northern Long Island, the son of second-generation Irish-Americans. After graduation from Catholic University in Washington, D.C., and service as a navigator aboard troop-carriers in the China-Burma theater at the end of the war, Killian joined the Trappist order. In the early 1950s, he arrived at Holy Cross in a bus from New England with the first batch of novices, Deep Spring farm having recently been acquired by the religious order.

"There are many ways to serve the Lord," Killian is now saying as we walk across the beautifully kept grounds. "Teaching, healing the sick, for example. But it was the life of prayer that attracted me, the life of study, the character of the monastic life, the fact that you went all the way when other people—well, in a sense, it didn't look like they were going all the way for the Lord."

The Abbot of Holy Cross sensed something special in Killian, and brought him along rapidly into positions of increasing responsibility. By the fall of 1965, Killian had been serving for some time as Novice Master, a position second only to the abbot in terms of real responsibility.

Even so, Killian had grown extremely restless. After all these years of focused effort, God remained maddeningly distant. Killian now feared that time was running out, that he would never close the seemingly infinite gap without a superhuman effort of some kind. Thomas Merton clearly had men such as Killian in mind when he described a monk as a "man so intent upon the search for God that he is ready to die in order to see Him."[1]

Killian's plan to enter a hermitage overseas had taken root in the early 1960s in Rome where he'd been sent to get an advanced degree in theology. One of his classmates, a French Trappist, said he was planning eventually to establish a hermitage in the Vosges, and asked Killian to join him. The idea immediately stirred Killian's imagination.

"The silence of the forest, the peace of the early morning wind moving through the branches of the trees, the solitude and isolation of the house of God: These are good because it is in silence, and not in commotion, in solitude, and not in crowds, that God best likes to reveal himself intimately to men,"[2] wrote Merton.

Killian returned to the monastery in Virginia afire with the plan. His mentor, the abbot, would hear none of it at first. Killian appealed to higher authority and finally was granted an unlimited leave of absence.

"A real essential note of the monastic life," says Killian, "is to live in separation for a meaning, for a purpose. When you come from 'the world' in the direction of solitude, you center upon God and prayer. When you move from the monastery into a hermitage, you move into an even greater solitude, a greater opportunity to come closer to God."

Killian and the French Trappist began their eremitic life in an empty farmhouse that had been made available to the French monk by a wealthy textile man in the region. The house was located in a fir forest on the western flank of the Vosges massif, seventy-five miles south of Nancy, and four or five miles from the hamlet of La Bourgance.

The men occupied rooms on opposite sides of the house, observing the monastic rule of silence except to communicate in time of minor emergencies. They led separate lives in fact; eating, praying, and working alone. Killian learned how to weave willow baskets for sale in the village, and the French monk wove cloth on a loom. During the first six months they lived on milk from a goat they acquired, and on sparse rations of coffee, cheese, chocolate, and bread donated by a local convent.

Killian was able to enjoy "the peace of the early morning wind moving through the branches of the trees," for only a few weeks. The Vosges is a place of austere beauty, but there's ferocity in its winters, and bitterly cold weather quickly closed in. "There's a saying that there are only two seasons in the Vosges: winter— and the end of winter," says Killian.

Raw winds whipped the mountainside and whistled through the hermitage. Snow fell endlessly in the fir forest. Temperatures during Killian's first winter plunged to 20 degrees below zero at night. The empty house had no heating system, no electricity, no inside toilet. The skin on Killian's hands cracked open from the cold. He suffered brutally from diarrhea. Sheer animal survival consumed all his physical and emotional resources. God, he says, became ever more remote.

At night, Killian lay on his hard bunk trying to ignore the sound of rats scurrying between the walls and in the rafters overhead. Doubts about his enterprise crowded in.

"I had come all this way to grasp God, and he wouldn't allow himself to be grasped. The harder I grasped, the further away he got. I lay there asking myself: 'Is this going to work out? Is it all worth zero? Am I just a fool?' "

With the end of that first winter, life became more bearable. The diarrhea which had tormented him cleared up. He established a vegetable garden, and walked into La Bourgance every now and then to visit with the local priest, and nod "Bonjour" to the villagers. But now a new problem arose: he and the French monk had developed cabin fever, the age-old affliction of two men living in isolation. Even though they were religious men accustomed to solitude and isolation, the monotony of their existence bred hostilities, and they tried to take each other's measure.

"There was a loneliness to this all by itself, to be alienated from the guy you live with," says Killian. "It was strange. You know the guy is there—you hear him moving about—and you take cognizance of him even if you don't like him at the time."

Late one evening the following winter, Killian's second in the hermitage, an event occurred which he found symbolic of his life's critical turning at that point. The milking goat had developed a skin irritation; she was in such pain that she couldn't be relieved of her milk. The French monk had been out in the forest most of the day and was tired, so it was decided that Killian should make his way to the nearest farmhouse, some miles away, and seek help for the animal. Killian's next words have an eery flavor of Dante.

"I knew that by the time I got midway to that farmhouse, it was going to be dark. So I took my kerosene lamp—that was all the light we had—and I remember very clearly that it was terribly cold and there was deep snow on the ground, and more coming down. And suddenly, it was very dark. And I was going through the forest—not knowing where the path was, really— and the lamp was giving off only two or three feet of light.

"I didn't know what was going to happen at that farmhouse— whether the people would be at home, or whether I could communicate, my French wasn't all that good; or whether they'd know what to do about the goat.

"There were an awful lot of question marks, in other words. And then again, I was going away from a guy who really didn't want me. I wasn't wanted at the hermitage, and I wasn't sure where I was going, or how I was going to get there.

"It was *really* dark. And then, suddenly, it was beautiful. Because I knew that every single step I took, the Lord was with me, because he was saying: 'One step at a time—I'll be with you —one step at a time.'"

After an exhausting hike, Killian found the farmer, who came back to the hermitage with him and successfully ministered to the goat.

That spring, the French monk left the mountain to found a one-man hermitage somewhere in Southern France, and Killian never saw him again. With the Frenchman gone, he was totally alone on the mountain.

Killian now began to experience what one psychiatrist has called "the naked horror" of loneliness; a depth of aloneness that most men fear more than death. Such loneliness is a form of separation anxiety rooted deep in our psyches, tracing to the infant's terror of being separated from its mother. It seizes us all at one time or another.

When Killian could no longer bear being alone, he would walk down into the village. And then other defenses began to give way. "After all those years of monastic life, sexual temptation started coming back. They soon became really vivid, really gripping. I wore a white habit, and I was aware that the villagers called me *Le Saint Moine*, 'the holy monk.' At the same time, I knew what was going on inside my mind, and it was just awful there for a while. And I remembered Saint Jerome in the Syrian desert:

" 'In the remotest part of a wild and stony desert burnt up with the heat of the scorching sun so that it frightens even the monks that inhabit it, I seemed myself to be in the midst of the delights and crowds of Rome.

" '. . . Many times I imagined myself witnessing the dancing of the Roman maidens as if I had been in the midst of them. . . . I tamed my flesh by fasting whole weeks. I am not ashamed to disclose my temptations.'[3]

"At this time, I was getting more and more insight into myself, and this was a shattering experience. I didn't like what I saw. Nor was I seeing God clearly at all. And now I was just kind of hanging on again, experiencing what the psalmists were singing: my enemies—my temptations—were all around me."

The temptations passed in time, but the loneliness persisted.

"I had forgotten how really lonely my teen-age years had been. And all of a sudden I said to myself, 'Well, hey now, these people are lonely! You're lonely, and they're lonely.' And then someone gave me a magazine and it had an article about lonely old people. And all of a sudden, it came to me: *everybody* is lonely.

"There was a fourth-century monk, Evagrius Ponticus, and he said something like this: 'The true monk is separated from all, and united to all.' In the hermitage I was separated from everybody, but precisely in that I was experiencing the deep things that people do experience, I was united to all. And I really do think loneliness is universal.

"If the young businessman, say, isn't aware of his loneliness, it's because he's busying himself with many things and is not in a state of reflection. But I feel now, after my experience in the mountains, that there is a depth to the human heart that we absolutely can't communicate to anybody. And it's only the Lord who can enter that depth, and it's precisely here where people feel lonely because they can't communicate this feeling to their spouse, their best friend, or anybody.

"When you're confronting your loneliness, not sort of avoiding it, and you are there before God with it, saying, as I did: 'Lord, I'm helpless. If you're not there, I just can't hack it.' Well, he certainly takes you through it. He took me through it."

On Killian's walks into the village in the fall of 1967, he started to take notice of a woman in her early sixties who lived alone in an old stone cottage on the edge of the community. She was often barefoot, disheveled, and distracted. One day when he nodded in greeting, she asked him to wait for a moment, then shyly handed him a basket of turnips from her garden.

Killian asked the village priest about the woman and was told that she had been raped by German—or French—troops during the war, and had given birth to a son, who had since grown up and moved away. She was poor, had no relatives and no real friends.

On Killian's next expedition to La Bourgance, he returned the woman's basket, filled with vegetables from his mountain garden. She invited him to have a glass of wine. They talked. And from that time on, the monk made it a point to stop and see her whenever he came down from the mountain.

"If it hadn't been for my own experience with loneliness, I never would have noticed that woman," he says. "I was in the same boat she was. I know my visits helped, because she always looked happy when I stopped by."

By Eastertime 1968, Father Matt was ready to return to Virginia. He was, he says, "psychically hollowed out." He had seen no visions on his mountain, no tongues of fire. One morning, he filled a basket with vegetables, took a last look around the hermitage, and walked down into La Bourgance. He had a last glass of wine with the woman in the stone house, and presented her with his basket.

After returning to Holy Cross monastery, Killian began to take on new life. There was the fresh-baked bread at dawn and the easy camaraderie of his fellow monks in the bakery; long walks over the fields; the mountains forever changing their shades of blue. He was home.

About six weeks after Killian's return to Holy Cross, he was praying alone in the small chapel one afternoon when he experienced an overwhelming sense of God's presence, as he puts it; a sense that has been with him ever since. What he'd gone to the distant, silent mountains to seek, he'd found here in the valley whence his journey had begun.

Notes

Preface

1. *Essays of Montaigne,* Charles Cotton, trans. (New York: Edwin C. Hill, 1910), pp. 28–29.

Chapter 1

1. Henry Wadsworth Longfellow, trans., *The Divine Comedy of Dante Alighieri* (Boston: Houghton Mifflin, 1882), p. 1.
2. Malcolm Cowley, "A Weekend With Eugene O'Neill," Oscar Cargill, N. Bryllion Fagin, and William J. Fisher, eds., *O'Neill and His Plays: Four Decades of Criticism* (New York: New York University Press, 1961), p. 115.
3. "The Lamentation of the Old Pensioner," *Collected Poems of William Butler Yeats* (New York: Macmillan Publishing Co., Inc., 1956).
4. Ernest Becker, *The Denial of Death* (New York: The Free Press, 1973), p. ix.
5. Becker, p. 26.
6. As quoted in Anthony Storr, "The Fear of Death," *Réalités,* August 1973, p. 33.
7. As quoted in Tanneguy de Quenetain, "The Dark Forces Come to Light," *Réalités,* May 1971, p. 54.
8. Elliott Jaques, "Death and the Mid-life Crisis," *International Journal of Psycho-Analysis,* 46:4, 1965, p. 506.
9. As quoted in Maggie Scarf, "Husbands in Crisis," *McCall's,* June 1972, p. 122.
10. John P. Marquand, *The Point of No Return* (Boston: Little, Brown and Company, 1949), pp. 537–538.
11. From James Baldwin's review of *The Arrangement,* by Elia Kazan, in the *New York Review of Books,* March 23, 1967, p. 17.
12. Carl Gustav Jung, *Modern Man in Search of a Soul* (New York: Harcourt, Brace & World, 1933), p. 107.
13. Catherine Drinker Bowen, "Five Against the Odds," *Horizon,* Spring 1974, p. 81.

Chapter 2

1. Richard E. Byrd, *Alone* (New York: Putnam, 1938), p. 6.
2. Byrd, p. 4.
3. Byrd, pp. 56–57.

4. Byrd, p. 8.

5. As quoted in A. L. Vischer, *On Growing Old* (Boston: Houghton Mifflin, 1967), p. 51.

6. As quoted by Tom Zito, *The Washington Post*, August 5, 1974.

7. Robert M. Pirsig, *Zen and the Art of Motorcycle Maintenance* (New York: William Morrow & Co., 1974), p. 98.

8. Pirsig, p. 91.

9. Zito.

10. Paul Gauguin, *Noa-Noa, A Journal of the South Seas* (New York: Noonday Press, 1957), p. vi.

11. Gauguin, pp. 33–34.

12. Robert Goldwater, *Paul Gauguin* (New York: Abrams, 1974), pp. 11–12.

13. Robert N. Butler and Myrna I. Lewis, *Aging and Mental Health* (St. Louis: The C. V. Mosby Company, 1973), p. 274.

14. Robert Manry, *Tinkerbelle* (New York: Harper & Row, 1965), p. 218.

15. Manry, pp. 217–218.

16. As quoted in Brian Inglis, interview with Carl Jung, London *Sunday Times*, 1962, quoted in *The National Observer*, July 30, 1962.

17. As quoted in *Cleveland Plain Dealer*, February 22, 1971.

18. As quoted in *Cleveland Plain Dealer*, August 18, 1965.

19. As quoted in *Cleveland Plain Dealer*, February 22, 1971.

20. Manry, p. 67.

21. As quoted in Loudon Wainwright, "The Old Pro Gets His Shot at the Moon," *Life*, July 31, 1970, p. 54.

22. Wainwright, p. 54.

23. Colonel Edwin E. "Buzz" Aldrin, Jr., *Return to Earth* (New York: Random House, 1973), p. 300.

24. Aldrin, p. 300.

25. Aldrin, pp. 308–309.

26. Malcolm Cowley, "A Weekend With Eugene O'Neill," Oscar Cargill, N. Bryllion Fagin, and William J. Fisher, eds. *O'Neill and His Plays: Four Decades of Criticism* (New York: New York University Press, 1961), pp. 41–42.

27. Constantine FitzGibbon, *The Life of Dylan Thomas* (Boston: Little, Brown and Co., 1965), pp. 227–228. Dylan Thomas verses from *The Poems of Dylan Thomas* (New York: New Directions Publishing Corporation).

28. Elliott Jaques, "Death and the Mid-life Crisis," *International Journal of Psycho-Analysis*, 46:4 (1965), p. 502.

29. Jaques, p. 503.

30. Jaques, pp. 505–506.

31. Henry Wadsworth Longfellow, trans., *The Divine Comedy of Dante Alighieri* (Boston: Houghton Mifflin, 1882), vol. 3, p. 166.

Chapter 3

1. William H. Sheldon, *Psychology and the Promethean Will* (New York: Harper and Brothers, 1963), p. 3.

2. Dr. Robert N. Butler, "Psychiatry and Psychology of the Middle Aged,"

in *Comprehensive Textbook of Psychiatry;* Alfred M. Freedman, M.D., Harold I. Kaplan, M.D., Benjamin J. Sadock, M.D., eds. (Baltimore: The Williams and Wilkins Co., 1974), p. 2397.

3. In "Male Menopause: The Pause That Perplexes," produced by National Public Affairs Center for Television (NPACT), original production June 24, 1974.

4. Bronislaw Malinowski, *The Sexual Life of Savages* (New York: Harcourt, Brace & World, 1962), vol. 1, p. 276.

5. NPACT, June 24, 1974.

6. NPACT, June 24, 1974.

7. "The Circus Animals' Desertion," *Collected Poems of William Butler Yeats.* Copyright 1940 by Georgie Yeats, renewed 1969 by Bertha Georgie Yeats, Michael Butler Yeats, and Anne Yeats.

8. Dr. George F. Vaillant, "The Human Life Cycle," *Seminars In Psychiatry,* November 1972, pp. 297–298.

9. Richard E. Byrd, *Alone* (New York: Putnam, 1938), p. vii.

Chapter 4

1. Dan Levinson, "The Normal Crises of the Middle Years," symposium sponsored by The Menninger Foundation, at Hunter College, New York City, March 1, 1973, transcript, p. 9.

2. Levinson, "The Normal Crises," p. 14.

3. Levinson, "The Normal Crises," p. 10.

4. Levinson, "The Normal Crises," p. 11.

5. Daniel J. Levinson, Charlotte Darrow, Edward B. Klein, Maria H. Levinson, Braxton McKee, "The Psychosocial Development of Men in Early Adulthood and the Mid-Life Transition," *Life History Research in Psychopathology* (Minneapolis: University of Minnesota Press, 1974), Volume 3, p. 248.

6. Levinson, "The Normal Crises," pp. 11–12.

7. Levinson, et al., "The Psychosocial Development," p. 249.

8. Levinson, "The Normal Crises," p. 11.

9. Levinson, p. 12.

10. Levinson, et al., "The Psychosocial Development," p. 252.

11. Levinson, et al., "The Psychosocial Development," p. 252.

12. William McGuire, ed., *The Freud/Jung Letters* (Princeton, New Jersey: Princeton University Press, 1974), p. 492.

13. *The Freud/Jung Letters,* p. 539.

14. *The Freud/Jung Letters,* p. 540.

15. Richard M. Huber, *The American Idea of Success* (New York: McGraw-Hill, 1971), p. 1.

16. As quoted in Maggie Scarf, "Husbands in Crisis," *McCall's,* June 1972, p. 120.

17. Levinson, et al., "The Psychosocial Development," p. 254.

18. C. G. Jung, *Modern Man in Search of a Soul* (New York: Harcourt, Brace & World, Inc., 1933), p. 108.

19. Jung, p. 112.

20. Anne Morrow Lindbergh, *Gift From the Sea* (New York: Vintage Books, 1965), pp. 84–85.

Chapter 5

1. Morton Hunt, *The Affair* (New York: New American Library, 1969), p. 29.

2. Dr. Harry J. Johnson, *Executive Life-Styles* (New York: Thomas Y. Crowell, 1974), p. 19.

3. John Updike, *Month of Sundays* (New York: Alfred A. Knopf, 1975), p. 33.

4. H. L. Mencken, *The Mating Game and How to Play It* (Kansas City, Mo.: Hallmark Cards, 1974), pp. 31–32.

5. L. Rust Hills, "What's Wrong With Adultery?," *Playboy*, May 1974, p. 198.

6. Johnson, pp. 23, 26.

7. Neil Simon, *Last of the Red Hot Lovers* (New York: Random House, 1970), pp. 32–34.

8. As quoted in Maggie Scarf, "Husbands in Crisis," *McCall's*, June 1972, p. 124.

9. Scarf, p. 124.

10. Dr. Albert Ellis, *The Civilized Couple's Guide to Extramarital Adventures* (New York: Pinnacle Books, 1972), p. 56.

11. John F. Cuber and Peggy B. Harroff, *The Significant Americans: A Study of Sexual Behavior Among the Affluent* (New York: Appleton Century, 1965), p. 97.

12. Joseph Heller, *Something Happened* (New York: Alfred A. Knopf, 1974), p. 195.

13. Nena O'Neill and George O'Neill, *Open Marriage* (New York: M. Evans and Company, 1972), p. 245.

14. O'Neill and O'Neill, p. 257.

15. Bertrand Russell, *Marriage and Morals* (New York: Liveright, 1957), pp. 140–141.

16. Dr. Leon Salzman, "Psychiatric and Clinical Aspects of Infidelity," in *The Psychodynamics of Work and Marriage*, Dr. Jules H. Masserman, ed. (New York: Grune and Stratton, 1970), pp. 127–128.

17. Norman Sheresky and Marya Mannes, *Uncoupling: The Art of Coming Apart* (New York: The Viking Press, 1972), pp. 36–37.

18. Sheresky and Mannes, p. 39.

19. Carle C. Zimmerman, *Family and Civilization* (New York: Harper and Brothers, 1947), p. 797.

Chapter 6

1. Anna Freud, *The Psychoanalytic Study of the Child* (New York: International Universities Press, 1958), vol. 13, p. 275.

2. *The Standard Edition of Complete Psychological Works of Sigmund Freud* (London: Hogarth Press and the Institute of Psycho-Analysis, 1955–1974), Vol. 13, p. 155.

3. Sigmund Freud, p. 155.

4. As quoted in Edwin A. Roberts, Jr., "A Mix of Brilliance and Arrogance," *The National Observer*, November 24, 1969, p. 16.

5. Dr. Gerald H. J. Pearson, *Adolescence and the Conflict of Generations* (New York: W. W. Norton & Co., 1958), p. 135.

6. Pearson, p. 177.

7. Dr. Wilhelm Reich, *The Sexual Revolution* (London: Vision Press, 1951), p. 80.

8. Drs. L. David Levi, Helm Stierlin, and Robert J. Savard, "Fathers and Sons: The Interlocking Crises of Integrity and Identity," *Psychiatry*, February 1972, p. 48.

9. Levi et al., p. 48.

10. Bertrand Russell, *The Conquest of Happiness* (New York: Liveright, 1930), p. 202.

11. Russell, pp. 200–201.

Chapter 7

1. As quoted in, "The Good Word: Cyril Connolly," *The New York Times, Book Review* (January 5, 1975).

2. René Vallery-Radot, *The Life of Pasteur* (New York: Doubleday, 1916), p. 342.

3. Dr. Nathan Shock, "The Physiology of Aging," *Scientific American*, January 1962, pp. 2–3.

4. Osborn Segerberg, Jr., *The Immortality Factor* (New York: E. P. Dutton & Co., 1974), p. 203.

5. J. Bronowski, *The Ascent of Man* (Boston/Toronto: Little Brown & Co., 1973), p. 317.

6. Edward Frankel, *DNA—Ladder of Life* (New York: McGraw-Hill, 1964), p. 43.

7. Rona Cherry and Laurence Cherry, "Slowing the Clock of Age," *New York Times Magazine*, June 9, 1974.

8. Segerberg, p. 253.

9. As quoted in Victor Cohn, "Can Science Extend Middle Age?" *Outlook* section, *The Washington Post*, March 16, 1975.

10. Cohn, p. C2.

11. Cohn, p. C2.

12. Segerberg, p. 243.

13. Pam Ginsbach, "Why Women Live Longer," *Marriage and Family Living*, January 1974, p. 3.

14. Ginsbach, p. 4.

Chapter 8

1. As quoted in, Mary H. Cadwalader, "How I Fight the High-Blood-Pressure Battle . . . And Sometimes Win," *Today's Health*, October 1974, p. 25.

2. Gilbert Cant, "Male Trouble," *The New York Times Magazine*, February 16, 1975.

3. Cant, p. 68.

4. Tavia Gordon and Thomas Thom, "The Recent Decrease in CHD Mortality" *Preventive Medicine*, June 1975, p. 115.

Chapter 9

1. Martha Weinman Lear, "Is There A Male Menopause?" *The New York Times Magazine*, January 28, 1973.

2. Dr. Hans Selye, "Stress and Distress," *Physician's World*, March 1974, pp. 25–26.

3. Anthony Storr, "The Case of the Unpleasant Boss." *Réalités*, March 1973, p. 31.

4. Lear, p. 65.

5. "Treating Menopausal Women—and Climacteric Men," *Medical World News*, June 28, 1974, p. 53.

Chapter 10

1. As quoted in Al Berger, "Aging," *Medical World News*, October 22, 1971, p. 46.

2. Paul B. Baltes and K. Warner Schaie, "The Myth of the Twilight Years," *Psychology Today*, March 1974, p. 40.

3. Baltes and Schaie, p. 35.

4. Marvin Schneider, "Johnny Unitas: The Six-Dollar-a-Game Quarterback," *The Sports Immortals* (Englewood Cliffs, N.J.: Prentice-Hall, 1972), p. 196.

5. A. L. Vischer, *On Growing Old* (Boston: Houghton-Mifflin, 1967), p. 12.

Chapter 11

1. James P. Gannon, "Man in Motion," *The Wall Street Journal*, July 3, 1974.

2. Don Fabun, *The Dynamics of Change* (Englewood Cliffs, New Jersey: Prentice-Hall, 1970), p. 13.

3. Cotton Mather, *A Christian at His Calling* (Boston, 1722), p. 37.

4. Richard M. Cohen, "Work Ethic Is Marriott Corporate Asset," *The Washington Post*, December 24, 1974.

5. Richard M. Huber, *The American Idea of Success* (New York: Mc-Graw-Hill, 1971), pp. 19–20.

6. Mary Bralove, "Was Eli Black's Suicide Caused by the Tensions of Conflicting Worlds?" *The Wall Street Journal*, February 14, 1975.

7. Ann Wood, "Wife Kills Hard-Working U.S. Aide and Self," *New York News*, February 19, 1975.

8. Eli Ginsberg, *Human Resources: Wealth of a Nation* (New York: Simon & Schuster, 1958), p. 138.

9. Arthur Miller, *Death of a Salesman* (New York: The Viking Press, 1949), p. 82. .

10. Miller, p. 56.

11. Walter Goodman, "Miller's 'Salesman,' Created in 1949, May Mean More to 1975." *The New York Times*, June 15, 1975.

Chapter 12

1. Roger M. D'Aprix, *The Struggle for Identity: The Silent Revolution Against Corporate Conformity* (Homewood, Illinois: Dow Jones-Irwin, Inc., 1972), p. 61.

2. Alan N. Schoonmaker, "The Tallest Decision Tree: Career Myopia," *The MBA Magazine* reprinted in *The HarBus News*, February 25, 1971.

3. D'Aprix, p. 62.

4. Joseph Heller, *Something Happened* (New York: Alfred A. Knopf, 1974), p. 13.

5. Studs Terkel, *Working* (New York: Pantheon Books, 1974), p. xi.

6. *Work in America* (Cambridge, Massachusetts: MIT Press, 1973), p. xv.

7. *Work in America*, p. 21.

8. Rush Loving, Jr., "The Automobile Industry Has Lost Its Masculinity," *Fortune*, October 1972, p. 268.

9. Loving, p. 190.

Chapter 14

1. Donald M. Frame, *Montaigne, A Biography* (New York: Harcourt-Brace & World, 1965), p. 187.

2. Frame, p. 183.

3. John C. Crystal and Richard N. Bolles, *Where Do I Go From Here With My Life?* (New York: The Seabury Press, 1974), p. 201.

4. Testimony before the House of Representatives Committee on Science and Astronautics as quoted in *The New York Times*, January 30, 1970.

Chapter 15

1. Alfred T. DeMaria, Dale Tarnowieski, and Richard Gurman. *Manager Unions? An American Management Association Research Report* (New York: American Management Association, 1972), p. 12.

2. Jay Robert Nash, *Bloodletters and Badmen* (New York: M. Evans, 1973), p. 62.

3. As quoted in, "Fired for Being 'Too Old'? Government Is On Your Side," *U.S. News & World Report*, June 3, 1974, p. 76.

4. U.S. Department of Labor, Employment Standards Administration, Wage and Money Division pamphlet, *40–65* (Washington, D.C.: U.S. Government Printing Office, 1974).

5. Frank P. Doyle, "Age Discrimination and Organizational Life," *Industrial Gerontology*, Summer 1973, p. 30.

6. Doyle, p. 31.

7. Carin Ann Clauss, "Sixty Suits Settled to Date," *Industrial Gerontology*, Summer 1973, p. 21.

8. 354 *Federal Supplement* 230 (Northern District Illinois), February 5, 1973, Hodgson v. Greyhound Lines, Inc., p. 239.

9. 354 *Federal Supplement*, p. 239.

10. Houghton and Brennan v. McDonnell Douglas Corporation, Transcript of Trial at p. 58. (Eastern District of Missouri) Civil number 73C 14(3), February 18, 1975.

11. Houghton and Brennan v. McDonnell Douglas Corp., Transcript of Trial at p. 73.

12. Houghton and Brennan v. McDonnell Douglas Corp., Transcript of Trial, at p. 78.

13. Houghton and Brennan v. McDonnell Douglas Corp., Transcript of Trial, at p. 112.

14. Houghton and Brennan v. McDonnell Douglas Corp., Transcript of Trial, at p. 22.

15. Houghton and Brennan v. McDonnell Douglas Corp., Transcript of Trial, at pp. 126–27.
16. As quoted in John Noble Wilford, *The New York Times*, July 16, 1975.

Chapter 16

1. Dr. Robert N. Butler, "Psychiatry and Psychology of the Middle-Aged," *Comprehensive Textbook of Psychiatry—II*, Alfred M. Freedman, M.D., Harold I. Kaplan, M.D., Benjamin J. Sadock, M.D., eds. (Baltimore: The Williams and Wilkins Co., 1974), p. 2397.
2. Merton C. Bernstein, testimony before the Special Committee on Aging, U. S. Senate, "Aging—Toward a Full Share in Abundance," February 17, 1970, p. 1477.
3. David Hapgood, *The Screwing of the Average Man* (New York: Doubleday & Co., Inc., 1975), p. 201.
4. Merton C. Bernstein, "Pension Act Cruelly Misleads," *Cleveland Plain Dealer*, September 19, 1974.
5. *The New York Times*, July 1, 1974.
6. Ralph Nader and Kate Blackwell, *You and Your Pension* (New York: Grossman Publishers, 1973), p. 123.
7. James W. Singer, "New Pension Reform Enacted; Law Gets Mixed Reaction," *National Journal Reports*, August 31, 1974, p. 1319.
8. Merton C. Bernstein, "Pension Act 'Cruelly' Misleads," *Cleveland Plain Dealer*, September 19, 1974, reprinted with permission Merton C. Bernstein.
9. Merton C. Bernstein, "Pension Losers: Women," *Cleveland Plain Dealer*, September 20, 1974, reprinted with permission Merton C. Bernstein.
10. Merton C. Bernstein, "Labor, Financial Interests Sank Pension Reform," *Cleveland Plain Dealer*, September 21, 1974, reprinted with permission Merton C. Bernstein.
11. Dr. Eli Ginsberg, "The Middle Years: Dimensions and Dilemmas," *Career Options and Educational Opportunities in the Middle Years* (Los Angeles: The Ethel Percy Andrus Gerontology Center, University of Southern California, 1974), p. 15.

Chapter 17

1. *The Complete Etchings of Goya* (New York: Crown Publishers, 1943), p. 10.
2. Dr. Robert N. Butler, "Why Retire at All?" *Modern Maturity*, December-January 1971–1972, p. 67.
3. Butler, p. 68.
4. Henry David Thoreau, *Walden* (New York: The Modern Library, 1937), p. 98.
5. Theodore M. Hesburgh, C.S.C., Paul A. Miller, and Clifton R. Wharton, Jr. *Patterns for Lifelong Learning* (San Francisco: Jossey-Bass Publishers, 1973), pp. 5–6.
6. Hesburgh *et al.*, pp. 5–6.
7. As quoted in Fred Hechinger, "Education's New Majority," *Saturday Review*, September 20, 1975, p. 16.

8. Don Fabun, *The Dynamics of Change* (Englewood Cliffs, New Jersey: Prentice-Hall, 1970), p. 17.

9. As quoted in Fabun, p. 18.

10. Staffan B. Linder, *The Harried Leisure Class* (New York: Columbia University Press, 1970), pp. 1–2.

11. Linder, pp. 1–2.

12. Linder, p. 10.

13. Walter Kerr, *The Decline of Pleasure* (New York: Simon & Schuster, 1962), pp. 136–137.

14. Kerr, pp. 153–155. Kenneth Fearing poem reprinted by permission, Simon & Schuster, Inc.

15. From "Prayers" by Michel Quoist, copyright 1963. Sheed & Ward, Inc., Mission, Kansas.

16. Linder, p. 850.

17. G. J. Whitrow, *The Nature of Time* (New York: Holt, Rinehart and Winston, 1972), pp. 18–19.

18. William V. Shannon, "The Death of Time" *The New York Times,* July 8, 1971.

19. As quoted in Dr. Alexander Reid Martin, "Leisure and the Creative Process," *The Hanover Forum,* April 9, 1959, p. 20.

20. Dr. Josef Pieper, *Leisure the Basis of Culture* (New York: Pantheon Books, 1955), p. 52.

21. Dr. Alexander Reid Martin, "Self-Alienation and the Loss of Leisure," *The American Journal of Psychoanalysis,* XXI: 2 (1961), pp. 157–158.

22. Alden Whitman, *The New York Times,* October 23, 1975.

23. As quoted in Whitman, pp. 1 and 40.

24. Whitman, p. 1.

25. *Play Factory Advocate,* February 1975, p. 2.

26. As quoted in Bill Gilbert, "Play," *Sports Illustrated,* October 13, 1975, p. 89.

27. Dr. Harold C. Goddard, *The Meaning of Shakespeare* (Chicago: The University of Chicago Press, 1951), p. 572.

28. Gene I. Maeroff, *The New York Times,* November 3, 1975.

29. Donald M. Frame, trans., *The Complete Works of Montaigne* (Stanford, California: Stanford University Press, 1958), p. 611.

30. *The Complete Works of Montaigne,* p. xiv.

Chapter 18

1. Albert Einstein, *The World As I See It* (New York: Covici Friede Publishers, 1934), pp. 20–21.

Chapter 19

1. Richard Huber, *The American Idea of Success* (New York: McGraw-Hill, 1971), p. 1.

2. John S. DeMott, "Is Bill Donaldson in Washington to Stay?" *The Institutional Investor,* May 1974, p. 132.

3. "Wall Street," Forbes, November 1, 1966, p. 40.

4. Chris Welles, *The Last Days of the Club* (New York: E. P. Dutton & Co., 1975), p. 337.

5. Welles, pp. 337–338.

6. DeMott, p. 65.

7. DeMott, p. 65.

8. F. Scott Fitzgerald, *The Last Tycoon* (New York: Charles Scribner's Sons, 1941), p. 163.

Chapter 20

1. Thomas Merton, *The Silent Life* (New York: Farrar, Straus and Cudahy, 1957), p. 76.

2. Merton, p. 38.

3. *Butler's The Lives of the Saints*, edited and revised by Herbert Thurston, S. J., and Don Attwater (New York: P. J. Kennedy & Son, 1958), Vol. III, p. 687.

Index

271